# WHAT IS KNOWLEDGE?

**SUNY Series in Latin American and Iberian Thought and Culture**

*Jorge J. E. Gracia* and *Rosemary Geisdorfer Feal,* editors

# What Is Knowledge?

*José Ortega y Gasset*

∽

Translated and Edited by
JORGE GARCÍA-GÓMEZ

STATE UNIVERSITY OF NEW YORK PRESS

Published by
State University of New York Press, Albany

For information, address State University of New York Press,
90 State Street, Suite 700, Albany, NY 12207

Production by Marilyn P. Semerad
Marketing by Anne M. Valentine

**Library of Congress Cataloging-in-Publication Data**

Ortega y Gasset, José, 1883–1955.
   [¿Qué es conocimiento? English]
   What is knowledge? / José Ortega y Gasset ; translated and edited by Jorge
García-Gómez.
      p. cm. — (SUNY series in Latin American and Iberian
thought and culture)
Includes bibliographical references and index.
   ISBN 0-7914-5171-2 (alk. paper)—ISBN 0-7914-5172-0 (pbk. :
alk. paper)
   1. Knowledge, Theory of. I. García-Gómez, Jorge. II. Ortega
y Gasset, José, 1883–1955. Ideas y creencias. III. Title. IV. Series.

   B4568.O73 Q42 2001
   121—dc21                                         2001031186

10 9 8 7 6 5 4 3 2 1

*This translation is dedicated to Sara, beloved wife and best friend*

# Contents

❧

# Translator's Introduction

## Jorge García-Gómez

Understandably, Paulino Garagorri, in his capacity of editor of the original version of this book,[1] was reluctant to offer the reader his own assessment of the work, preferring to defer to the reader's unprejudiced consideration.[2] Accordingly, he confined himself to taking a look at it from a vantage point internal to Ortega's "entire philosophical work," and on that basis he came to the conclusion that, "[a]s to the intellectual significance of the new book," one could appropriately say that "it is destined to be one of the most important parts of his legacy."[3] I certainly concur with him in that, and yet I cannot rest my case with a simple acknowledgment of agreement, if for no other reason than the fact that Garagorri, following Ortega's own choice and his usage of terms in this work,[4] has chosen the Spanish equivalent of *What Is Knowledge?* as the title for the book. But that decision, in my opinion, may prove misleading to the reader, for it seems to suggest that this work of Ortega's should be understood as if it were a mere effort on his part to arrive at a further articulation of the longstanding philosophical preoccupation with knowledge and as his particular contribution to the field that has come to be known as epistemology or theory or knowledge.[5] That however would be, in fact, a fatal misinterpretation of his intent and a failure to appreciate its radicalness. Let me attempt to show that this is the case.

## Some Epistemological Traditions

As a first approach to the philosophical discipline in question, one could say that epistemology "is a branch of philosophy which is concerned with the nature and scope of knowledge, its presuppositions and basis, and the general reliability of knowledge."[6] Yet this material-descriptive formulation is both too broad and vague to do it justice and consequently to be of much help to us, failing as it does to identify any formal point of view from which cognitive questions are to be philosophically examined. It is no wonder that the author of the formula felt obliged to differentiate the theory of knowledge from psychology, inasmuch as the latter, as opposed to the former, cannot say "whether the beliefs [human beings hold] are based on good grounds or whether they are sound."[7] Ortega did certainly share this opinion, even though, in his view, the epistemological task so characterized is only a derivative endeavor, dependent as it is on the determination of the nature of knowledge as such and of its origins.[8] Even an analysis of knowledge seeking to identify the logical conditions it would have to meet would fall short of being a satisfactory philosophical account of knowledge, because it does not achieve its intended goal for the same reason, presupposing as it does the phenomenon of knowledge—i.e., the human cognitive effort to come to the truth—as a mere fact. Moreover, Ortega also dismissed logic as not being competent to discharge that task,[9] but, in so doing, he placed himself squarely under the obligation of rendering an account of knowledge, an endeavor he indeed undertook, as we will have an occasion to appreciate. Yet the task in question cannot in principle be carried out, if epistemology is identified with the theory of science, a valid form of inquiry which, again, is not radical enough, since a theoretical examination of scientific praxis in general, or of that which is proper to a particular scientific discipline, would prove wanting for the same reason.[10]

A first step in the right direction would be—to put it negatively—temporarily to set aside such explicative or theoretical-constructive concerns, for the purpose—to express it positively—of carrying out a "simple intuitive analysis"[11] of cognition as actually experienced, that is to say, of the phenomenon of knowledge itself which underlies all such attempts. At that basic level, it seems that knowledge can be characterized as the interplay of three factors, namely, the subject, the object, and the position adopted with regard to the object, to wit: the subject's "knowing, or failing to know, that something is or is not."[12] In other words, knowledge seems fundamentally to comprise a relationship established between subject and object, in which the subject strives to connect itself with the being of an object and thus essentially to arrive at the truth. Ortega, once more, would concur with this thesis, which, however, he would consider insufficient, because it still proceeds on the basis of unavowed presuppositions, albeit to a lesser extent than the prior contentions, as we will learn to appreciate in some detail later.

If we take a look at the history of philosophy, we soon enough come to the realization that the cognitive relationship in question has not been understood univocally. Abbagnano, for one, argued that there have been two basic interpretations of it, namely, one in which subject and object are considered either identical or similar, and another in which subject and object transcend each other.[13]

Ortega concurred with Abbagnano in principle, but also in identifying, as the originary interpretation of knowledge, the one which "reduced" the subject to the object, an interpretation that first took hold with the Greeks and was assumed to be valid into the nineteenth century.[14] Ortega further agreed with him in breaking down the period during which it prevailed into two phases.[15]

The first phase is realism, where one finds the pre-Socratics, Plato, and Aristotle, among others. At this developmental stage, the subject—it is assumed—assimilates itself to the object or unites with it.[16] This interpretation came to its essential culmination with St. Thomas Aquinas, when he contended that "the known . . . is in the knower after the fashion of the knower,"[17] a point that served, by balancing the weight of the subject against that of the object,[18] to temper somewhat Aristotle's thesis that knowledge in act is identical with the object in act.[19]

The second phase is idealism, where one finds Descartes, Leibniz, and Kant, to mention only some of the salient figures. At this developmental stage, knowledge, still considered a matter involving assimilation, moved from dealing primarily with the objects of cognition to focusing on the order they constitute.[20] Indeed, this was so much so that in Descartes, for instance, the assimilation and the identification of the *order* consisting of ideas and that comprised of the objects of cognition are proposed and pursued.[21] Even Kant's so-called "Copernican revolution" was not so radical as to have been capable of transforming the classical conception of knowledge, except to the extent of admitting that the "objective order of things is modelled after the conditions of knowledge, not vice versa."[22]

The second basic interpretation of knowledge, typical of many philosophers of the twentieth century, consists in taking cognition to be a phenomenon of transcendence, amounting as it would to being in the presence of, or at least to pointing to, an object.[23] As Ortega himself did acknowledge concerning such an interpretation,[24] the cognitive initiative belongs with the subject, and cognition is "directed toward making the object present or manifest, toward rendering reality itself evident."[25]

Perhaps it was Nicolai Hartmann who arrived at the clearest formulation of the notion of cognitive transcendence, focusing as he did—to use Hessen's words—on the *relation between the content of thinking and its object*."[26] His point of departure was then the phenomenon of knowledge, and he sought to work out, as the foundational preliminary to his examination thereof, what Müller took to be, as already mentioned, the "simple intuitive analysis" of it.[27] Accordingly, if we now turn to Hartmann's own treatise on the matter,[28] we will find that the results of the analysis of the fundamental phenomenon of knowledge qua act of apprehension are as follows:

1. In cognition, a knowing subject and an object known confront each other, being as they are opposite to each other in reciprocally transcendent terms. "The *relationship* existing between the two is knowledge itself."[29]

2. Such a relationship is essentially a *correlation,* for the subject is constituted as a subject only in relation to an object, and an object only in relation to a subject.[30]

3. Not only are the roles of subject and object constituted reciprocally, but they are, as well, necessarily different, inseparable, and irreversible, all of which determinations are themselves given within the relationship of knowledge.[31]

4. "The subject's function consists in grasping the object, and the object's in being graspable and actually grasped."[32]

5. The act of grasping, or apprehension, amounts to the subject's self-transcendence toward, and entry into, the sphere of the object.[33]

6. Consciousness of the opposition between subject and object is an essential dimension of the consciousness of the object, being as it is an indestructible component of it, despite the union between subject and object that is brought about by knowing.[34] Cognition is effected in three stages, so to speak, for the "subject first comes out of itself, [then] it places itself outside itself, and finally it returns to itself."[35]

7. Knowledge amounts to transferring the characteristics of the object to the sphere of the subject, a process that does not alter them but limits itself to reproducing them by means of an image of the object, the *content* of which *image* is identical with that of the object.[36] "The object, therefore, is not modified by the subject; rather, it is the subject which is modified by the object."[37] Hessen gave expression to this point as follows: "Knowledge, then, may be defined as the *determination of the subject by the object.*"[38] If Hessen's interpretation of Hartmann is correct, this formulation has the advantage of rendering explicit a presupposition on the latter's part, namely, that *cognition is perception,* a point that Ortega rejected for good reason.[39]

Despite the fact that, according to both Hartmann and Ortega, the "subject" is the only active factor in cognition, it is nonetheless true, as it turns out, that the product of knowledge, namely, what Hartmann calls "image" *(Bild)*, would be the mere result of the subject's passivity or receptivity, his characterization of it as a construction or creation *(Gebilde)* in the subject notwithstanding.[40] No doubt, such a conception would serve to safeguard the externality and independence of the object with regard to the subject,[41] a notion that is essential to Hartmann's idea of knowledge, inasmuch as it involves the necessary reciprocal relationship of *transcendence* between subject and object, although the object considered in itself does not belong to the subject's makeup.[42] But it does so at a price, namely, that of taking the being-in-itself of the object for granted and of confusing being with thinghood. If so, Hartmann's position would—at least in part—imply a reversal of his original stance, an obscure manner of relapsing into the first interpretation of knowledge, an implication that would place him at odds with his insistence on the reciprocal transcendence of subject and object in cognition.

However, this is not the most serious objection that could be raised against Hartmann's notion of cognitive transcendence. In fact, the most troublesome aspect of it, even if one grants that it is the correct formulation of an adequate—but *static*—essential phenomenological description of knowledge, is that it takes the relationship of cognitive transcendence and its termini for granted. Ortega directed our attention precisely to these matters, when he pointed out that, in works like Hartmann's, "it is still held that the problem of knowledge has been posed when one has asserted that it is the apprehension of *being,* then to proceed, without further ado, to analyze the consequences of that definition."[43] But this will not do at all, if one is in pursuit of complete clarity and certainty concerning the essence of knowledge, because "neither the fact that human beings strive to apprehend being nor the *being* apprehended [by them] raises any questions for Hartmann."[44] To that end, one must engage in three different, albeit necessarily interrelated, accounts, namely, an inquiry into the motives leading human beings to strive to apprehend being, an investigation of the meaning of being, and, lastly, an examination of the question of "how it is that a subject is capable of grasping an object,"[45] which is, or so it seems, the only dimension of knowledge of significance to Hartmann.[46] In what follows, I propose to deal only with the first two of the questions mentioned,[47] and to do so in light of Ortega's analyses.

# The Genesis of Knowledge as Transcendence

Let me turn, first of all, to what Ortega called the "historical character of knowledge,"[48] in the special sense that he assigned to the expression, and which remains to be determined. This is just one step, albeit a decisive one, in the direction of grounding the concept of cognitive transcendence and thus of overcoming the epistemological concerns—in the usual sense of the term "epistemological"—that have prevailed in the philosophical tradition.[49] This is to say that Ortega did not take the phenomenon of knowledge for granted or as a matter of course, but that is not the same as asserting that he denied it reality or existence. On the contrary, it means only that, to him, it had become problematic, that is to say, that he was not "altogether convinced of its opposite being true."[50] To overcome the *dubium,* to escape the oscillation intrinsic to the essential or radical doubt,[51] one must ascertain whether or not the problematic reality in question (in our case, knowledge) is endowed with a genuine essence and, if it is, to establish what it is. However, one thing must be clear from the outset: Ortega did not attempt, except where it was important to his reflective effort, to retrace the steps, or to reiterate the results, of the *static* phenomenological analysis of knowledge that we were, just a moment ago, concerned with; rather, his endeavor amounted to developing—in a sense yet to be determined—a *genetic* phenomenological account of it.

The essence of something—no matter what it is—lies concealed "[behind] its trappings and its masks"[52] which, in our dealings with the thing in question, keep it out of sight "unfailingly and of necessity."[53] One must therefore be prepared not to confuse the essence of the thing in question, "the 'thing itself' in its selfhood"[54] with its trappings and its masks, when one engages in the effort of determining it. Now, not just anything would be a suitable candidate to bring about the covering up of the essence of something, but only "those phenomena that '*have to do with* . . . *[the thing]*' but are not of it,"[55] phenomena which are all the more insidious the more intimate and enduring their connection with it is.

The first order of business would then appear to be the identification of the various sorts of concealment relevant to the thing under scrutiny. In other words, one must be, according to Ortega, able to determine which things "have to do" most intimately with the phenomenon in question, without however really constituting it. In the case of knowledge, there have been, and continue to be, three identifications responsible for the concealment. In what follows, let me both formulate them (by way of theses) and suggest, in principle, the grounds for their refutation:

1. *Knowledge is the work of certain psychological mechanisms:* When one seeks to know, one no doubt engages in thinking,[56] but the "question 'what is thinking?' is apt to be answered with a description of the psychic mechanisms that function when a man is thinking."[57] This is hardly an evident proposition. According to Aristotle, for example,

"[a]ll men by nature desire to know,"[58] and this seems to mean for him that the mere possession of intellectual and other, related faculties automatically triggers cognitive activity, "just as looking consists in using [the power of vision]."[59] Now, this is not the case at all, since the possession of faculties and our engaging in the execution of their acts, however spontaneous this may be, are "not knowing itself."[60] And they are not, first of all, because, obviously, "in order to make use of an instrument, it is not enough to possess it,"[61] and, secondly, because the mere possession or use of instruments or faculties provides one with no assurance that one will adequately come to the intended result, which in our case is knowledge.[62] Something else is needed which would move us in the direction of some definite goal, in reference to which the possession and use of such faculties just constitute the *conditio sine qua non*.

2. *Knowledge is logical thinking*: Logical thinking is prescriptive or normative.[63] Accordingly, no manner of thought would be acceptable as leading to the truth, except that which is "characterized by certain distinguishing features: identity with itself, avoidance of contradiction, exclusion of a third term between 'true' and 'false.'"[64] But this approach is affected by two disadvantages:

A. It limits the "rich morphology of thinking" to one sort by reducing it to an "abstract pattern"[65] satisfying the above-mentioned conditions. But the scope of thinking is much wider. In fact, it is coextensive with imagining, its various forms being specifications of the activity of our mental capacity to constitute "ideal" worlds, such as the religious, poetic, scientific, and other realms. They arise as correlates of our different ways of exercising thinking in our attempts to deal with the circumstance, and logical thinking turns out to be just one of them.[66]

B. Logical thinking is not an actuality, but a "mere ideal."[67] Indeed, it is nonexistent,[68] inasmuch as the conditions thinking would have to meet so as to be logical cannot be completely fulfilled.[69] But, if this is so, then either knowledge, as the pursuit of the truth, would have to be abandoned, or it would have to exceed the boundaries of logical thinking.

3. *Knowledge is coextensive with thinking*: No doubt, cognition is thinking, but not "all thinking is a cognitive act,"[70] as has already been suggested. Such a contention serves to obscure its nature, since its distinctiveness, arising as it does by contrast with other manners of thinking, would become impoverished or simply unavailable. Accordingly, one would have to say that this thesis is no thesis at all, but a

mere hypothesis, and a false one at that, namely, "that man whenever he has set himself to thinking has done so with the same end in view: to ascertain what things are,"[71] to determine the being or essence of things. But this intellectual exercise[72] depends on conditions that are seldom fulfilled in human history, conditions that may be summarized by means of this formula: being placed in the "firm pre-rational belief that there is being."[73]

Having removed the various manners in which knowledge becomes covered up by, or confused with, something else, Ortega was at last free to propose his own definition for it. In attempting to do so, he began at the simplest, least compromising level of approach, suggesting as he did that thinking is a human occupation, a manner of doing, something that we do, among many other things, in our lives.[74] Like anything else one does, it requires the employment of certain instruments (for example, the faculties and activities of "seeing, remembering, reasoning").[75] To be sure, such faculties and activities are of primary importance when cognition is the style of thinking we are engaged in, and yet, quite in general, they are used or triggered automatically and thus are insufficient to bring about the doing or action in question.[76] Faculties (or the activities proper to them) which are essentially relevant to a form of action constitute only the necessary conditions thereof and do not figure, therefore, in the picture, except as functions in the service of other factors that may be at play. Accordingly, Ortega argued that there was more to action than that, and contended that the structure of doing in general (and of thinking in particular) was fourfold, amounting as it does to "[1.] *something* done . . . [2. *because of* ], [3.] *for* [*the sake of* ], and [4.] *with* something."[77] In other words, in Ortega's view, the structure of any kind of doing or occupation (and, therefore, of thinking as one of its forms) consists of what we actually do; the motives for what we do (both as rooted in the past, i.e., the "because of" dimension of the action, and as projected towards the future, i.e., its "for the sake of" dimension); and, finally, the instrumentalities (and the performances thereof) that are relevant to it (i.e., the "with" aspect of the action). Furthermore, the motivational constituents of doing clearly point to one essential aspect thereof, namely, its "aspir[ation] . . . to justify itself not only before other people but in the eyes of him who is *absorbed* in it."[78] This aspiration is neither a matter of choice nor a normative dimension of doing; "it is done, wittingly or unwittingly"[79] and is, therefore, a necessary concomitant of it.

Let me now approach cognition or knowledge as a special sort of thinking, and let me do so from the vantage point of its motivational constitution. Normally, human beings are not inclined to engage in knowing, unless they find themselves no longer *placed* in a belief; that is to say, that they would do so only when a belief "fails [them] . . . , and [they have] nowhere to *abide*."[80] This sounds implausible, because one cannot live without making decisions at every turn, and one cannot do that unless one is already possessed by a certain belief or beliefs, which constitute the operative ground for life's settlement or abidingness and thus for the possibility of its ongoingness or continuous action.[81] However, to understand this position in Ortega's precise sense, two remarks, it seems to me, are in order.

First of all, a belief is not in force and does not function as the spontaneously uncontested basis of our lives whenever we come to doubt it (and thus it ceases to work as our unmediated access to reality). But this is true only if we do not take the term "doubt" in its ordinary sense, namely, as a state of mind resulting from a deliberate action, to wit: an act of reflection, as is the case, say, with Descartes's universal, methodical doubt[82] or with Husserl's *epokhé*.[83] Rather, it must be a pre-reflective state in which we have come to find ourselves, a condition into which we have indeliberately fallen.[84] The origin of this *radical* form of doubt is not then our will or intellect, but rather the antecedent socio-historical problems and difficulties that we have encountered in our life, and which, in their severity, have served to dissolve our belief or beliefs. This set of problems and difficulties constitute the *because-motive* of our radical doubt.

Secondly, since life's decision-making capacity—whether activated spontaneously or deliberately—is rendered moot in such a condition or state, it follows that the meaningful ongoingness of life would strictly depend on our being successful in overcoming the radical doubt. Following Ortega, I will call any such endeavor "thinking." However, the kind of thinking in which one would engage in such a situation is not always, or necessarily, cognition. As Ortega put it, "[w]hatever . . . a human being then resorts to is thinking,"[85] and thinking may take different forms and accordingly yield different resolutions to the doubt (e.g., prayer,[86] poetry, or scientific propositions).[87] The "modes of satisfying . . . [the] need [of thinking] . . . are in principle unlimited,"[88] but they do not constitute an established stock of paths permanently available to the doubter. Rather, human beings "must *invent* them and train . . . [themselves] to handle them, experimenting with them . . . and, in the end, always coming up against their limits."[89] These range from error to total failure, including possible meaninglessness or even death, inasmuch as human beings proceed, at the moment of crisis and of subsequent invention, without significant precedent or assurance of success. The meaningful continuation of one's life depends on belief, which is *no permanent possession* but "a state of mind [or conviction] at which . . . *[human beings have] arrived,*"[90] just as we have arrived at the radical doubt of which a belief, as the *consolidated* result of successful thinking, is the negation and sublation.

Now then, this analysis, if correct, would require that we drastically change our idea of knowledge or cognition. Far "from being an inborn faculty of man," as was the case, say, with Aristotle,[91] or a permanently available disposition, as was true, for example, for Dilthey,[92] cognition must be reconceived, in light of the preceding, as "a *historical* form evolved by human life as a result of certain previous experiences."[93] This could be brought about "by simply taking into account the *precognitive implication* . . . at the back of cognition,"[94] namely, the *because-motivational nexus* constituted by the dissolution of the beliefs in which one was placed and the "state" of radical doubt following in its wake.

It is now clear why Ortega was not satisfied with the notion of cognition as the *relationship of mutual transcendence* between subject and object. Correct as far as it goes, such an idea is however just "an *abstract concept* made up of *abstract constituents.*"[95] The formula indicating that knowledge is "any attempt made by . . . [human beings] to adjust . . . [themselves] intellectually to . . . their environment"[96] is merely an algebraic expression,[97] the nature of which is purely *occasional* in Husserl's sense of the term.[98] In other words, it is one in which the blanks—i.e., the *Leerstellen* formally identified as "abstract human being, an environment no less abstract, the abstract necessity of adjustment between the two, and the notion of a likewise abstract intellectual activity"[99]—would have to be reinterpreted historically whenever the situation in which human beings find themselves living changes significantly, so as to be able to determine the concrete values corresponding to them. In light of this, one can now fully appreciate what Ortega meant by his attempt to account for knowledge in terms of its historical character.[100]

However, this phenomenological genetic analysis of knowledge is incomplete in one important respect. Ortega has, I think, given an apt reply to the question, why?[101] about cognition, but the question "what for?" has yet to be raised, let alone answered successfully.

Once motivated by the condition of radical doubt or perplexity, one would set out to inquire into whether or not there could be any abiding ground upon which to settle and by means of which to guide our lives. If obtainable, this could be the result of that special form of thinking called "knowing," not of believing, which had entered into a state of crisis. For anyone to be able to engage in such an endeavor, even in such critical conditions, at least "two presuppositions must be fulfilled," said Ortega, namely, the following.

"*First*, a belief must obtain that [,] behind the confusion and chaos of the world as it appears [,] there lies concealed a fixed and stable figure on which all changes depend."[102] We do *not* know *what* and *whether* such a figure might be, although to inquire into it we must *believe* that it has a particular nature and that it exists.[103] In light of this, cognition as such is defined by Ortega as the "ascertainment of the *being* of things,"[104] where "being" is, to begin with, just the name for that figure.

Given that the inquiry in question is a "conceptual pursuit,"[105] not an affair of perception,[106] the "*second* implication without which . . . [such a] pursuit . . . would be absurd is the belief that this *being* is of consistency akin to the *natural* gift called intellect."[107]

Accordingly, if Ortega is right, one would have to assert, in brief, that the "for the sake of" motive of knowledge—the one urging us along in the cognitive enterprise—is none other than our dual belief in the competence of our existing intellectual capacity to discover and determine being.

Now, if successful in discovering being, a human being would gain—and for good reason—a new *ideative* "life settlement" upon which to abide, and, if further rational grounds and confirming experiences abound, its consolidation as a *belief* as well. Whenever that comes to pass as the outcome of the human cognitive behavior, "a state of . . . [tranquility] and certainty"[108] would result concerning the particular "worldly" or "subjective" area primordially affected by the radical doubt or perplexity.

The human cognitive effort, if carried to its ultimate consequences, becomes the search for absolutely first—i.e., universal or pantonomous and indubitable or autonomous—grounds for living.[109] This is the endeavor which, at least since Plato, has been called philosophy, i.e., "the *lógos* of reason" or "of truth," amounting as it does to "*àlétheia* . . . [or the] discovery of hidden being which is once and for all."[110] The phrase "ultimate consequences" just employed suggests that philosophy, because of a requirement forming part of its nature, must strive to take nothing for granted, and that, of course, includes even itself as a finite, contingent rational endeavor permanently *open* to the possibility of its own extinction. Thus any philosophy that is not so determinable is incomplete and only *in via* towards itself.[111] Ortega called it "naïve or unjustified" because "it leaves outside its doctrinal body the *motives* from which it springs"[112] (what he, as I have already pointed out, characterized as the "because" and "for the sake of" motives).[113] The first principle of philosophy must therefore be its *self-justification*,[114] and any given philosophical system must be taken as having fallen short of itself, to the extent that it has failed to include "what impels . . . [human beings] to philosophize . . . as part of the philosophical theory itself."[115]

# The Metaphysics of Knowledge

The genesis of knowledge as transcendence, as we just had an occasion to see, is a demonstration of the "historical character of cognition."[116] However, an endeavor of that sort was not, for Ortega, a mere appeal to, or the construction of, the empirical history of knowledge, and it was not that because he was concerned in his inquiry with the structures that play an essential role in motivating a human being to know, not just with determining the link existing between particular theses, thinkers, and dates. The account in question involved the establishment of the "because" and "for the sake of" motives of doing or action, of which cognition is a particular form. To put it succinctly, Ortega's is a "logico"-motivational elucidation of historical experience and, on that basis, of knowledge. Therefore, it implicates neither a skepticism of sorts (the *aporiai* to which such an attitude may lead had been examined by him quite early in his philosophical development[117]), nor the particular form thereof called historicism (and the special difficulties it involves concerning the nature of truth[118]).

Indeed, his conception—and practice—of philosophy, as the pursuit of ultimate knowledge, is incompatible with skepticism and relativism of any kind.[119] This clearly was his position when, in his attempt to consider the conditions that truth in the full sense of the word is to fulfill, he asserted that metaphysical truth "presupposes no other truths";[120] in other words, what he was seeking after was a form of truth that is unproblematic *de jure,* not merely *de facto.*[121] This is possible only if philosophy, as opposed to science, does not in the final analysis proceed, however systematically, on the basis of assumptions, including that of the validity of its own practice, since, as he put it, the first principle of philosophy is its own self-justification. In other words, philosophy, in contradistinction to any other form of knowledge, seeks only incontrovertible certainty or truth.[122]

Now then, if such a declaration is not to remain on the plane of mere claims or proclamations, then it must be shown that there is some fundamental reality, the intellectual possession of which truly satisfies such strictures. Such a reality, if it exists, must fulfill a twofold condition, as we will be able to appreciate in due course, namely, to be intuitively available, and to be so accessible as a self-articulated totality. This can be so if, at least, cognition in general—and metaphysical knowledge in particular—is conceived as a modality of life qua self-positing activity, not as a primordially reflective affair.[123] Philosophy, then, would ultimately proceed upon the "acknowledgment of life as primordial reality . . . ," which is precisely the "first act of full and incontrovertible knowledge."[124] Life (or anything else for that matter, insofar as it lies within life)[125] exists absolutely; that is to say, it exists *for me* already in immediacy, or by virtue of my spontaneously counting on it.[126] Accordingly, this indefeasible awareness does not require any reflective analysis for confirmation, being a matter of ongoing self-validation.

This view presupposes that life, as the first "object" of philosophical cognition, is conceived as consisting of doings or actions,[127] such that, in its midst, I, as the actional and actual totality of reciprocity comprised of myself and my circumstance,[128] find *myself,* as a matter of course but necessarily, "in need of [being occupied] . . . with that which is not *myself.*"[129] In other words, life presents itself, to begin with, as the unreflective awareness of *itself* as the *ongoing* confrontation of self and circumstance.[130] Accordingly, philosophical thinking, as any other manner of thinking, consists in "react[ing] to a reality *already present* [to us; that is to say, it consists in] interpret[ing it]."[131] And yet this formally intellectual way of being occupied with things or "self" is a distinctive style of thinking, inasmuch as, therein, things or the components of the "self" are "not taken as utensils or obstacles but in respect of their being."[132] In this sense, science and philosophy are not different from each other, except in two important respects: in degree or quantitatively, since the philosophical endeavor would achieve its goal only when it does so in the absence of any presupposition;[133] and qualitatively, because, despite appearances to the contrary, the question raised by philosophy is in kind other than the one raised in any scientific investigation, for the form of the specifically philosophical question is "'what is the being of things?' in general,"[134] while the form of a scientific question properly so called is, "what is the being of this or that?"[135]

There is no denying that philosophical knowledge is of a paradoxical sort, if its point of departure is to be life's unmediated access to itself. On the one hand, as Ortega has insisted, life is only correctly understood—or understands itself—as performativeness or performative being, i.e., as the ongoing actional awareness of itself;[136] and yet philosophy, as a theoretical—and thus as a reflective—performance of and in life, would have, as its fundamental theme and origin, pretheoretical reality as such, i.e., "life as self-performance."[137] The possibility of philosophy, therefore, essentially hinges on the possibility of carrying out the task of examining such a reality without effecting a *metábasis eis allo génos.*[138]

To summarize: philosophy, or absolute knowledge,[139] is to be, of necessity, the intuitive grasp[140] of life's self-articulation. But if so, philosophy, at its metaphysical or foundational level, would consist in carrying out the categorial analysis of life. To verify this claim, let me now proceed to the presentation, in principle, of such an analysis.[141]

The most evident character of life, argued Ortega, is its absoluteness,[142] i.e., its being self-positing in the performative, not in the objective
sense.[143] In other words, "life is an absolute event happening to itself;"[144]
it is straightforwardly, as opposed to objectively, entitative.[145] If this is
correct, life is self-present, or exists for me, to begin with, performatively,
not as perceived or objectively.[146] Life would then be "absolutely continuous,"[147] since it does not require, for it to be present to itself, any perceptual or objectivating interruptions, to which of course it is always open.
Therefore, since life is an entitative, not a mediated, presence to itself,[148]
philosophy, as one of the doing modalities of life, would have direct access to it and basically amount to the systematic descriptive analysis and
critical exposition of the articulated series and totality of forms that life is
comprised of "before its very eyes."

Moreover, my life must be regarded, at the most fundamental of levels,
as an "all-encompassing reality of reciprocity"[149] that consists of myself
and my circumstance, and amounts to the "actuating and functional co-
existing with that which is not me"[150] (i.e., things, animals, and people),
and vice versa. But this means that the subject of life (as performative self-
presence) is "neither myself [i.e., the objectivating ego or first 'I' of
Ortega's basic formula] nor the other [or circumstance] but [something
more primordial, namely,] life itself, my life."[151] Indeed, my life is tantamount to "my counting on myself and, at once, on something other than
myself . . . [i.e., my circumstance]. . . ."[152] This is a thesis which serves to
keep in view two fundamental characters of life, to wit: spontaneous self-
attendance and actuality.[153] But this implies that the classical categories
of "substance" and "accident" do not apply to life, for "I am the one who
is in need of the so-called 'things' in order to exist."[154] Similarly, things
are such as to be in need of me in order to be actualized for what they basically are in life, namely, facilities and difficulties for my living, i.e., instruments and obstacles for what I need and want to do with myself.[155]
The reason for this is, as Ortega argued, that the "primordial reality [of
anything real] would be whatever it is as lived by me,"[156] that is to say, its
way of functioning in my life.[157] This is what he called "evidence," a term
to be understood—as used by him—in its etymological sense, i.e., as ex-
pressing the character of anything that lies right before our eyes, a feature
Ortega took as having its foundation in "life's altogether pre-intellectual
act of self-attendance or self-realization."[158]

Now, life is ongoing perplexity or insecurity.[159] This is due to two essential conditions of life: its haste (given not only its temporal-vocational reality, but its temporal finitude)[160] and its neediness (an aspect to which I
shall return).[161] As Ortega insisted, life "is being absolutely at a loss [in the
midst of things]."[162] This is a decisive point, for it gives expression to the

root of our need to know, since, as he also said, "for that very reason, it obliges us, willy-nilly, to engage in an effort . . . to save ourselves from being at a loss. This effort is knowledge."[163] What is then the aim of that effort to save ourselves? It is "to know *what* [we can] livingly abide by."[164] Now then, for us "to be," i.e., to live, is to strive after "security, clarity about how to abide by each thing and . . . the world."[165] In one word, the purpose of knowing, at its most fundamental and consequential level, is to be able to persist living and to survive *(pervivir)* meaningfully.

Let me return to the problem of knowledge now that we have a sufficient grounding in Ortega's metaphysics. At this point, I believe it is possible to pose it not only correctly, but satisfactorily. In Ortega's opinion, it is "superficial to formulate the problem of knowledge in the usual fashion,"[166] i.e., in the way Hartmann and others seek to come to terms with it, for it is not enough to reduce it

> to the question of how the intellectual subject or consciousness is capable of grasping being, as if consciousness and being pre-existed apart from each other, and the only thing were . . . to effect the passage from being to consciousness or vice versa.[167]

On the contrary, even if cognition involved a relationship of transcendence between subject and object, and it does, it would still remain to be seen why it is, in the first place, that the relationship in question would have to be established. In other words, in order to produce a full account of knowledge, one would be required not only to describe the relationship between subject and object and the cognitive consequences thereof, but, as well, to present the reasons why a human subject would be moved to engage in knowing and to show what the nature of being is, which the knowing subject is seeking to determine thereby. Or in Ortega's own words: "[both] the [subject's] cognitive act of apprehension and the apprehended being . . . emerge as the radical edges of something prior, namely, life,"[168] which is, as we have seen,[169] the ultimate subject of any of our doings. Let me now attempt to carry out a brief examination of each one of the two edges in question and to do so in the order prescribed.

Cognition or knowledge is a form of thinking, and thinking is a form of doing. Now, cognition seems to begin with a question, a question I pose to myself, namely, "what is the being of things?" Generally speaking, one thinks or utters an interrogative phrase[170] for the sake of doing. In other words, thinking is that form of doing one engages in when other forms of doing make us end in a perplexing or problematic situation. To put it succinctly: if need be, one would think, and would do so for the sake of doing.[171] Cognition, as a form of thinking, is no exception.[172] Accordingly, the expression "to ask a question" would not refer to a kind of behavior the sense of which is merely grammatical. In fact, it reaches much further, for, "[i]f I ask a question, . . . it must be that I am in *need* of doing so,"[173] although I may not know, or actually focus upon, the need involved. This is so because "the need is not found expressed or declared in the question, remaining as it does prior to it,"[174] i.e., in those past decisions and choices, both positive and negative, I have already made, and in the figure of a man I have come to cut in the world—in other words, in what constitutes the "because of" motivational structures of my life's present.

But what do I do "when I think or speak to myself"? In Ortega's view, what I originally do then is to "perform the operation of rendering [something manifest which] . . . was hidden and secret to me before [I thought of it]."[175] As is the case with any other form of doing, thinking cannot be adequately understood unless one sees it as arising from a situation in which one finds oneself, a situation which, likewise, cannot be adequately understood unless one sees it both as coming from and as moving towards something else.[176] A word, an utterance, a thought cannot therefore be separated from its "surroundings" with impunity, for

> the surroundings of a word are an essential part thereof . . . and the word is an activity [i.e., a doing, not the act of a mechanism], something purely dynamic, a pressure exerted by the surroundings on it and by it on the surroundings.[177]

For the purposes at hand, the import of this passage may be assessed in light of two remarks. First of all, the concept of linguistic "surroundings" must be seen as a generalization, on Ortega's part, of a notion that was formulated much earlier by Wilhelm von Humboldt when he asserted that in "the grammar of every language there is a part expressly signified and another unspoken and to be added in thought *(still schweigend hinzugedachter Theil)*."[178] Secondly, one must bear in mind the point made by Ortega himself as a way of prefacing the remark quoted earlier, and that point is that the word "surroundings" signifies something which, to begin with, is a mere context comprised of words.[179] But this understanding can be generalized, in turn, to mean the context of the situation in which the utterance is made (i.e., its "because" and "for the sake of" motivational structures), on the grounds that utterance or thinking is a form of doing, and doing is a response to a given situation. Accordingly, we respond to the pressure exerted on us by the situation and its surroundings, upon which, in turn, we exert pressure by thinking, for my life is a mutuality existing between what befalls me and what I do. Concerning this contention, one should note two things:

1. The concept of "linguistic context," which is comprised of words, utterances, or thoughts, is accounted for by reducing it to a species of the genus "surroundings."

2. The scope of the sphere of the surroundings includes, or so it seems, something *ideal,* as is obvious in the case of words, insofar as they are endowed with sense. In light of this, it is reasonable to introduce a distinction between someone's living situation and the linguistic or thinking context within which he or she gives expression to the situation, and which, as such, can only be constituted by abstracting from the situation.[180] But, if this is so, one could speak of an ultimate ideal dimension of the surroundings, viz., the "world beyond," or "world of being," to which Ortega referred and to which we will be turning our attention in due course.[181] Such a dimension could potentially arise—in a special way yet to be specified—as an aspect of the surroundings of my situation, indeed as something that would be the counterpart of my active engagement with problematic things and situations, as a determinant of my situation within the totality of my life, and thus as something capable of exerting its own pressure on me, just as I am able, by my thinking of it, to exert pressure on it.[182]

In light of this, let me ask again, what do I do when I engage in knowing? A preliminary answer would be to say that I "begin . . . to pose an essential question, namely, 'what is this or that thing?'"[183] But why is it, in the first place, that I initiate this line of inquiry, let alone pursue and sustain it? Curiosity, as some would have it, is not enough.[184] It is not even plain ignorance, for there are many things I am ignorant of but whose determination I do not care to pursue.[185] In order to engage in knowing, we must be "in a state of confusion, in which we are face to face with something hidden,"[186] since without being in such a situation and without gaining such a clarification, respectively, it is impossible to live, i.e., to persist in living and to survive meaningfully. Now then, "being" is the name given by Ortega to that which lies hidden but needs to be known in a situation of crisis, and yet one does not seek after it unless "one senses that one is lacking it."[187] In other words, it is ignorance of what we need to know concerning that which we need to do[188] in the given situation that motivates and supports our cognitive effort. This is the "most genuine presupposition of knowledge."[189] However, in this connection, it is important to avoid a simple misunderstanding. Ortega was not speaking of our ignorance about this or that, no matter how needful the thing of which we are ignorant may be in our lives. He was making a larger and more far-reaching point concerning the formal[190] essence of human life, to wit: "[o]nly an entity ignorant by nature is capable of setting itself in motion by engaging in the operation of knowing."[191]

The reality of things is manifest to us; it is given to us non-mediately in everyday experience. At that level, there is no "evidence" whatsoever of being. Being is not part and parcel of the actual (or even possible) inventory of the world or the self at any given time. Why is it, then, that one speaks of being? What are its origins and placement? Or expressed by means of Ortega's own words:

> How is it possible for human beings not to be content with what they encounter before themselves, with the world of immediacy, but to go after the world beyond, or world of being . . . , of which they do not have the slightest inkling?[192]

To answer this question, let me now take a step back and attempt descriptively to present the way we live in this world, at least so far as it is convenient for the purposes at hand. There we are engaged in dealings with things, by means of which—or against which—we fashion our lives by carrying out our designs. "Things are found";[193] we encounter and use them, but we do not come across being as if it were another thing in the "world." At best, being is sought by us,[194] and yet it would be sought by us only when the things of this "world" will not do for what we want and need to do. If our execution of *particular* projects, if our implementation of our global program of being, leads us to apparently irremovable problems and stumbling blocks, that is, to those the overcoming of which requires but does not find—in our perceptual acquaintance with and anticipation of things—sufficient grounds leading to successful action, we would go in search of further clarity, a clarity of which there is no trace in the world. Such clarity—let me call it the "clarity of being"—is, to say it again, not found but sought by us, for it is not of this world.[195] To put it in technical terms: being, or the clarity it would afford us, is, to begin with, just the "for the sake of" motivational determination of our lives, when we come to live in a situation of crisis and seek to overcome it critically and radically.

It is reasonable to wonder why this is so. Things may ultimately fail us because they come and go, they arise and perish; their behavior leads us to discover, time and again, that they do not measure up to any apparently permanent determination we make about them.[196] In fact, things are never identical with what is predicated of them, and they are not because the predicates are self-identical, while things are not.[197] Indeed, it was the awareness of this factual condition of things, as already developed by the pre-Socratic thinkers among the Greeks, which "led Plato to making the most paradoxical, astonishing, daring, and fruitful of discoveries, namely, that things taken by themselves are *devoid of being*."[198] In other words, if we are striving to find something ultimately permanent that would accordingly permit us to obtain abiding clarity about reality, we undoubtedly would not and could not find it here, but would have to look for it elsewhere. As given in perceptual experience,[199] things even fail us as the means to enter into the sphere of what lies beyond, if anything, and certainly to arrive at "our discovery of . . . being."[200]

It would seem that we will always be at a loss as long as we live in this world, and by means of the things of this world, for, on the one hand, things do offer us no ultimate support, and, on the other, there is no sign of total clarity and abidingness in any corner of this world. To think so, however, could only be the outcome of our failure effectively to come to terms with the things of this world and to arrive at an adequate, essential description of what we truly encounter in the world (and of the consequent flavor of our lives therein). Since, after all, we manage, for the most part, to survive, and even to flourish, in such a world, it must be, then, that at least something trustworthy about this world is *given* to us in our actual experience of it. And no doubt this is so: when we attempt to carry out our life projects (both global and local), the things of this world appear, in light of such projects, as *prágmata* [201] or importances. In other words, they present themselves, for the most part, as exhibiting a determinate countenance in response to the pressure we exert on them by means of our endeavor to carry out our projects. They appear as favorable (facilities) or as hindering (difficulties) or as indispensable (necessities). We surely count on them in such terms, since we would soon enough discover our folly if we ignore or falsify their countenance as we strive to bring our projects into effect, for, while "[n]o world already predetermined is given to human beings," the "sorrows and joys of life,"[202] or the "subjective" counterparts of *prágmata,* are assured constituents of our lives, and it is under "their guidance . . . [that we] have to invent a world."[203] According to Ortega, this leads us to the realization that "reality," as presently given, is an *interpreted* reality, a reality covered up by layers of sedimented interpretation[204] produced earlier by other human beings in their effort to survive upon encountering a circumstance that is neither transparent nor readily pliable to human designs. Now then, if we take this realization to its ultimate consequences, we would then be taking the first metaphysical step, the final aim of which is to produce an account of "things" as they fundamentally are, a step requiring that, first of all, we strip reality of all coverings and reduce it to what it is purely and simply, i.e., a set of direct responses to our dealings with it. "To come across . . . [genuine and primordial reality] as it is in its actual nakedness, it would be necessary to remove [from reality as it is actually lived contemporarily] . . . all present and past beliefs."[205]

Now, where are we to find any sign of being, if none seems to be identifiable in this interpreted world? How would knowledge then be possible, understood as the pursuit of being, if we have nothing that points in its direction? As Ortega has argued, only in situations of crisis are we prompted to go beyond this world, precisely because it fails us so far as our basic purpose of surviving meaningfully is concerned. Hence, in such situations, nothing is given to us except being, but only as a question, to wit: what is this or that?[206] In fact, originarily being is available to us exclusively in the form of "is," i.e., as an ingredient of such a question. To begin with, we know nothing about it, except that; whatever else it may be beyond that—i.e., whether or not it exists beyond the question and what its nature might be—remains indeterminate. On this basis alone, we should soberly and reasonably abandon the quest for being before we even start on it, except that the situation of crisis promoting it persists in spurring us to pursue being. Our need to survive is the ultimate "because" motive inducing, indeed urging, us to seek after being, which is the "for the sake of" motive of our lives at that point, for "being" is conceived, should it exist, as the formula that would cast light on our critical situation and allow us to continue to live.[207]

But if originarily being exists for us only in the question we pose about things when they drastically fail us in our attempt to lead our lives, then, as an *answer*, its status is, at best, that of a hypothesis we propose to solve our problematic situation.[208] Although our lives would then be at stake, the only thing open for us to do would be merely to postulate[209] being as a problematic means to deal with the situation.[210] This is not, however, a matter of choice, for, in such a predicament, the only alternatives left to us, if we refuse to ask the question concerning being, are either biological or biographical death. To put it bluntly: either I invent such a solution[211] or I am "done for." The cognitive effort thus starts with a postulate, a hypothesis,[212] or an invention of my own, and it is therefore not assured of success.

But, if not in this world, in which it cannot be found, where is the being located that I postulate? Things, even those that we are in dire need of, are sometimes missing or beyond our reach; often, too, they are there at our disposal; but they need not be there, in which case we go after them in order to be able to effect our survival. Their "absence therefore is accidental."[213] As opposed to this, not just at this point of our lives but always, the being of things is absent from the world, for it is *never* a component thereof: "the being of things [is characterized] by its *essential* absence and *transcendence* . . . ; one *must* go, *necessarily* . . . , in search of it."[214] Hence, the idea of the cognitive relationship of transcendence, according to which knowledge is conceived as a dynamic correlation between a needy self and the things of the world, must ultimately be abandoned for the sake of another in which the relationship is seen as established, instead, between the self and being.[215]

Let me now approach the matter from the opposite end, that is, from the standpoint of the presumptive result of cognition. In conformity with this, one may inquire into what becomes of things, which originally displayed themselves basically as *prágmata* or importances, when they are regarded in the light of their being or essence (assuming, of course, that we have identified and demonstrated it). According to Ortega, they are transformed into *entities,* and a thing qua entity could then be defined as a system of importances *unified* under the concept of being or essence.[216] A thing properly so called is thus an *essentially interpreted* reality; while originally it was nothing of the sort, but rather a mere function of my life, i.e., of my needs and projects (as, for example, a light primarily is that which illuminates me when I need and allow it to do so).[217] It must be acknowledged that this concept of being is an oddity, as Ortega himself recognized when he said that the "being of a thing . . . does not contain the thing, but precisely the *relationship* the thing in question bears to us and, therefore, its way of functioning within the economy of life."[218] In other words, the being of a thing is not a component of it, just as equality is not an ingredient, say, of any apples that are equal to each other.[219] We should take to heart the point that the place of origin of being is the question we ask about things when they critically fail us; hence, we should not be surprised if it eventually turns out that being is a response or reply to our question and, therefore, something different from the thing we asked about. Without our questioning things, being would not arise, just as equality would not emerge, except when we compare things. The process of inquiry thus involves three factors: a subject who inquires, a thing inquired into, and the result of the inquiry. Consequently, being (or equality or anything of the sort) depends not only on the behavior of the thing, but also—and decisively—on the inquirer's. Being is not constituted at all, save as a response of the thing involved to the essential question posed about it by an inquiring subject. From whence does being emerge, then? As Ortega emphatically put it, "[t]here must be another source, a source other than things, from which to derive our cognizance of genuine being."[220] But since self-identical, invariable "entities" like being, whiteness, equality, etc., which we justifiably may predicate of things, cannot be found in any part of the world, then one must only be able to find them within us.[221] Here lies precisely the reason for Ortega's *rejection* of the *equation* of knowledge and perception. As he put it,

> I must have nothing to do with the data reaching me from without [i.e., via perception] and withdraw into myself; I must enter into and abide in myself *[ensimismarme]* and, in my sole company *(auté kath'aute hè psykhé)*, discover in me the concept of justice . . . [or that of equality or whiteness or being, or the like].[222]

In conformity with this, Ortega asserted that "it is I who endow or supply . . . [things] with the being they are devoid of."[223] However, he was careful to introduce his conclusion by means of the qualifier, "*[i]n this sense*," by means of which he was desirous to give expression to the point that, despite the fact that being is *both* a component of *and* an answer to my essential question concerning things, being (or equality or justice or the like) is definitely *not* a mere "subjective" determination of the inquirer's mind, although, no doubt, that may occur in the case of error or any other form of falsification. On the contrary, in the case of the success of one's inquiry, that is, when one arrives at the truth, being, proposed as it is by the inquirer as an essential formula for the thing, is nonetheless the thing's own.[224] Hence, Ortega's final conclusion was this: "To know . . . is [in principle] to enter into and abide in myself."[225]

Finally, let me insist on a point which has been made before, but deserves greater attention. A thing properly so called is not an object of non-mediate experience; rather, it is the result of the transformation undergone by a thing as lived, a living thing, when it is considered in the light of the concept of being. We have, on the one hand, the things "out there,"[226] that is to say, the circumstance, the "world" of non-mediate experience, or the set of things that "consist . . . solely and exclusively in acting upon me with living evidence."[227] We come, on the other hand, to a *world* comprised of "imaginary elements," about each one of which, by contrast with the living things, the following characteristics may be predicated: self-identity, failure to contradict the other elements of the same world, and relatedness to those elements without benefit of alteration.[228] Let me refer to the attributes in question as the reality criteria that anything must meet in order to be a member of such a world, as opposed to the non-mediate circumstance. "Interpreted *as* an element of that world and, therefore, as possessing such characteristics, a 'thing out there' is said to be an entity,"[229] and its being or essence is anything pertaining to the entity which is so characterized. Without much exaggeration, this could be taken as a position close to, if not identical with, Aristotle's way of understanding the "things out there", or of saving the phenomena metaphysically, rather than physically or mathematically. That notwithstanding, and employing the same reality criteria, one could also arrive at an opposite assessment of the same things, by attributing "being" (so under-

stood) only to the "elements" of such a world, and thus by reducing phenomena to the status of appearances, for "[not] everything there is can be
said to *be* if by *being* one understands *Being as* . . . [*entity* ]."[230] This interpretation could be considered as the sense of the Platonic way of dealing
with the "things out there," which are thus set in opposition to the Ideas
as the genuine entities *(óntos òn)*.[231] Evidently, this move would effect a
reversal in the order of discovery and be responsible for an upset in reality assessment, wherein Ideas would be taken as coming first and as being
fundamental, while the "things out there" would be taken as coming second and as being derivative. Such a reversal and upset is mediated by the
*identification* of the real and the conceptual,[232] identification which, despite the clarification just made, can be taken either *simpliciter* (as in
Plato) or *secundum quid* (as in Aristotle). In conformity with this, one
can see that "being as entity" is not a primordial condition, for, even if the
Platonic or the Aristotelian or some other similarly grounded scheme be
considered valid, the condition in question would still have to be demonstrated by some process of derivation from what "things out there" are as
given in living experience,[233] which is precisely what Ortega is striving to
show in this book. Or as he has formulated it elsewhere:

> "being" [and] "entity," *to begin with and in the primordial sense,* do not
> refer to the being of things [i.e., the things "out there" or living things], but
> to a need [felt] by human beings and, therefore, to a manner of being of
> human beings. But this can also be formulated as follows: human beings
> need that something be (with genuine being).[234]

This is the fundamental (i.e., non-mediate) notion of being, namely, its indubitable sense *as question,* which must not therefore be confused with
its sense *as answer* or *solution,* which lies only in the realm of possibility
and for which there is no a priori assurance.[235] The latter sense of being is
what Ortega called "essence" in this book, and it should be distinguished
from others like real existence, logical existence, etc., but above all from
"entity," when it signifies the "manner of existing" of an entity or the
"manner of being" of an existent, interpreted in light of the essence.[236]
The primordial sense of being (as question) would therefore correspond
to, be motivated by the sort of human being I have already become (or the
ensemble and tissue of decisions I have made), and be prompted by what
"things out there" are livingly or non-mediately (i.e., by their provocation
and response, whether positive or negative, to our life needs and projects). This is what has been conceptualized by Ortega, at least in part, on
the basis of his notion of *Prâgma* or importance,[237] of which I have
availed myself more than once and which does not coincide with what a

thing would be by itself and apart from me.[238] Instead, it is "something I handle for a particular end, something I deal with or avoid, something I have to count on or disregard; . . . an instrument or obstacle *for*. . . ."[239]

Wolfgang-Rainer Mann has recently published a book that seems to have a direct bearing on the question at hand, namely, the *philosophical status of things,* whether one judges it in light of the provocative title of his work,[240] his theses, or the rigorous and insightful analyses he carries out about the subject. Simplifying matters in view of my prior discussion, Mann's basic position could be summarized by means of the two following contentions[241] about the status of things:

1. We have the position he calls the "Aristotelian priority claim."[242] It allows him to formulate the thesis concerning Aristotle's discovery of things by means of the twofold claim that "bona fide things are particular objects . . . ; and, conversely, that particular objects are the only bona fide things there are."[243] This is clarified by his statement that the "discovery of things amounts to the discovery of objects, to the discovery that all entities need to be divided into particular objects on the one hand, and whatever belongs to those objects on the other (including . . . their species and genera)."[244]

2. We have the position he calls the "Platonic priority claim,"[245] which amounts to saying that "[a]mong the 'beings' or 'entities' *(tà ónta),* . . . only the Forms *deserve* to be called *ousíai,* because only the Forms satisfy the criterion—ontological priority—for being fundamental entities, for being *ousíai*."[246] As opposed to these, one finds the "things out there," or the participants in the Forms or Ideas,[247] such participants not being interpreted by Plato, however, as Aristotle later would, namely, as particular objects having features.[248] The criterion to establish the difference lies in the "associat[ion of] being with the Forms, and [of] becoming with the participants,"[249] a statement in which, presumably, being is that which is eternal, self-identical, and unchangeable, while the participants are not so characterizable.[250] Mann goes as far as suggesting, even if it be only heuristically, that, if Plato is taken "in some ways [as] a quasi-Anaxagorean," one could understand the status assigned by Plato to things qua participants in being (i.e., in the Forms or Ideas) as that of "bundles or clusters of Form-instances, rather than as bona fide objects, or things,"[251] that is, as particular objects having features.

Cutting now through this opposition, but without trying to mediate between its terms or attempting to evaluate Mann's penetrating analyses at its basis, let me simply indicate that Ortega's thought on the matter of the metaphysical status of things moved, or endeavored to move, on a plane, or in a direction, more radical than Plato's or Aristotle's. One way of seeing this is to point to the Parmenidean element both have in common. Despite their differences, Plato and Aristotle sought to identify in reality, following in the footsteps of Parmenides, that which truly is, whether it is possessed of a quasi-individual status (as is the case with Plato's Ideas)[252] or is, in general, something that abidingly pertains to a particular sort of object (as is the case with Aristotle's second substances).[253] As I pointed out earlier,[254] this stance is, according to Ortega, the product of taking as the really real only that which is, in some sense, commensurate with logical concepts (e.g., the *ón* of Parmenides, Plato's Ideas, and Aristotle's substantial forms),[255] inasmuch as sense-perceptual experience only discloses, without mediation, what is "confused and diffused—in brief, what is inexact"[256] (that is, the extra-logical or non-conceptual).[257] In an effort to overcome the distress that human life is thus brought to thereby, those who were significantly dependent on the Parmenidean tradition left the "things out there" behind—either *simpliciter* or *secundum quid*—by primarily re-interpreting them in the light of the concept of being. The net result was the concept of thing qua entity, the formula for which would be the outcome of the synthetic conjunction of the notion of "thing out there" and the concept of being,[258] the product in question allowing two possible, general specifications, to wit: one according to the "Platonic priority claim," another according to the "Aristotelian priority claim." But whichever option is adopted, the consequence is clear: an obliviousness to or a neglect of the "things out there," which could not be philosophically more damaging, for things qua entities are neither original (they are not encountered first) nor originary (they are not primordially given, requiring as they do a special process of derivation on the basis of what is primordially experienced—i.e., the "things out there," in Ortega's sense of the expression—which is thus presupposed by them). Accordingly, and so contended Ortega, if metaphysical inquiry is to be pursued radically, one must transcend the plane of things qua entities by constituting them out of the basic significance that "things out there" primordially have, to begin with and always, in our lives, that is to say, on the grounds of their fundamental sense of *prágmata* or importances.[259] To carry out such a project is precisely the ultimate sense of knowledge, in which all its other layers of meaning are rooted, and on the basis of which they can be accounted for and legitimated at the fundamental rational-experiential level.

# Notes on the Translation

Let me now bring this introduction to its conclusion by devoting a couple of words to the translation. First and foremost, I would like to underscore the fact that the essay, "Ideas and Beliefs," does not form part of the original work, *¿Qué es conocimiento?*, presented here in English. I found good reason, however, to include it as an appendix thereto, and I hope the reader will learn to appreciate my decision after going through the body of the work and the essay itself. Moreover, I have tried to make this fact and others apparent by adding, in the notes, a number of references and cross-references which, in my opinion, are pertinent to obtaining a correct or fuller understanding of the various sections of the book. In passing, let me point out that all translations, both of this work and others, are mine, except when it is otherwise indicated and only when they are somewhat extended. Moreover, for the purposes of clarification, I have made, here and there, additions to the text, additions which are in every case indicated by the use of brackets. I want to caution the reader, however, about the fact that, unless it is otherwise indicated, all notes are my responsibility. Any problems or obscurities affecting the translation, at least those that I am aware of, have also been addressed throughout the book by use of the notes.

The last point notwithstanding, I would like to take the opportunity here to single out one of the difficulties I encountered in translating *¿Qué es conocimiento?* I have in mind the locution *hombre,* when it is used universally or to refer to the human race as such, something that occurs frequently in the work, since philosophers, given the nature of their *métier,* are given to generalizations. In keeping with contemporary American usage, I have rendered the word, when it is so used, as "human being," although the literal and idiomatic thing to do is to translate it as "man." Nevertheless, this practice is not without difficulties—logical as well as moral and political in character—which Ortega himself took on, let alone those which often enough result in stylistic clashes and awkwardness, for which the author is certainly not responsible. Here I will confine myself to a brief consideration of the logical problems involved, which, in my opinion, are ultimately or philosophically the most important and, in fact, the grounds or sources of the rest. Ortega brought them up when he spoke of the rationalistic interpretation of abstraction that consists in thinking of a reality, as he put it, by "bearing in mind the least [common denominator]," which is just what is being done when one ignores, as in the case in point, the necessary fact that the "species [in the logical sense of the term]—and the species is that which is concrete and real—reacts on the genus and specifies it."[260] When this happens, a failure in cognitive thinking occurs, if indeed its essential purpose is the certain grasp of the truth, or of the reality under consideration, in its *essential* plenitude, which in this case, where such a prescription goes unobserved, has led to the faulty "hypothesis of the abstraction 'human being.'"[261]

Last but not least, I would like to avail myself of these concluding remarks to thank my wife, Dr. Sara F. García-Gómez, who, as in previous occasions, has read and revised the results of my work as a translator and has provided numerous and invaluable suggestions, very often redounding to the improvement of the clarity and accuracy of the final product.

# Spanish Editor's Note*

## Paulino Garagorri

In the daily *El Sol [The Sun]*, Ortega published a series of articles entitled "What Is Knowledge? (Excerpts from a Course)." They appeared on January 18 and 25, February 1 and 22, and March 1, 1931. To date they have never been reprinted, except in the journal *Humanitas*,[1] but are now, for the first time, making their appearance in book form in this new volume of the collection, "Works of José Ortega y Gasset."[2] They are presently being brought out as part of the entire course—as yet unpublished—from which they had been taken, at points which I will specify later [by means of footnotes]. But in this new book, belonging to his posthumous work, I also include the text—unpublished as well—of two other courses, one given before and another afterward. I chose to do that because they are interrelated, even though this is so, to some extent, by chance. I have adopted *What Is Knowledge?* as the title for the new book, not only because it was the one already employed by the author [for his series of articles], but also by virtue of the fact that it is suitable for the totality of its contents.

As is known, the closing of the University of Madrid forced Ortega to continue his 1928–1929 public course, *What Is Philosophy?*[3] "in the profane precinct of a theatre."[4] However, the period during which the university was closed proved long, and Ortega was determined not to have his

---

*In his concluding remark to this Note, the Spanish editor stated that "[a]ny contribution for which the editor, not the author, is responsible will appear in brackets." In the text, I have omitted this sentence because, in order to avoid confusion, I decided not to abide by his practice; instead, I have employed footnotes clearly identified as belonging to the Spanish editor. By contrast, those which are of my own making will not be labelled at all, unless they appear to give rise to some misunderstanding. Accordingly, any brackets will indicate my own additions.

teaching activities interrupted. This led him to resume his classes in the following academic year (1929–1930); he did so before a small audience in December, 1929 at the locale of *Revista de Occidente,* the journal and publishing house he directed. The text of the course appears in Part I of this book, to which, given its subject, I am assigning the title, "Life as Performance (Performative Being)."

The reopening of the university allowed Ortega to resume his classes there at the beginning of April, 1930. In that venue, he made the announcement that he would be offering a mini-course—it was, of necessity, to be brief—that would be called, "Concerning Radical Reality."[5] Its text is found in Part II of this book.

The subsequent (or 1930–1931) course was entitled, it seems, "What Is Life?," and its text is to be found—split [in two]—in Parts III and IV of this book.

For the benefit of the reader, let me reiterate what I said at the beginning of my edition of Ortega's 1932–1933 course, *Some Lessons in Metaphysics,* to wit: that what is here transcribed are the notes he usually drafted for himself in preparation for his courses.[6] [Let me point out that] the scattered condition in which the manuscripts for this book were found has forced me to engage in the laborious effort to bring order to them. I trust that, in the end, this endeavor of mine has met with reasonable success. It is true that the text is abbreviated here and there, but, for the most part, its composition is finished and the exposition complete.

As to the intellectual significance of this new book by Ortega, I believe that, when considered in terms of his entire philosophical work, it is destined to be one of the most important parts of his legacy. His fashioning of new concepts, the inner "road" of his very innovations, and the (inapparent) construction of the method by which he arrives at them are set forth in these courses with dramatic acuity. The presentation of one of Ortega's unpublished books is not, however, the proper place to advance judgments or to impose them on the reader, who should come to them on his own without pre-judgments.

# PART I

# LIFE AS PERFORMANCE
## (Performative Being)

# Problems*

1. Who is the subject of life?, i.e., who am I, Mr. So and So?

2. What is the meaning of the possessive word "my" in [expressions like] *my* body, *my* soul, *my* book, *my* things, and so on? [Where is] the line of demarcation between that which is mine and that which is not?

3. Why is it incongruous to place life—a life—in the world? Because the world in question belongs to my life, because it is the performative *[ejecutivo]* or absolute[1] world for me, while it is nothing of the sort for a life impervious to my world, for a life which, in no sense, is *found therein*.

4. The error or insufficiency of every form of idealism consists in proceeding on the basis of the [would-be fact that] the mind or consciousness reflects itself, on the grounds of *Selbstbewusstsein* [self-consciousness]. But there is no such thing as *Selbstbewusstsein*. An act performed by reflecting consciousness is not itself reflected; it is always other [than what is being reflected upon]. Therefore, there is neither an act of reflection properly so called nor anything like *one's self [sí mismo]*[2] either. Like anything that engages in objectivation, *Bewusstsein* [consciousness] severs itself from its object, whether the object in question is itself or something else. True "self-reflection" is given only in life. It is odd, indeed, that it be *possible* for the mind to reflect itself—a fact (?) on the basis of which phenomenology proceeds—and yet for it not to *have* to reflect itself, not to consist in doing so. Life is essentially self-reflection, and yet reflection is not just intellectual in nature; rather, it is, more generally, [life's] way of affecting itself. A belief, or a believing, not only succeeds in regarding itself, but in *believing*[3] itself as well.

5. Phenomenology leaves out of consideration the performative character of an act, which is precisely what renders it a living act, rather than a

---

*Ed.'s N: The set of notes bearing the title "Problems" seems [to have been] an exercise in reflection to be done before the course.

mere act (or fact). This is our novel theme: the performative character of every act.

6. Life is valid for itself—it is definitive, it is that which is definitive. It is the radical[4] "reality" not just *for* philosophy; rather, it consists in being the absolute standpoint, since everything in it is absolute. *That which* someone else believes is for me something relative to him or her, but what I believe is absolute. If I were to apply as well to myself the relative character I attribute to my neighbor['s life], I would thereby relinquish a vantage point that is living or vital;[5] I would be turning my back on it and see everything as a *fact*,[6] not as a performative finality. However, what I must do is the opposite: I must see my neighbor as an operative subject, that is to say, as I would see myself if I did not objectivate myself—in other words, [as I see myself] when I do not objectivate myself, when I live. Therefore, life is absolute always, and not just when or because it is *mine*. In ratiovitalism,[7] I propound, over against any form of idealism, that the ego is not possessed of theoretical privilege of any kind.

7. Life is absolute positing *[posición]*. However, this must not be construed as if the absolute positing of life were a philosophical outcome. If that were the case, as any fact or *positum*[8] considered as such, it would be relative. A fact or *positum* can be radical at best, never absolute. Life is absolute positing, and it is so not from a philosophical [point of view], but in itself, by nature. This character originates in the fact that life is performative and definitive for itself or in itself. If we make our way into life on the basis of that character, which is the one most evident to us, and seek to determine why life is absolute, we will discover that it is so because it is always *unique:* it is being, or what the unique one is. Now, the being of the unique one is having to be unique, having of absolute necessity to refer to itself (and to refer everything to itself); it is operative unicity *(werktätige Einzigkeit)*.

[However,] the unique one is not the same as the *only one*, for there may be an infinite number of unique ones, each and every one of them being no less unique than the next.[9] Yet, by the same token, the unicity of life renders it impervious, non-communicating, and exclusive. By virtue of its uniqueness, *my* life cannot—none of its parts can—belong to you or to anybody else. By reason of its uniqueness, it is altogether different from any other thing and any other life. My life is one of a kind, and this is true in such a radical sense that its *uniqueness* surpasses God's unicity, inasmuch as the latter is not internal to God but [a determination] grounded in our own reasons. Only insofar as God were living would He be truly unique.

Hence, in ratiovitalism concepts are occasional.[10] Accordingly, all lives are such because, in each one of them, *life* signifies a different reality, even if all their attributes, without exception, were the same. But to acknowledge this would force us to turn around the *principium identitatis indiscernibilium* [principle of the identity of indiscernibles][11] and affirm the opposite, namely, the *principium de discernendo identico* [principle of the discernment of identicals].[12]

This points to the fact that, in ratiovitalism, concepts are indeed transcendent in character, since they themselves indicate how the logical laws having validity for them have no validity for the "real" which they [allow us to] think.

Life's unicity is, therefore, its absoluteness.

Living is having to be unique.

Life's being consists, first of all, in *having to be* and, secondly, in having to be *unique*.

# December 19, 1929

8. I am not certain yet whether life's absolute positing is equivalent to its absolute existence; there is no doubt, however, that the latter is one of the sides of the former. To live is to exist absolutely. But this is not so as in the case of the Cartesian ego which exists *because* it thinks, that is to say, because thought exists;[13] rather, to live is, non-mediately and by itself, to exist. Life, therefore, is endowed with existence in a more radical sense not only than the ego, but even than thought itself in Descartes's system of ideas. It would be possible for thought not to exist because it is an object of mine, but it is not possible for life not to exist because life is not life insofar as it is an object of mine; rather, it is an object to the extent that thought[14] thinks it as being a non-object for me, as being, instead, that which is for itself. Here one can clearly appreciate the novel way of looking at things proper to ratiovitalism. Life is the performative as such; therefore, regarded precisely as life, it is that which exists. It is not possible for the one living not to exist, because it is not possible, for itself, not to exist.

In accordance with our novel point of view or manner of looking at things, an object is defined not as it is for us, insofar as we are engaged in thinking of it, that is to say, as what it is objectively, but rather as what the object is for itself, as the subject of itself. Thus the existence of life does not signify here that it exists for us, but that it exists for and by itself.

But even this formulation proves insufficient, for my thesis is not that life exists for itself because it regards or encounters[15] itself or, therefore, because it turns itself into its own object. To assert that would be to relapse into idealism. Life is not its objective existing for itself, but its active existing for itself. This is, in my judgment, a novel and radical turn of thought, because life is *Being for itself*. This, however, must not be construed as it was in idealism, in which Being = being an object, but rather by taking *Being as Be-ing*, Being as Entity, as entitative Being. One may understand this more clearly when one realizes that the Being of life is a *fashioning*[16] or, better yet, a *self-fashioning*. The self-reflection belonging to everything vital is not intellectual in character or an objectivating sort of reflection, but an efficient, operative one; it is the [act of] *self-fashioning*, of carrying *itself* out, of *self*-performance, of self-endowment of being, of self-subsisting. That is why, strictly speaking, the idea of "positing" [or] "self-positing" is not valid, because in it activity is reduced to positing and [thus] presupposes the posited, as if the latter had a nature of its own apart from its being-posited. (Hence, the confusion and contradiction found in [the notion of] *Sich-selbstdenkende* [the one-thinking-itself-by-itself].)

Life *is for itself* because it is by its own effort; it is that which it makes of itself.[17]

9. Performativeness is the most evident character with which life, this novel reality, appears to us. Of it I say that it is performative in nature, that its being is performative being. Let me explain what I mean by that.

Performativeness is the note most suitable [to describe] something when it is in the nature of an act and is considered as such, that is to say, as carrying itself out, as fulfilling itself, as operative. Now then, [to say] that implies that it is possible to consider an act otherwise, in such a way that its being would not be [given to us as] performance. This other manner of consideration is one in which one does not refer to an act for what it is, *internally,* or as a performance taken *from within,* but rather as it makes its appearance before us, as it is, therefore, for another or from without.[18] Accordingly, when one says of it that it is an act, one is saying something about it which it is not when it is being regarded *internally*. The act of seeing [for example] is not an act for itself; it is not cognizant of that because it is not engaged in reflecting upon itself; it does not see itself as an object or [as it would be] "from without." In order to be clear to each other, let us then speak of the "internality" and "externality" of an act, or of its "internal" and "external" being.

We see then that the concept of performative being is formed in contradistinction to that of objective being, and it must be understood as a function of and in reciprocity with it.

The act of regarding [something] *internally*, or in [terms of] its internal being, does not turn itself into its own object. What is more: *no act is capable of being its own object*. This is the reason why idealism is not cognizant of performative being, since it is based upon reflection, wherein an act is observed from [the standpoint of] another act. [Accordingly,] what is said of it [therein] is *just* that which the act shows of itself in such an alien consideration; the act shows just its external being.

On the other hand, what is the meaning of [speaking of] the *internality* or internal being of an act? Obviously, that which the act would be to an eye internal to it, what it would see if it saw itself.

But suppose that "seeing" is understood as usual or in the sense it normally stands for, namely, as an act of objectivating consciousness. One would then incur contradiction, for the meaning of objectivation, or "consciousness of,"[19] is to stand outside of something and take it as the terminus of an act. The object of a conscious act is precisely that which the act is not; it is, instead, that at which the act terminates.

Performativeness, then, presupposes that an act *is for itself* and yet, at the same time, that this *being for me* does not signify the same as objectivation, or the consciousness properly so called that the act would have of itself.

*Being for itself*[20] is a category belonging to idealism, the one defining thought in its ultimate ontological peculiarity. Thought was presented as the only object for which to be an object is sufficient to be absolutely or to be real (= being *for* itself or *in* itself). It is odd indeed [to believe] that this feature of thought is not constitutive of it, even though it is so decisive for it and endows it with its ontological rank, but rather [to contend] that it must be *possible* for the "I think" to accompany all my representations,[21] that is to say, that it must only be possible for it to do so. Reflection or self-consciousness is a possibility for thought, but it is not constitutive of it.

In idealism, apart from that strange situation, it is presupposed that thought or "consciousness" is peculiar in that, by its very nature, it would be at once *in itself* and *for itself*. Such a peculiarity would be responsible for its being, at once, an object for another and an absolute entity—in fine, for its being [both] performance and object. But it does not seem so; rather, the absolute or performative being of thought or consciousness is—ontologically speaking—neither more nor less distant from itself than anything else. Phenomenology—for which it would be so important to establish that point—only succeeds in showing that there is continuity between the act engaged in reflecting and the act reflected upon, that is to say, that there is continuity between acts belonging to the same "mental stream" or *Bewusstseinsstrom*. Now, the mental stream transcends each act, and every act is at best continuous, but never identical, with another act, even the one immediately next to it. Hence, what is arbitrary about the *being for itself* of thought does not lie in the *being for,* but rather in the *itself.* There could be genuine self-reflection (and thus *one's self [mismidad]*), only if an act reflected itself. But it so happens that it is not so: act *A* is endowed with external being for act *B,* but it is not possessed of internal being *for itself.* One must then subject the idea of "one's self" and "being for itself" to correction.

Either a toothache hurts someone or it is no ache at all. The event of "hurting someone" is a "being for another," and yet it is not so in the way of an object. My ache hurts me but not qua object of my consciousness or *cogitatio;* rather, it is absolutely and in itself as "it is engaged in being for me." Its internal being is in no need of being turned into external being in order to be-for-me. Or equivalently stated: it is for me as engaged in being for itself. But the converse is true as well: its being for me is, at once and identically, being for itself. I may pay attention to it or not; I may observe it, think it, remember it—and all of that will yield to me its "being for me," in the usual sense of objectivation. The ache I am thinking about does not hurt me, [however]; it *is* objectively, but *is* not performatively.

Here we have, then, a presence of being before me which is not of an objective sort, but rather of a straightforwardly entitative kind. Therefore, it is a reflection of the reality "ache" itself, one which is not endowed with the (already special) character of consciousness, but originarily constitutes that very reality. The said reflection is no mere possibility but something inseparable from the real, an indefeasible dimension of it, one that does not come to be superadded to it by my *cogitatio*.

Now then, that which I call "I" is present to me constantly and indefeasibly every moment. This is so much so that it makes me be what I am, that it indefeasibly forms part of my very existence. I am present to myself without having to perceive myself; on the contrary, when I perceive myself, my performative or inner I, my internal being is neither more nor less apparent than when I am not engaged in carrying out an "immanent" or "internal perception." And just as this is true of the "I," so it is too of each and every one of my "acts." And just as it is true of my "acts," so it is too of the entire "world" upon which they are usually directed. (Those "acts," which are thus present to me, are not the "acts" resulting from psychological objectivation, nor is my "I" the psychological one, but rather they are my *living* I and acts.)

Here we are dealing with the strange and unavoidable presence that life in its entirety is endowed with for the one who lives it, the presence in virtue of which only that which is possessed of it is part of my life (and, in consequence, of the real).

If by "me" one understands consciousness properly so called (and, therefore, a particular act thereof), then one may not say that the presence in question is an "act of reflection in me," for the latter does not exist for me. In other words, such a presence is not, in turn, present to me.[22]

That is the reason why one may say that to live or exist is, for me, to do so within a universal presence, the "subject" of which is not me, properly speaking. Rather, both I and the world participate in that presence. Reflection, then, is not in me (= consciousness), but a "reflection in itself" of everything. The reality called *life* is the realm of reflection in itself, wherein everything is "engaged-in-being-for-itself" absolutely. *I* am not the locus in which reflection occurs; rather, I find myself, as a matter of course, immersed therein, as it were, in a medium of light. Life is self-illuminating, and everything in it is possessed of self-illumination, of self-luminosity.

# The 1929–1930 Course*

~

## First Day

We are going to do philosophy. [To that end,] the plentifulness of the "past" has its drawbacks. What others have thought they embodied in formulae that weigh upon us. Accordingly, in what I said before, the word "philosophy," summarizing as it does a long past, does not prove helpful but rather leads us astray. Now, *our* task is this: to do philosophy. The word in question, however, does not incite us to do it ourselves, but to go instead in search of what others have thought under that name.

[There is] a way of avoiding that. For us, "philosophy" does not refer to what *has been*. Rather, it is a term for a virginal task we are to discharge. We are going to assign the name philosophy to an occupation of ours; later there will be an opportunity to determine whether or not that occupation is coincident with others which before have borne the same name.

One may ask the question, what is this? say, about a headache or a storm. In the corresponding attitude or state, we find ourselves postulating, seeking after another state, which may be given expression by saying, "it is such and such." The prior state is balanced by the subsequent one, [for in it] we find rest, tranquillity. That which soothes us we call "truth," i.e., a mental state or situation fixed and sufficient, characterized by bringing restlessness and endeavor to term, and marked, therefore, by the exclusion of a return to restlessness. A "problem" is restlessness. In biological parlance, we would say that the truth is that which regulates an organism (and, consequently, an imbalance internal to it).

Now then, there are two kinds of rest and, therefore, of "truth," to wit: thoroughgoing restfulness and the restfulness of resignation.

*The Spanish editor added this title and the designation "first day."

To seek after the truth concerning something leads one to seek the truth about everything else.

I make my departure in search of a problem, and this one poses other problems to me. The series comprised of problems is continuous, uninterrupted.

If I stop, it is not because I have achieved rest, but because I am unable to reach it. [This would be] resignation.

[The condition of] "being unable to" is of two sorts: one that is a matter of fact and another which is a matter [well-]founded or *de jure*.

If the latter is the case, then my departure in search of the truth, as well as the urge motivating it, is altogether satisfied when I find a truth such that it makes no sense to continue the search. [This would be] a well-founded manner of resignation or interruption.

[Let us recapitulate our] results: Anyone in search of the truth about something is obligated—in principle, before him- or herself—to seek the truth about everything. Or, to put it otherwise: a truth implies all others.

Searching for the truth is called "science" or "knowledge."

A science does not deserve to be called a science, to the extent that its [consideration of] problems is arbitrarily interrupted.

Every particular science presupposes [the existence of] further problems. [It is possible to distinguish between] the truth proper to each science and truth in the full sense of the word. In physics, the locution *truth* refers to the fact that the predictions made about the operation of its instruments are fulfilled. This is the [sort of] rest achieved in it.

But that is a conventional way of resting [one's case], resulting as it does from the fact that an entire series of problems has been relinquished. [It is said: there is] only one field. But how does such a field arise? Why? What for? Moreover, what is the sense of calling it the truth? What grounds are there to justify the pliability of instruments to predictions?

Physics is not true if it is just physics. For it to be true, it has to ground its proper truth in the fullness of the truth.

Every particular science is in search of truths proper to itself, of arbitrary [points of] rest, but it implies a search for the fullness of truth, for a well-founded rest.

To seek after truth in the full sense of the word, that is to say, to seek after the conditions [it is to fulfill]—that is what philosophy is. To do so is to seek after rest by meeting all its requirements. The only truth deserving the name derives from[1] accepting problems without the prior delimitation [thereof] and the elimination [of some]. It is not known whether a truth like that is possible.

[In seeking after the truth in the full sense of the word,] one does not begin with method, as is done in physics (i.e., with the measurable), but with what is problematic.

[To propound] exactitude and sense-perceptual confirmation as attributes of the truth is arbitrary.

A truth, taken in the full sense of the word, is one which presupposes no other truths; it is one presupposed by all other truths.

Now we can refer to history in order to simplify matters. In the past, the two great positions [have been]:

1. *Realism* [or the doctrine in which the thesis that] *some thing* (or extra-mental item) exists is acknowledged as the first truth. There is nothing that is not problematic. [But such a thesis is] impossible, for it cancels itself qua first truth. If anything extra-mental exists, a mind also exists which thinks of it and exists outside of and in relation to it.

2. Hence, [the doctrine of] *idealism,* to wit: the truth that something extra-mental exists, if indeed it is a truth, presupposes another truth, which is prior and more certain, namely, that a mind, a subject thinking it, exists. [The existence of] mind, spirit, or *cogitatio* is more certain than [that of things]. I can doubt that . . . [things exist], but I cannot doubt that thought exists, because to doubt is to think.[2]

The most favorable interpretation [of idealism is as follows]. Thought, consciousness, or subjectivity exists. [The status of] the table apart from me is doubtful, but not [that of] my seeing it. My seeing exists. I beg to disagree: it is not just that the real table is other than my act of seeing it, but as well that the table seen [by me] is other than what is mine in my seeing [of it]. Let it not be said, then, that [just] a seeing subject exists, but also that a seen object exists.

Seeing does not posit existence, but co-existence.

# Second Day*

Anything one may decidedly characterize as an error or substantial deviation in philosophy, and [thus] as the origin of its periods of decadence, amounts not so much to [the existence of] internal doctrinal differences as it does to something prior, namely, to being oblivious or ignorant of what philosophy qua intellectual occupation is.

Every human action (and every intellectual action, as one of its spe-

*Added by the Spanish editor.

cies) is determinate. Or equivalently put: it is one among many which are possible. If we carry out a given intellectual action (say, if we think a proposition), we do so in view of a determinate purpose, of an objective we intend. Every proposition is born, then, according to a determinate mental direction which excludes all others. To say it otherwise: the sense of every proposition has a vectorial dimension. If the one listening to me, or reading what I write, is not cognizant of my goal, he will be oblivious to it and, in consequence, unable to understand the sense of my proposition.

Now then, a proposition does not usually render manifest the goal serving to guide it, that is to say, the ultimate intention of the one thinking it. The ultimate intuition[3] in question lies behind the proposition. It is the ground on the basis of which it is thought.

The first proposition of any science thus presupposes the general intention of the science in question. (For example, mathematics speaks of numbers, while a practical man speaks of numbered things, [and this provokes] a misunderstanding of the mathematician on the part of the latter. The same obtains in art: every work of art is made from the standpoint of a given convention or intentional presupposition.)

Some conventions or presupposed intentions are sometimes known to everyone; they are, so to speak, in the air, but others are not.

Physics was not understood in the Middle Ages. [There were] those who wanted to "save the phenomena."[4] [Consider] the reverse: since 1850 the "intention" constitutive of philosophy begins to disappear from the "air," to become arcane. (Please note that I am not referring here at all to internal doctrinal differences among philosophies.)

What is proper to philosophy qua intellectual project has never been more mindfully and clearly seen than among the post-Kantians. This is the reason for the special nature of their works, which were the most properly philosophical in character ever produced.[5] But, by the same token, nobody [could] understand Hegel twenty years after his death, and to this day his writings, as well as those of Fichte and Schelling, have proven hard to decipher.

It is, then, no vague assessment of mine to assert at this point that, for the first time in precisely a century, philosophy is truly making a beginning again. Once more have our eyes become accommodated to philosophical vision, to its presupposition and genuine intention.

As we had the occasion of seeing the other day,[6] an intention of that sort is the simplest of all. It is just our being ready for boundless curiosity. Curiosity is the [state of the] mind [when it] shapes itself as a question mark. It is [itself] the question. [The formulation of] any specific question in the form "what is this?" would lead me—if I do not violently cut its unfolding short—to the posing of a question universal and ultimate in content. Physics—and, like it, any other particular science—comes to be constituted by means of a restriction in the exercise of theoretical curiosity, that is to say, by virtue of the conscious, deliberate relinquishment of countless questions and problems, by keeping to the delimited realm of the questions which are defined in terms of measurability.

Now then, a question formed as the result of excluding other questions is, obviously, less simple than an unbounded question. Taken in this sense (and we shall see in subsequent days in what other and more profound and essential senses as well), philosophy is a more natural intellectual occupation or activity than any particular science. This notwithstanding, today philosophy indeed is the least natural, the most unusual of intellectual activities. [The examination of this] weighty subject would lead us to discover the very tragedy of culture and civilization. Readymade and established cultures and civilizations are received and imposed as pseudo-natures.

What, then, is philosophy as the project of an intellectual occupation? Every question is tantamount to being aware of a problem.

But every question which is in the nature of a problem leads us, in unbroken continuity, to an infinity of problems or, equivalently, to the awareness that everything is problematic. The admonition that there is nothing which of itself is unproblematic—that there is no firm ground, therefore, upon which to stand—makes us feel vitally lost, makes us fall into an abyss consisting of problems.[7] This is the state of mind out of which philosophy is born. Now, we do not conduct ourselves as philosophers to the extent that something presents itself to us as unproblematic, as firm, that is to say, as *incontrovertible*. Such a thing would be a matter of *faith*. In other words, it would be a conviction a human being finds in himself exhibiting an automatic character proper to it as such, namely, its being uncontroverted and incontrovertible.[8] A physicist who takes for granted the truth of physics without allowing for its controvertible or problematic character is not a practitioner of theory, but someone who has faith in physics, a believer. Except for the radical theoretician or philosopher and the believer, there are no two other kinds of human being that resemble each other more and are, nonetheless, in greater opposition to one another. Both are, vitally speaking, "radical," aboriginal, and non-floating (i.e., not *deracinés* [uprooted]).

When human beings feel theoretically at a loss, and find nothing upon which to stand, an instinctive movement in the opposite direction takes place in their minds, namely, one by means of which they seek after something they can hold on to. But that is what philosophy is—a soaring by means of which someone, sensing him- or herself falling, tries to counter-act the event. It is an effort to build for oneself, to find in the void, some-thing solid upon which to stand.

Since every question is [the equivalent of] the admonition that each and every thing is problematic, one could pose the opposite question, that is to say, that which would be tantamount to the creation of an "artificial" problem, to wit: what must something be like for it not to be problematic?

[Consider] the perspective encompassing that which is problematic and that which appears as "certain" or "earnest" in spontaneous life. How does spontaneous life, having arrived "in earnest" at the "earnest" or "certain," come to discover that it is not so? [One finds] a different per-spective and sense of rank in theoretical reconstruction—the "ridiculous-ness" of philosophy. ([From] Parmenides to the young Socrates.)

The unproblematic or the truth—*àlétheia:* this is the name given to the first philosophies.[9]

The unproblematic will have to be an ultimate and comprehensive truth:[10] it will have to be ultimate, that is to say, a truth that does not re-quire or presuppose any other in order to be a truth itself, and it will have to be comprehensive, that is to say, a truth the value of which—vis-à-vis and in conjunction with any other truth—is not left indeterminate. If it is true that there are numbers and that there are dogs as well, then the fact that there are numbers—i.e., the there-being or existence of numbers—is left indeterminate vis-à-vis and in conjunction with that of dogs. No one knows which of these two modalities of being—so different from one an-other—is fundamental in respect of the other. In brief: a truth is ultimate which does not implicate or presuppose another,[11] and a truth is compre-hensive which is definitively true vis-à-vis each and every other possible truth (a condition that may be fulfilled only if every other possible truth implicates or presupposes it). The first truth brings [us] salvation but at once imprisons [us], by virtue of the fact that it is the *matter* out of which one must fashion everything else.

Implicative thinking [is of two sorts]:

A. Analytic (or by way of division), [and]
B. Synthetic (or by way of composition)—synthetic implication or com-plication.[12]

The thesis that "cosmic reality exists" (or that things or the world do) co-implicates[13] another proposition which is at least of equal rank, namely, the proposition in question taken as such, that is to say, as a thought.[14] Therefore, the said thesis requires [us to accept] the conjoint one.

Thought exists:

Figure 1

This duality requires that the relation between the two—the world and thought—be determined. It is discovered, soon enough, that they are not co-ordinate; it is found, instead, that thought is a priori with regard to the world. The world—of which I say, "it exists"—is that which I think; indeed, the attribution of existence is likewise a thought.[15]

The *realist* thesis, therefore, becomes subordinate to the idealist thesis. Or equivalently stated: it is necessary to derive the existence of the world from the existence of thought.

The *idealist* thesis is simpler, not more complex, than the realist thesis, which, in the final analysis, adds thought to the world. Idealism does nothing but subtract the thesis of the *world* as something unnecessary. And, in so doing, it thinks that the existence of thought does not imply that of the world.

The idealist thesis seems to be exemplary qua ultimate and comprehensive truth, for it seems to imply only the thought by means of which one thinks it. And yet the thought in which I think the existence of thought is already part and parcel of the thesis in question.

# Third Day
## (Tuesday, January 28, 1930)

Let me continue by summarizing what I said the last day.

The admonition that every problem found by us is itself encompassed by other problems, while these, in turn, are encompassed by an ever wider sphere of problems, has the effect of producing in us the awareness that everything is problematic. Or equivalently stated: that there is no actual belief at all which is ultimately firm. Consequently, we find ourselves at a loss in a void of theoretical certainty. The latter—I contended—is the state of mind out of which philosophy is born. No one is a philosopher who does not feel that he is, from the standpoint of theory, absolutely lost. This will later surface again, but in a more profound and, at the same time, more specific sense.

Now, the awareness that one is falling and becoming lost in an absolute abyss of uncertainty automatically induces in the mind a movement in the opposite direction, one marked by the greatest intellectual activity. To fall and become lost is a passive condition. To become lost absolutely in the midst of absolute theoretical uncertainty—i.e., not to *find* anything firm—is responsible precisely for provoking in us a manner of theoretical activity which is absolute. These two mental modalities are reciprocal, and their equation could be formulated as follows: the height [reached] in positive theorization, or the [degree of] firmness of the truth arrived at by each person, is a function of the depth of the lack of firmness, or uncertainty, into which one has fallen. Or to put it otherwise: each one knows as much as he has doubted.

As for myself, I will admit to you that the first and most decisive impression I get of every intellectual person I meet is that of the profile or range of his or her doubt. What he or she *apparently* "knows" is of no significance to me because I know it is pseudo-knowledge; I measure the narrowness or breadth of his or her wit by the scope of his or her capacity to doubt and feel at a loss.

Now then, the maximal theoretical activity sets itself moving as one suddenly proceeds from the mere realization that each and every thing is problematic to the *creation* of a new problem *for oneself*, a problem that is not given as those problems were, for it is artificial or instrumental, in fine, something fashioned by the mind. And that problem is as follows: how must a proposition be for it not to be problematic, for it, therefore, to be absolutely true?

Some of the conditions to be met suggest themselves at once to the mind. First of all, if a proposition is to be firm, it will not require the support of another; rather, it will be necessary of itself, it will be self-substantiating; in short, its eventual truth will not depend on any proposition except itself. Secondly, every other true proposition will depend on it, that is to say, every other proposition will implicate it. We may give expression to these two conditions [in combination] by saying that an absolute or altogether firm truth is to be ultimate and comprehensive in character.

When a mind finds a proposition that fulfills these two requirements, it ceases to fall into the void of absolute uncertainty; it absolutely is in its own depth, that is to say, it attains salvation by way of theory. This is the state of intellectual bliss or happiness. Most human beings—even those who are religious "believers"—are intellectually unhappy. When their occupation and vocation are also intellectual in nature, such unhappiness points to a sense of ultimate and radical failure, which only with great difficulty does not turn into resentment. That is why the latter is a chronic condition among persons of an intellectual sort, and not the result of empirical reasons pertaining to their character.

Among intellectuals, only the philosopher is happy, because he is the only one who is certain or abides by what is firm. All others live in the painful awareness that, as intellectuals, they live like sleepwalkers.[16]

But those two conditions that a fundamental truth is to fulfill, as well as the said advantage, are responsible for producing a result that may appear to be a disadvantage. Once a philosopher has attained his salvation[17] in the truth as if he had reached a small island, he would have to "stick obstinately" to it and lead there the life of a consummate Robinson [Crusoe]. This would be so because a truth of that sort cannot suffer to share its rank with other ideas. He or she would have now to go in search of all other truths about the countless problems in which he or she had lost his or her way, and do so on the basis of the fundamental truth, the only one in his or her possession that is absolutely firm. Every further truth will implicate the fundamental one and only the fundamental one; therefore, it has to be fashioned out of *matter* belonging to it.[18] To put it differently: philosophy would take on the obligation of developing in a strictly systematic fashion, inasmuch as it goes in search of an ultimate and comprehensive truth and proceeds on its basis. We will soon consider examples of that.

Implication [is of two sorts]:

A. Analytic (or by way of division), [and]

B. Systematic (or by way of composition) or co-implicative.[19]

I will call "truth" any proposition that fulfills the conditions specified above; in other words, a proposition which in our estimation is absolutely firm. Here "truth" signifies, then, that one "holds something as firm." But this formula cannot be interpreted psychologistically,[20] for, even though "firm" is employed here to refer to a firmness capable of withstanding every criticism or counterproof and is thus a subjective state of firmness or certainty, it is [nonetheless] one which lives precisely on the objective firmness of the proposition. Or expressed otherwise: we do not say that something is true *because* we subjectively hold it as firm, but the other way round: we hold it as firm *because* we believe we are seeing the grounds for its firmness.

I have said this not because it is of relevance to what I am about to say, but in order to avoid straying on that path, which would be a sheer waste.

It is evident that not every conviction, or subjective state of belief, is such that one is therein convinced of, or believes in, what is objectively true. It is [likewise] evident that every full, objective truth is given as constitutively encased in a subjective conviction or belief.

Let *thesis* be the name for [the act in which one] holds a specific proposition as firm.

As we sense that we are losing our footing in the realm of the absolutely problematic, an opposite movement stirs in us [by virtue of which] we go in search of what is firm. *Skepsis* means to be lost in doubt, and *thesis* to shed one's doubts, to encounter what is firm.

What *thesis* will save us from the absolutely problematic?

First of all, we attempt to hold on to what is in our surroundings and say: the world, cosmic reality, exists. This is the realist thesis.

But neither is this proposition sufficiently ultimate nor can it stand by itself or be comprehensive, because it implicates at least one other thing, to wit: itself taken as a proposition, as a thought or mental act. When I have affirmed that "the world exists" and inquire whether in effect everything I may surmise to exist is implicated therein, I discover, soon enough, that not only does the world exist, but so does my thinking of it too.

For the proposition "the world exists" to be true, it is necessary that it be constantly given in conjunction with another proposition, namely, "thought exists,"[21] which is the other side of the coin. Here, then, we are dealing with the essential co-implication of two truths.

Such a duality imposes on us the obligation of determining the nature of the relationship between those two "things" (i.e., world and thought). Therefore, the realist thesis, far from being unproblematic, poses a problem for us, viz., whether thought is a part of the world or lies outside it (or, rather, envelops it). We soon come to the realization that neither the former alternative nor the latter is admissible, and that there is no doubt, once the question is formulated in that fashion, that the thing called thought encompasses, somehow essentially, the thing called world. The world of which I say that "it exists" is the one of which I think as the world, the attribution of "existence" being a thought as well.

The realist thesis is thus subordinate to the idealist thesis. Or to put it equivalently: one must derive the existence of the world—which is secondary—from the primary existence of thought.

Judged by its contents, the idealist thesis is simpler than the realist thesis, for the latter, when all is said and done, means that thought is being added to the world. Idealism just subtracts the unnecessary portion (i.e., the world) and leaves the rest (i.e., thought) intact, by reason of its belief that the existence of thought does not imply that of the world, while the existence of the latter, on the contrary, implies that of the former.

In passing, please note how idealism is nothing but the realist thesis itself, once the portion of it called "world" has been subtracted. In saying this, I am anticipating something we will only see clearly on another ocassion, namely, that the so-called idealism is nothing but the *realism of thought*.

But can we attain salvation by means of the idealist thesis?

In fact, it seems that its truth value is that of an exemplary truth, i.e., of one which is intrinsic [ultimate?] and comprehensive, for the only thing that seems to be implicated by the proposition "thought exists" is the act of thinking by means of which one thinks it, and it is evident that such an act is already part and parcel of the thesis in question and adds nothing new to it.

The idealist thesis is unquestionably the firmest one known thus far.

But is it the case that it implicates nothing else? Is it the case that the thesis that "thought exists" implicates nothing but the existence of the act of thinking it?

In order to answer this question, we must come to a clear understanding of the nature of what we call thought.

The [consideration of a] difficult matter is about to begin for every one of us.

We may be seeing this room, for example; or, again, we may be thinking of the Himalayas. Any one of the two is called a *cogitatio* or thought, in the broad sense of the word.

Now then, when we are engaged in seeing the room, we are not engaged in seeing our seeing of it. In the thought "seeing the room," nothing is found but the room, which, by itself or in itself, is no thought.[22] But if we close our eyes the room ceases to be; therefore, the room is not what it is by itself but [only] in conjunction with our eyes. If there are no eyes, there is no room. But apparently what is important is not our being dependent on the eyes, but the fact that, if we were to entertain the thought that nobody were here, that no one, no subject, were to—or could—be found [here], then the room would not be, i.e., would not be what it is. By contrast, if a subject, finding him- or herself in Peking, were to see this room, it would be because he or she is hallucinating. In other words, for a room to exist it is not necessary that it exist for itself or in itself; rather, it is sufficient that a subject exist. This leads us to affirm that the reality of the room does not reside in it, and that it is not, *in the final analysis,* identical with the room; but that the final quality of such a reality is, instead, what we call "subject," for lack of a better word. We call "appearance" any reality which, despite being a reality, is not a reality in the final analysis. In effect, this is true because it is the [sort of] reality which consists in really *appearing* to be what it is, without however being so [in fact]. Appearance is a way of being something, though not in itself but in a subject to whom it appears or seems to be so.

Therefore, a subject and "someone to whom something appears" are one and the same thing. Now, given that a subject of this sort would not be either except for its capacity to make its appearance before itself, we find that every reality is reduced, ultimately and finally, to the reality referred to as "appearing." This is what we call "thought."

At this point, we can define thought more strictly by means of a formula which, as a formula, is altogether novel, to wit: thought is that entity which always *seems* to be something other than itself, but which is endowed with the capacity to *look like itself,* though subject to that condition.[23]

This is the precise definition of thought I would propose; however, because of its difficult character and the fact that it is unnecessary for what we are about to do, let us look for a clearer one.

Something is a thought when that which does not seem to be the thought is, truly and ultimately, nothing but the thought.

Idealism is the philosophical doctrine which affirms that only thought is possessed of ultimate existence or quality, and which is committed to showing that everything that does not seem to be thought is just thought.

Equipped in this fashion, let us once more raise the question as to whether or not the thesis "only thought exists" *implicates* any other existence that is irreducible to thought and *prior* to it.

In effect, the thesis "thought exists," as any other thesis, implicates the existence of a "thesis." A thesis as you will remember[24] is [the act by which one] "holds a given proposition as firm," believes in it, or is convinced of it.

*Thesis* "signifies"[25] a firm or full position [or positing]; *hypothesis* is a feigned or non-firm position [or positing]; "antithesis" a counter-position [or counter-positing]; *synthesis* a combined position, com-position [or com-positing]; and "prothesis" a pro-position, or content offered or presented for a possible thesis, position, [or positing].

However, the Spanish word *posición* has lost its active sense [of positing] in living speech. Why? The causes [responsible for it] are more serious than one might suspect. Spanish is incapable of taking cognizance of the fact that every being or thing—therefore, that everything static and inert—presupposes a prior *action,* that every matter presupposes a *dúnamis* [or power], that every fact presupposes a *fashioning.*[26] In view of this, instead of *thesis* I will speak of *conviction,* a word that has preserved more of an active significance [in Spanish], though not too much—a Spaniard does not *change* his convictions; they are final and inert states, quasi-things.

The one who says "thought exists," and means it as true, is convinced of the fact; that is to say, to him or her thought exists absolutely.

The idealist thesis—no more and no less than any other—necessarily implicates another, to wit: that *a thesis or conviction exists.*

By that I mean to say that if the reality or thing called "thought" is of a sort, nature, or structure other than that of cosmic or bodily reality, then what I call "conviction" is a reality radically different from "thought" by virtue of its nature or structure.

Now, the idealist would say in reply to us that a conviction is nothing but thought—that is to say, that we find ourselves in the same situation as that in which a realist was when he or she was constrained to add the existence of thought to that of the world. But that served as the occasion to establish a contrast between thought and world, for the purposes of identifying the manner of their relationship and determining which of them contained the other.[27]

Yet there is a difference, [since,] for better or for worse, all of us were cognizant of the nature of the "world" or "cosmic reality," on the one hand, and of that of thought, on the other, while on this occasion you are cognizant of the nature of thought, but not of that of *conviction*. Here lies precisely the *radical* innovation [I am proposing] in relation to no less than the entire philosophical past.

Fortunately, we have to carry out one and the same task to see what novel measure of reality there is to a conviction, on the one hand, and to contrast my thesis with that of idealism, so as to be able to overcome it once and for all, on the other. I say "once and for all," for, in so doing, not only would we overcome idealism but also realism, its opposite, at the same time. In other words, we would thereby avoid and transcend the disjunction "realism or idealism." Moreover, you will be able to appreciate the commonplace simplicity [with which it is brought about].

Imagine that [I am] in a situation that would prove most favorable to idealism. Say that I, Ortega, see an ichthyosaurus before me. My conviction is that there is such a thing before me. This is the conviction we are going to subject to analysis.

However, Fabre, an idealist, asserts that I am suffering a hallucination, that there is no ichthyosaurus there, that there is only one of Ortega's thoughts, although, in this case, [he would assert the same thing] even if he were no idealist.

Let us analyze that situation, [which one could call] the *fact Ortega*. In it this is what we find: I am face to face with an ichthyosaurus. There is me and the ichthyosaurus, as well as the world enveloping us both. ([But] now disregard the world, which is irrelevant, [for] one could equally have said that there is a world within which there is an ichthyosaurus before me.) The conviction in question contains my existence and that of the ichthyosaurus, both existences taken absolutely. I am absolutely convinced that I exist and that the ichthyosaurus does too, neither more nor less in either case. Don't ask me *why:* it is of no consequence; there is not even a need for a why. The question at hand is not whether the said conviction is [well-]grounded or not; the example of the ichthyosaurus is a symbol of that, and it has been chosen to underscore it. But, be that as it may, we are dealing with a conviction, and what is of concern to us now is this: to grasp that which is at work within it.

To reiterate it: in the conviction [under scrutiny] I and the ichthyosaurus exist absolutely. In it I find no thought whatever; there is nothing but the absolute existence of the ichthyosaurus and my absolute existence.

This "I"—the one that is afraid of the ichthyosaurus and runs away from it—is not the "I" [spoken of] in idealism and [playing a role] in knowledge; it is not the "I" that is engaged just in thinking and knowing, but the one made of flesh and blood and many other materials, the "one that my friends usually call" Ortega. It is the "I" that a savage or the man in the street would refer to. The nature of such an "I," its precise definition, would be the outcome of hard work on our part, and yet in my conviction the question is not about defining myself, but about coming to a simple and absolute encounter with *myself,* or to encounter that *I* as it faces the ichthyosaurus. Neither do I *"know" what* the ichthyosaurus, its definition, is, just as the "brag" does not know, in the final analysis, what the bull he is running away from is. He is only certain that what he gives that name to is there, and [that] it holds immediate consequences for him.

Let us now take notice of what is happening according to Fabre. [His is] as much a conviction as is mine, but its contents are different. Strictly speaking, [they are] two convictions [occurring] in succession: the one is negative in quality (namely, that the ichthyosaurus does not exist); the other, the one that matters to us, is positive in quality (to wit: that Ortega's thought exists or, equivalently, that the ichthyosaurus thought about exists).

Permit me to simplify matters. Ortega's conviction is that the ichthyosaurus is real ($I^R$),[28] while Fabre's is that the ichthyosaurus is one of Ortega's thoughts ($I^T$).[29]

[Let *F, O, I, R,* and *T* stand for Fabre, Ortega, the ichthyosaurus, reality, and thought, respectively.] What exists for *F* is not $I^R$ but *O* . . . who is thinking *I,* or *I* as thought by *O,* i.e., $I^T$. How is it possible for such a substantial change to have taken place? It is very simple. *I* is $I^R$ as seen from *O,* that is to say, as seen in light of *O*'s conviction insofar as the latter is at work as such, or insofar as it is being performed by me. When I perform something, I say that I "live it." By contrast, *F* does not perform or live my conviction; rather, what he does is as different from that as it can be, namely, he contemplates it or turns it into his object. And so it happens that both *O* and *F* are right: *I* exists absolutely for me who is living the said conviction; *I* does not exist as *R* but absolutely as *T* for *F*; *F* also lives his conviction performatively, the object of which is my conviction, but, inasmuch as the latter is [for him] only an object, he regards, assesses, and qualifies it, that is to say, he objectivates it as *T*. But that my *T* exists is also an absolute positing for him.

([Now consider] the case that later *F* comes to think that my *T*, in turn, is nothing but a *T* of his own. There you have the idealistic thesis. That, however, is another conviction which, though possessed of a different content, is just as much a conviction as the former.)

We thus arrive at an observation of the greatest importance: that performativeness is a standpoint—let me call it that at this juncture—altogether different from objectivation. For us to objectivate something, or to see it as an object, we must *not* "see it" performatively.

At this point, let us set aside the fact that this twofold employment of the word "see" is troublesome; later you will be able to appreciate what exceptional novelty lies behind such a use.

That notwithstanding, how is it that you have understood at some point what *I* was for me, if *I* only is $I^R$ when I performatively live my conviction? It is very simple: because, instead of being content with an act of mere contemplation (i.e., one by means of which you would look at something from your own respective standpoints), you availed yourselves of a fictive or complex modality of contemplation, [a characterization in which] the word "fictive" is not to be taken pejoratively. In other words, instead of seeing what you are seeing, viz., that there is no *I*, you have feigned the abandonment of your standpoints and translated yourselves to mine, that is to say, to the object I am. But since I, like you, am someone who is living, it so happens that the object *Ortega* itself envelops a standpoint, that it *is* [a] standpoint because it is a performer, and performativeness is and implies a standpoint.

(The wall is an object which is standpoint-free; its being is not performative in character. Accordingly, its being is not vital or living, but the being of a thing or matter.)

Let it be clearly understood, then, that a conviction is not a thought. The being of a conviction is, exclusively and yet necessarily, a being *for itself,* not a being for another. *By contrast, a thought is never [a being] for itself.*

What remains for us to do now is to show that, since a conviction is not *T*, it is prior to *T*, that is to say, that *T* implicates it. But it is evident that this follows precisely from what has been said.

# Sixth Day*
## (Tuesday, February 18, 1930)

We have seen how the proposition "the world, cosmos, Nature, or matter exists" implicates itself qua proposition; in other words, that it presupposes the pre-existence of itself, that is, of thought.

The proposition "thought exists" presupposes as well the intellectual act by means of or in which it is thought, but this is not to implicate, but to imply.

Nonetheless, the idealist proposition is not ultimate in character either, nor does it fail to be involved in strict co-implication. In other words, it too presupposes the pre-existence of a sort or form of reality other than, and prior and primordial in regard to, itself, a formulation in which "prior" and "primordial" do not signify a temporal arrangement, but rather a hierarchy in the order of truth and being.

In effect, as is the case with any other, the idealist proposition is a firm judgment, involving as it does a claim to be true or something in which one believes; in fine, it is a settled, firm thesis or positing, one that is performatively in force for the one adopting it.

Therefore, one must place the thesis that the reality called "thesis" or conviction exists prior to any other in which one affirms or denies something. Now then, such a reality does not simply involve the existence of thought (the one given expression by the proposition), but also the fact that someone, upon thinking a thought (say, matter exists or, again, thought exists), takes as firm what the thought proposes, which is for him or her something posited with finality, something which he or she absolutely counts on. The content of the proposition, whatever its sort, is then of no consequence. What matters is that someone be irremediably convinced of a thesis when he or she constitutes it. This state of conviction or certainty may be grounded in reasons or be arbitrary; it may be rational or irrational. Such differences would only lead us to divide theses into kinds, say, into rational and irrational, or into sensible and absurd. But theses of both sorts would be theses nonetheless, that is to say, they would be tantamount to "having someone count on something absolutely."

The reality in question, namely, the existence of someone counting on something absolutely, is prior to any other. If I say "thought exists," I do it because I have realized that it is so, discovered the existence of thought, or become convinced of it. All of that has been verified within a reality that is

---

*The fourth and fifth days were devoted to class discussion. [This remark is the author's.]

prior to the one named by the proposition, which is just a result and aspect thereof. And what is more: if a true proposition or theoretical judgment is to exist, it must originate in and live on a pre-theoretical reality that would produce and support it in being, that would endow it with being. Someone must actually believe in it. [To take] "believing" and "counting on" as "thought" would always be, in turn, an act of "believing" and "counting on"; it would be, therefore, a particular determination of that basic reality, or one content among countless possible ones therein. Accordingly, such a reality would be something other than thought; in other words, it would be, at best, problematic to say that it is [in the nature of] thought.

Among the various ways in which I have expounded this system of ideas, there is one that I have often availed myself of in my university courses of recent years, and which I employed in the public course I taught last year.[30] With utmost brevity, it can be formulated as follows: philosophy is a theory that sets itself to solve the absolute problem, not one that has been delimited and restricted before the fact. Every problem presupposes a datum, in the absence of which there is not even a problem. Since the problem dealt with in philosophy is absolute in character, so will its datum or data be. Hence, philosophy must make its beginning by finding the radical datum it counts on. A datum is something that is unproblematic to us. Hence, the first positive problem encountered in philosophy is that of identifying *that which* is unproblematic to us. Idealism [is the doctrine that] maintains that the existence of thought is unproblematic to us. Its path or method is this: if the existence of thought is problematic to me, then I doubt the existence of thought, but if I doubt, I exist; that is to say, the doubt exists, and the doubt is thought, and thus everything it presupposes, such as the "ego," exists too.

Suppose we set aside the most flagrant error committed by Descartes in his interpretation of that path or method, namely, his assigning of a role to the idea of substance therein, as he did when he applied it, as a matter of course, to the "ego." Even then, and adopting the most favorable formulation of it (which I just advanced), the original idealist method would [be found to] involve most serious errors. One can understand that, so far as the first truth is concerned, every false co-implication or implication—as is every one that is not strictly or unavoidably drawn—is a most serious error.

The primordial and precise sense of [the proposition] "if I doubt, I exist"[31]—or of "I doubt, I exist," if we remove its conditional form, as Descartes does sometimes—can only be the following: something must of necessity exist for me, for the one who is engaged in doubting everything; in other words, something is indubitable, or there is something absolutely, namely, my doubting. This is the unquestionable, absolute reality, [a formulation] in which absolute = absolutely real. Therefore, at this moment, there is for me no reality in the universe except an [act of] doubting, and this reality exists absolutely. Every reality narrows to this one reality alone.

It would have been natural for Descartes to have said to himself immediately that, "since I am fortunate enough to have found an absolute reality, let me inquire into its being, or nature; let me attempt to determine what it is, endeavor to define it, or take hold of its nature." Or to say it as Sancho [Panza] would have: "To pull in your heifer, run along with your rope."

But Descartes did not do that. He introduced a superfluous complication, to wit: [the contention that] the "doubt" is "thought," instead of remaining content with putting together, as one must, the fact that I doubt and the acknowledgment that the *efficacy* that my doubt may have for any theory implicates its absolute existence. (The doubt is nothing but the existence of the problematic. The first unproblematic truth would be that everything, except this truth, is problematic. We will have an occasion to see the positive sense these words have.)

It is already peculiar and significant that Descartes never tells us what thought is, even though he turns thought, in the order of method, into the *primordial reality*. He is content, instead, with listing a series of realities, each and every one of them deserving the name "thought," to wit: seeing, judging, willing, being joyful or sad, etc.[32]

In the decisive situation in which we find ourselves presently, we are to proceed with the utmost care. If we have discovered, at last, that there is an absolute reality (namely, the doubt), and then, without nexus or transition, we are told that the absolute reality in question is "thought," it should come as no surprise that we should prove resistive and say: let us tread softly and inquire whether they are one and the same reality. The slightest modification in such an absolute admission would mean being radically thrown off the tracks.

What is thought? We could arrive at a definition marked by maximal abstractness, but we would find it difficult to understand. For our purposes, it will suffice to define it as it has in fact been defined in historical idealism, to wit: the reality called "thought" lies in the fact that indeed there is an entity—let me call it a "subject"—which consists exclusively of its (own) states, wherein it refers to objects that do not exist outside of the said states and, therefore, of itself. In other words, the objects of thought are not possessed of reality absolute and for itself, but only of that which is derived from the subject's. [For example,] the table I am seeing is not itself, accordingly, a table absolutely speaking; rather, it is, absolutely speaking, a state of mine.

Allow me to compare that with doubting, the only absolute reality [identified] thus far. If doubting exists for me absolutely, what absolute ingredients would it contain? Let us keep in mind what I just said, namely, that if thought is what exists absolutely, then nothing but the thinking subject or subjectivity exists absolutely, and nothing which is not strictly identical with it would exist absolutely. But if the reality called "doubting" exists absolutely, it would be the case that: (1) I the doubter exist absolutely; (2) a burdensome reality exists absolutely, namely, the one I describe as actual doubting, as actually being engaged in doubting; (3) the doubtful, no less than those two things, [also] exists absolutely.

The "doubtful" is endowed with an absolute existence different from my own. I cannot actually engage in doubting, except to the extent that a reality exists absolutely for me which, in itself and for itself, is doubtful.

The reality called "doubt" is, then, radically broader than—and different from—the reality called "thought," since not only does the so-called "subject" exist therein, but, no less than the subject, so do both the so-called "object" and the relation obtaining between subject and object, the latter relation constituting, as it does, an absolutely real area within the compass of which "subject and object" exist. Since in the case of the doubt the object is constitutively the "doubtful," it would be advisable now for us to substitute another situation for that of "doubting," one which would be possessed of the same absolute significance, inasmuch as the "doubtful" is not a name that serves clearly to express the extra- or trans-subjective nature of the character [meant]. If indeed the enthymeme "I doubt, I exist" is valid, so would be—and to no lesser degree—this other one: "I see this light, I exist."

The absolute reality we now find is [the event of] "seeing this light."[33] What is there absolutely in that? [I would say:] I who see and the light I see, the two being different from one another. In the universe, then, there are absolutely two things, which are irreducible to, and radically different from, each other. But, if there are two, then there is [as well] that special distance or distinction between them, their existing "outside each other." Now then, [being] "outside" [or "external being"]—i.e., my existing or being outside of the existing or being of the light—is a reality at once other than me and other than the light; it is a sheer area of being for itself. We both are supported and enveloped by this [being] *outside,* by this external being or metaphysical distance, which [thus] renders it possible for the two not to be confused, i.e., for the light not to *be* me, and for me not to *be* the light.

Let us now take a small step.

It is false [to assert] that, if [the proposition] "I am seeing this light" is true, then only that would be true. This is so because I see the light among

other things, one of which is my body. In other words, [the reason for it
is] that I see a plurality of things before me, things that are different from
one another and yet the same, to the extent that none is I myself. That
plurality of things forms a structure which surrounds my body; [but,
since] I am placed in my body (though I do not know how) and also am,
at least, *my* body, I am therefore surrounded by it [too]. That which envelops me I call "circumstance" or, if you will, "world." Now, let it be clearly
understood that all of that exists absolutely.

Accordingly, the radical datum[34] is neither thought nor subjectivity,
but another infinitely broader reality that consists of the existing of an I
and, also, of the existing of its surroundings, which are radically different
from it. Furthermore, the reality in question amounts to the fact that my
existing consists in finding myself *in* such surroundings, in my being directed upon, busy with, and acted on by them. And, conversely, the said
reality amounts [as well] to the fact that the existing of the given surroundings consists in surrounding me, in presenting me with problems
and necessities, in making me suffer or enjoy. Such a reality[35] I must call
"my life." My surroundings and I constitute an indivisible and absolutely
existent organism.

It is now that we can say, in all strictness, that "my life is the absolute."
The radical datum or absolute reality is, then, no monomial, no mono-
logue, as it was in idealism (*der Sich-selbstdenkende*[36]), but a binomial or
dialogue.

In saying this, I have referred, by way of anticipation, to an aspect of
that reality, a reality that is different from all those known in the history
of philosophy. Now we can return to the "doubt" in order to show how it
is that the *integrum* [or whole I call] "my life" comes out of it, just as it
did out of [the proposition] "I am seeing this light."

As I have already said,[37] when the "doubt"[38] exists, that which exists
absolutely is this: I who doubt, the doubtful, and the distance between the
two. I am doubting, and this means, first, that I find that I do not exist
alone, but, second, that my existing presently consists in doubting everything, and, third, that what I have called "everything" is nothing but the
ensemble of my opinions, which are about many things, including myself.
Let us now set aside the portion of my doubting that concerns myself,
since it is just one of the countless components of my universal doubt. [At
present,] I am calling into doubt the opinion of mine according to which
the room surrounding me amounts to a material reality independent of
my thought. Now, that means—if I express myself broadly, though not
without the rigor befitting precisely our needs at this point—that what I
am casting into doubt is the philosophical definition that I can provide,
with assurance, of that which lies in my surroundings. In fine, my[39]

doubting now consists in not finding any theory to be sufficiently firm or true.

If I did not construct theories, if I did not theorize, I would not be doubting in this fashion. My existing as a doubter is, then, nothing but an action belonging to—or just one component of—my broader existing, of my existing as theorizer. My casting everything into doubt implies, then, that I do not cast the fact of my theorizing into doubt, since only as a function of it does my doubting have sense. But theorizing is something I do *because of something*.[40] If I were a theorizer only, I would not even be a theorizer. I theorize *because* I am something broader than, and prior to, my theorizing, something in which my theoretical activity originates and in which such an activity finds its motivation and is endowed with sense. To theorize is to produce a determinate thing, namely, conceptual truth or precise knowledge. Therefore, I am a being possessed of a conceptualizing function, of an intellect properly so called. That I am so endowed is an absolute fact implied by my doubt [and] rendering it possible. I the doubter am, without a doubt or absolutely, an intelligent being who employs his intellect or sets it in motion *because* he is in need of it.

The intellect, by itself, neither can nor needs to be employed. Or equivalently expressed: it is an activity or gift that cannot exist in isolation. The ego, or being to which it belongs, must be constituted by something that is prior to the intellect; moreover, that which is prior to the intellect and to its theorizing must set the said faculties in motion, must motivate and endow them with matter, must bring them to understand *something* and *for the sake of* something.

In effect, I theorize because of the fact, which takes precedence over my being intelligent, that I am an entity whose being or existence[41] consists in finding itself surrounded by other things (minerals, animals, and people), which in turn exist as absolutely as I do. The existence of my self (or I) does not consist in existing apart from such surroundings or circumstance, but, on the contrary, in conjunction with all of that. My existing now consists in being here, among these pieces of furniture, surrounded by this room, reading by this light which is not convenient, and doing so before you, whose opinion matters to me, whether I like it or not, because my existing depends—to a lesser or greater degree—on it. If today you think that I am an imbecile, my existing would be other than if you thought that I am not an imbecile, but a man whose work is possessed of sense and seriousness. Let me repeat it: my existing does not consist in existing apart, but in existing in conjunction with this room and with you. But the expression "in conjunction with" does not serve to convey well the absolute dimension of the absolute reality which my relationship to the room and to you is. It is not true that I exist and that you do too, as if my existing were [taking place] side by side with yours and yours with mine. Rather, the case is that you are ingredients [found] *in* my existing, that my existing depends substantially on you, that my existence is essentially interlocked with yours; in fine, that the very "substance" of my existing is, certainly, an actuating and functional co-existing with that which is not me.

But the other way round [too]: the existence of this light and of this room and your existence do not amount to being there, apart from me; rather, they amount to [being] *exclusively* that which you, the light, and the room are [respectively] in my existing or for me. That this light is not very convenient, that it is placed there, that it is turned on and located precisely so far from me—all of that is due to the fact that *I* want to see these pages *in order to* read them. As a function of my will and purpose, i.e., *in order for me to* read [something] to you, does the light exist there and show itself to be inconvenient. And the other way round [also]: if you exist, as you do here and now, and if your existence amounts as it does presently to hearing, and not to being at a nightclub, it is because I have summoned you [here], I who am Mr. So and So and display, as I do, such and such conditions and attributes, which are proper to this most individual existence. Let us mark it well: your absolute existence is the existence you have *for* me—this is the grain of truth contained in idealism. But the *me* in question, the one I am, in turn exists for *me* too and only for me, and yet its existence consists in depending, in part, on you. Therefore, it consists in existing for me no more and no less than you do. And this is the grain of truth contained in realism.

The absolute existence of the doubt, which is a theoretical activity, presupposes or implicates, then, the absolute existence of a reality I describe as the "actuating co-existence of myself, or of this I, and the circumstance or world." I am the one who has to exist here with you, and you and here are those things with which I, Mr. So and So, this unique, most individual being, have to co-exist. This co-existence I call "my life."

The circumstance or world, then, consists exclusively of the determinate correspondence to that which I, Mr. So and So, happen to be.

Please note the strange condition with which the absolute reality of *my life* certainly presents itself to us:

I am, to begin with, the one who exists, but my existing (and therefore I) consist in co-existing with the other, with the world. In other words, I am the one who lives, but to live is to maintain myself, to perdure existing in the world. My life, then, depends on what the world might be like. But this world is not an entity [that exists] apart from my life and, therefore, from me, from the one who is living; rather, it is, formally and exclusively, "that with which I co-exist"; consequently, its nature, its being, its ontological profile depend on who the one living in it might be. If I am blind, the world is altogether different from what it would be if I were sighted; if I am an artist, otherwise than it would be if I were an economist; if I am an [African] black, otherwise than it is if I were a Spaniard; if I am Ortega, otherwise than it would be if I were someone else. Is this not a vicious circle? My life will be in accordance with the way the world in which I live might be, and the world in accordance with what I, the one living in it, might be. But, even if it ultimately proved to be a vicious circle, we would be forced into it and to acknowledge it as the plain truth. It is at this point, however, that the term "my life" begins to render its good services to us.

I am not in possession of a being, or existence, apart from my life, and neither is the world. Therefore, both [I and the world] are only abstract components of the radical reality "my life" is.

[Being] a philosopher, for example, is one such abstract component of "my life," one that *I* am when considered abstractly. The world belonging to "my life" will consist of the ensemble of facilities and difficulties, aspects, and characters that "that which is not me" places at the disposal of someone who, like me, is in need of existing as a philosopher. "My life" may turn out to be of minimal philosophical significance. I could have been born to a tribe in the Congo. In fine, I am not *my life,* but only an element of it.

Considered abstractly, *I* am a philosopher, but, of course, I am many other things, even when I am still being regarded abstractly: for example, I am a man. But to my being a man corresponds the other abstract element of my life, namely, the world or circumstance which is being constituted as possessing certain characters. As a man, I find myself assigned to a male body with which I have to co-exist in immediacy and which imposes on me the ensemble of its instincts, bodily faculties (some excellent, some defective), clinical temperament, illnesses, etc. I am not my illness, which is one of the absolute characters of the world I happen to encounter and have to count on in order to exist. The pathological or medical concept of illness is the theoretical definition of an absolute reality, the primordial concept of which is to be given by metaphysics.

Therefore, inasmuch as *my life* is the absolute reality, the element thereof I call surroundings, circumstance, or world *originarily* consists of three fundamental categories or worldly modalities (to wit: necessities, facilities, and difficulties), not of what we will later call things, when we come to adopt a one-sided, secondary, and relative (i.e., non-absolute) vantage point. Since my life amounts to my existing in co-existence with the other, the other will consist of that which I have no choice but to do or of that which I must needs count on in order to exist; consequently, [it will be comprised of] "necessities," [as well as of] the "facilities favoring my existing" and the "difficulties hindering it."

For the time being, this will suffice for us to have a glimpse of that aspect displayed by me and the world when one engages in the attempt to think them as absolute elements of the absolute reality *my life* is.

My life, then, is possessed of two essential dimensions consisting in encountering difficulties and facilities. Therefore, my life or existence is easy, but it is also hard. For the purpose of casting light on the essence of life, few things will do better than availing oneself of the hypothetical constructions of what life would be if it were just easy and what it would be if it were just hard. The two constructions in question, by virtue of their opposition, would render apparent to us, or would make us see and conceive, though in a way already free of construction, what real life is, namely, simultaneously necessitating, easy, and hard. (We will later have, as well, an occasion to appreciate the radical significance of our constructive capacity or pure reason.[42])

But presently I will content myself with [saying] just this: among the difficulties I encounter [in living], some originate in the fact that my psyche fashions ideas or opinions about things, that is to say, that it finds a world constituted not only by absolute realities, but by ideas about them as well.[43] It finds, for example, an illness, a toothache, the sea, cold, heat, the need to feed oneself, other human beings (both taken individually and collectively); but it also finds an idea about the nature of illness and physical pain, another about the nature of the deep, [and still others about] the nature of nutrition, our neighbor, society, etc. Now then, such ideas or opinions intrinsically are novel difficulties, because they are intrinsically problematic. I have to live or exist with my ideas, which should serve to support me, and yet they do not prove to be firm, solid, certain; I lose my footing in their midst, I doubt.

Self-doubt is one of the intrinsic dimensions of life, and self-doubt is doubt about the ideas life has of itself. Or equivalently stated: living is also theorizing, doubting, endeavoring to overcome doubt, and, therefore, it is, ultimately, radical doubting and radical theorizing, i.e., philosophizing.

(Here I could repeat all I said, by way of introduction, about our philosophical purpose, something which then seemed to be vague or arbitrary. Now it reappears in its entirety, but endowed already with the character of a determination intrinsic to philosophy itself and as a dimension of the absolute reality my life is.[44])

Let me say it again: my life is myself and my circumstance,[45] with which I exist by way of co-existence. Since my circumstance, at least in part, is comprised of difficulties, my existing is difficult. Now then, for an *I* that is inescapably intelligent, that is to say, one whose manners of existing include understanding and thinking, a difficult circumstance is transformed into a new kind of difficulty. In other words, the originary and real difficulty turns into a problem, or intellectual difficulty, as well. Like it or not, I have to solve the intellectual problem my circumstance— i.e., my theoretical culture[46]—poses for me; I have to reabsorb[47] my circumstance, my life, in the theory [I formulate].

I do not live *because* I think (as idealism would have it), but I think because I live, [and do so] at a more radical level than that of thinking. My living sets my thinking in motion and forces me to think about my life.

In saying this, I have only intended to anticipate, in very broad strokes, a landscape consisting of absolute reality, one which, in a more earnest fashion and step by step, we would have to conquer methodically.

I was in need of giving intuitive embodiment to the concept of life and absolute reality, which the doubt posits and places in anteposition with regard to any other thesis or positing.

But let us now take up our path or methodical progression again, without, however, repeating anything except the following:

When Descartes said, "I doubt, therefore I exist," he committed an error (and with him so did every form of idealism, including Husserl's), an error consisting in *supposing* that the doubt is in the nature of thought. But thought or *cogitatio* is a concept that has been fashioned about a reality, namely, the doubt, as it appears to one who is engaged in theorizing, who thereby places him- or herself outside of it. Thought is not, therefore, a radical datum; rather, it already is [an artifact of] theory, a theoretical determination [functioning] formally as such, and thus something which is born, arises, and is produced already within the confines of theory. Now then, anything that is already a theory is a sediment left behind by a prior, actual, performative occasion of theorizing, which every theory, every particular thesis presupposes and implicates. But such an occasion is not yet a theory, but rather a radical modality or component of a broader structure, namely, life.

The radical character of the way in which philosophy proceeds in elaborating a universal theory makes us realize that every theory is conditioned, and [allows us to discover] the particular conditions to which it is subject. To put it otherwise: there is no theory *ex nihilo,* that is to say, the content of every theory or thesis presupposes the said theory and thesis, if taken as actuation, as performance, as life. But the content in question serves inadvertently to posit life as an absolute reality, as the only one *in* and within which the content or theorem can exist (with a secondary manner of existence), or *be,* as what it claims to be, namely, as true.

But this presents us with the *paradoxical* task of constructing a primordial theory, one the theme of which must be pre-theoretical reality as such. The possibility of philosophy depends on whether or not that is possible.

Now then, theorizing is thinking, and thinking is turning something into an object; it is [the act of] regarding something and, therefore, of placing oneself outside of it, of grasping [only] its visage. In fine, it is [an act of] objectivation. [Accordingly,] the pre-theoretical reality of something will be what it is when it is not being regarded or objectivated, when it is not *for* another, but by itself and for itself. This is what something is as self-performance, as performativeness.

The most fundamental distinction possible is that obtaining between objective being and *performative being*.

We have to undo the objective conception of the "world"—the one naïve thought provides us with—and retrace it to a conception of the "world," or of the real, as performativeness. As a conception, ours will be an objectivation as well, that is to say, a thought we carry out. Yet, in contradistinction to what happens when we employ thought naïvely, we are going to make it look upon reality from the vantage point of the latter.

Our theme, then, is the exact opposite of the theme of phenomenology, and our method is, consequently, the opposite of the method of phenomenology. When it describes an act, phenomenology eliminates or *reduces* its performative character.[48] [By contrast,] we busy ourselves *exclusively* with it. We do not take the act as it appears qua object of reflection, but the other way round: we suspend our reflection, since it is artificial.

# Seventh Day

We went in search of something firm, of an incontrovertible certainty or truth. The possession of such firmness, or the awareness thereof, we called "theory, science, knowledge." It is already ours, and it amounts to the following: every theory, even the doubt which is its incipient form, has been acknowledged to be a modality of a reality that precedes it and is broader than itself, namely, what I call "my life" or "life." The firmness of the existence of such a reality, or [of the proposition that asserts] "it is a reality," exceeds the firmness of any other conceivable proposition, even [that of] the very reality of doubting, which is endowed with reality only in life and as a living actuation.

Consequently, the acknowledgment of life as the primordial reality is the first act of full and incontrovertible knowledge. Science or knowledge thus begins with the intellectual positing of life as primary reality. Such an act, then, is an absolute positing advanced within the realm of opinion.

Or equivalently stated: we know absolutely that life is a reality, that there is life, that life is the primary reality implicating no other prior to itself, and that every other reality implicates it as its presupposition. In effect, every other reality, different as it is from my life, is made known by some modality of my life. [Even] God Himself,[49] should He exist, will begin to be for me by existing somehow in my life.

But then we come to the realization that life is not only absolute in the sense that we have to acknowledge it as absolutely real, but also in that it serves as the foundation of all other realities and envelops them. In the final analysis, every other reality will be a reality *in it*. This is what I was talking about these last few days. A philosophy that arrives at the discovery of such a reality has no choice but to stick obstinately to it, never to abandon it. Or to express it equivalently: it is not just that there is life or that it exists absolutely, but [also] that it is the absolute by virtue of its content. It is at least one first absolute. It leaves no room for anything which could be said to lie outside it. We shall soon have the occasion to appreciate that this is so at a new level of meaning and truth.

It is of great importance to bear always in mind what that basic reality is, to wit: *my life exists absolutely,* or *there is my life absolutely*. Therefore, I who live exist, and so do my surroundings, co-existing with which is the nature of my existing. At present, I do not *know* sufficiently who I am, but the existence of my *I* does not depend on my knowing myself, if "knowledge" is taken to mean theoretical knowledge, or even what is usually called practical knowledge. I am not even in need of perceiving myself, in the precise sense of the term, if, as it is customary, self-consciousness properly so called is understood to be inner perception. To exist I do not have to perceive myself.

That notwithstanding, my existing consists, certainly and radically, in existing for myself. Whenever one attributes existence to life (or to any of its components, no matter which), such an attribution must be taken as qualified by the character "for me." I exist to the extent that I exist for me, and my existing—that is to say, my life, or anything that I do or that befalls me[50]—only exists insofar as it exists for me. This is likewise true of my surroundings, without which I would not exist, because my existing consists in co-existing with my surroundings, in seeing or thinking them, in moving in them, [and] in desiring, loving, or hating this or that about them,[51] [for] my surroundings[52] exist only insofar as they exist for me. ([For our purposes,] it would be advisable to avail ourselves of fewer "psychological" examples and of more non-mental actuations, such as building, grasping with one's hand, founding an industry, or getting married.)

The odd [character] "for me" thus appertains universally and ubiquitously to my life; it is an integral component of it, whether one regards life as a whole or in terms of any of its smallest parts. This reference or relationship to me, which is a constituent of everything that exists, turns it, without exception, into life, and life into "my life." Life is a reality that essentially belongs to someone who is an *I*. Strictly speaking, every life is "mine."[53] To date, the character "for me," which unquestionably belongs to reality, [has not fared well]. It was not theoretically acknowledged by ancient and medieval realism, and only a glimpse of it was found in idealism, though it was erroneously *interpreted* by it (that is to say, the concept formed by it to respond to the glimpse in question was not valid). In effect, it was thought that the relation "for me" was identical with the one between consciousness and *cogitatio,* i.e., between a thinking subject and the object thought about. [That] something exists "for me" was taken, then, to be the equivalent of its being perceived, thought about, imagined, etc., [all of them] modalities of consciousness or *cogitatio.* But this implies that I and *what* exists for me are severed and separated from each other, that there is a distance between a subject and its object. However, [consider] a toothache: it exists or is for me without there being any distance [between it and myself].[54] Here "being for me" does not mean "being an object for me," or an object that I perceive, think about, imagine, etc.; rather, the relationship between the toothache and me is straightforward, and it does not consist in its being my object, but in its hurting me absolutely and without mediation. Moreover, the other way round [is the case too]: the I of my hurt is not a perceiving but a hurting I, an I who feels the hurt of the toothache. The relationship between the toothache and me does not amount to a mere "realization" [of the toothache], or consist in just "adverting" to or "seeing" it, but precisely in *hurting me,* which is an extra-intellectual relationship. And yet, as part and parcel of [the phenomenon of] hurting me, one finds a pre-intellectual ingredient,[55] namely, "my seeing the ache" or the "ache's regarding itself."

The same is true about belief. When I am engaged in believing, I am not thinking of my believing, but I am engaged, instead, in straightforwardly performing the extra-intellectual act of believing, within which lies [the phenomenon of] "seeing-the-act," or [of] the "act's seeing itself." I do not *see* but perform my belief; I *am* my belief. (Or equivalently stated: the light I am seeing is not, primarily speaking, an object for me. I do not see the object called light; rather, for me the light is straightforwardly the reality consisting in illuminating me, not in being my object.)

This prompts us to hold in abeyance the traditional validity of concepts like "consciousness," "*cogitatio,*" "subject," and "object" and to postpone our examination thereof to another suitable occasion. If they are nonetheless going to resonate in what follows, let it be noted that it is just in order to place the sheer reality encountered by us in contrast with the content of those concepts, and to show the lack of congruence—at least in part—between the former and the latter. The case of a toothache is a most flagrant example [of that], and it is for this reason, of course, that I have brought it [to your attention]. But, as we proceed, we shall have the occasion to appreciate that the same happens with anything pertaining to life. Vitally speaking, my "I" does not exist for me either, of necessity, as something known or of which I am cognizant. But it does not exist for me even as perceived; if that were so, I would not exist for me except insofar as I pay attention to myself, the result being that my life would be discontinuous.[56] But my life is absolutely continuous. How could it be otherwise, since it is the only reality, and no distance can separate any of its parts from another? There are no gaps in my life; it is absolutely compact. A dream one does not remember does not, as such, pertain to my life, unless it were meaningful to say that a cell found in my body (but which I do not see), the far side of the moon, or Alcalá Street[57] (when I am not concerned with it) pertain to my life.[58] The fact of the matter is that, in my life, I am constantly present to myself, such a presence being, without fail, part and parcel of my existence.

The vital [relationship] "being for me" is the odd kind of presence that my life has before itself. My life is comprised only of whatever is present to me in this fashion. Consciousness, perception, thought: these are special powers belonging to the universal and constitutive presence exhibited by everything which my life truly is. My life is an entitative presence, not that of an object before a subject.[59] *The latter,* namely, *cogitatio* or conscious presence, *is just a species of the former.* For the purpose of giving expression to the odd non-intellectual, non-noetical, and [non-]objective presence my life has before myself, and thus to reduce to a minimum, by my choice of words, the disturbing effects of an idealist interpretation, let me say that the "existence of something for me" is [equivalent to] "my counting on it." My life consists in my counting on myself and, at once, on something other than myself, that is to say, on what I will call the "other" (the circumstance or world).

The terminological expression "counting on" has the advantage of serving to remind us, simultaneously, of [two] characters exhibited by my life, to wit: permanent self-attendance and (the new note of) *actuality,* which pertains to my life both as a whole and so far as any of its parts is concerned.

If I am nothing but "the one who counts on something," then it is evident that I am not except insofar as I act. "Counting on" is a manner of acting, of "doing"; [it is] a dynamic character never possessed of [self-]re-alization or consciousness properly so called. (It is questionable whether "seeing" is endowed with living reality, since it does not exist for itself, while looking, on the contrary, is.) Considered in terms of my absolute reality, I am not a thing, whether material or spiritual; I am not a substance, not even an act; rather, I am the *performance* of my act. Similarly, the sur-roundings—which are other than myself—do not exist, are not, except insofar as they act on me. Considered as an absolute reality, this light is not a thing that subsists by itself and apart from the operation [it carries out] on me; instead, it is, only and radically, that which is now illuminat-ing me. Considered as an absolute reality, each and every one of you is a most determinate something that is imposing on me, willy-nilly, a deter-minate actuation or manner of conduct, *because* that something is a de-terminate actuation on me. Matter is that which resists the movements of my body; each and every one of you is, likewise, a resistance—of a differ-ent character in each case—to my tendency toward my being "myself." Anything else you might be, you would be *a posteriori* in respect of the only thing you are, primarily speaking, namely, the actuation in question, so that any further [manner of] being of yours will be grounded in your primary being.

The absolute reality [called] "my life" consists in being *pure actuality*. Living amounts, always and exclusively, to my doing *with*, and to my being acted *upon* by, the other, or that which is other than myself. The other is nothing but what is acted upon by my doing and that which col-laborates or works with my being acted upon. ("Doing" is not being used here correctly, [for] there is such a thing as performativeness and actual-ity outside [the sphere of] doing, as it happens in the mineral world.) Consider the example of my being illuminated by a light. A light is not a "thing." "[Being a] thing" is an objective interpretation of the primary being of the light, an interpretation which is false for that very reason, since it claims to give expression to its primordial reality. The primordial reality of the light consists in actually illuminating me. Such is its reality in my life.

Let us, then, hold in abeyance—please note I only say "in abeyance"—all traditional categories which have been employed to "say"—*katêgo-rein* means "to say"—what reality is. Our endeavor consists in breaking loose from them, so as not to be hindered by them in our intellectual ap-prehension of what that reality is presenting us with. Only by holding the past in abeyance in such a fashion will we be placed in the clear for the purpose of creating new concepts better adapted to that which appears to us as reality itself. We have to philosophize in the way in which the

Hebrews reconstructed Jerusalem—with [both] the mason's tools and our defensive weapons, with one hand pouring the lime upon the stone and with the other resisting the past that assails and tries to enslave us.

The proof of it lies in the fact that the only expression I have kept that belongs to traditional terminology,[60] namely, *pure actuality,* is, at least, equivocal and insufficient.

It is at this point that I should turn to the historical study of the emergence and vicissitudes of the term[s] "act" and "actuality" in the philosophical past. But I did promise—and I believe with good reason—to reduce every allusion to the history of philosophy to the barest minimum.[61] I will confine myself, then, to saying that the term "actuality" corresponds to Aristotle's word *ènérgeia*.[62] The most exact and lively way of translating the term into Spanish, [as well as into English,] to convey most precisely what the Greek locution signifies, is to say things like "bringing about" *[poner por obra],* "working out" *[obrar],* "operating." [But] this implies that that which is to "be brought about" pre-exists the [process of] "bringing about," which accomplishes nothing other than the transposition of something pre-existent to a new way of being or existing. The origin of the word is clear: my idea of doing something pre-exists my doing of it; the "doing [of] something pre-conceived" consists in "bringing it about"; therefore, *ènérgeia* means "execution."[63] As always, Aristotle projects an anthropomorphic concept on the absolute reality, and proceeds on the supposition that the possible being of something is an ontological state preceding its actual or actuating being. The fact is that, in [both] Aristotle and Scholasticism, [we find that] act and potency are inseparable, even though, by virtue of an inexorable dialectical necessity, it later turns out that, in the final analysis, actual being is primary and the presupposition of every being that is merely possible.

The expression[s] "performance," "performing," and "performativeness,"[64] which, as we have seen, are lexically equivalent to *ènérgeia,* possess the advantage of not having been officially employed in the history of philosophy.

That is why, instead of saying, as I just did, that the absolute reality called "my life" consists in being pure actuality, I will now say that it "consists in being *pure performativeness*." Life, and everything therein, is performative in character; it consists in being self-performance and just that. The idea of substance is thus held in abeyance: a being or reality is not substantial in character, if we take the term "substantial" in Aristotle's sense of "substrate."[65] It is not the substrate of actuation (as the form is)[66] or of passivity or possibility (as matter is).[67] But neither is it, like Leibniz's monads,[68] an actuating substance or a being consisting of sheer activity. Activity is not actuation or performativeness.

# Eighth Day*

As you have seen, the idea of performativeness has led us to [form] an idea of "entitative reflectiveness"[69] as pertaining to everything real.

Let us go over the stations we have passed on our way to it:

1. My life is the totality of what exists for me, including my own existing.

2. Now, the "existing for me" which absolute reality is does not amount to something existing objectively—or as an object—for me. It is not an objective but a performative presence. It is the primary presence of an ache insofar as it is hurting me, of a light insofar as it is illuminating me, and of myself insofar as I am hurting and insofar as I am being illuminated. Consequently, [the character] "for me" does not signify that the ache and the light each are [first] endowed with a being in itself, and that, later, they would enter that other entity which my consciousness is, and in which they would acquire a new being or manner of being, i.e., its "being for me." Far from that being the case, the "I" or "me" for whom they are is, instead, only insofar as it "counts on" the ache and the light. Or to put it otherwise: I am the one to whom [something] happens absolutely, [namely,] aching, being illuminated, or stumbling on a stone. My existing consists in existing *for* the ache, *for* the light, *for* the stone. The existing for me of those so-called things is one and the same as my existing *for* them.

3. But this means that the presence constitutively attendant upon everything that is, is not [the same as] the participation of things in me, since it involves—to no lesser degree—my participation in them. It does not consist in my being their subject, inasmuch as I am, so to speak, also their object, contributing, as they do, to making me someone who hurts, is illuminated, or stumbles. If in order to understand such a presence, we want—instrumentally or metaphorically—to employ the idea of subject (that is to say, the idea of someone before whom that which is present presents itself), then we would say that the subject in question is neither myself nor the other (or world), but life itself, i.e., my life.[70]

   For, in fact, when I speak of myself and say that I exist, [that means] that I have had to go *intellectually* in search of myself, and that I have found myself not in me, but in a reality prior to my-being-apart. I have found myself to be a segment of a broader reality that was present to itself before I was present to myself partitively. *Life* is

*Added by the Spanish editor.

the reality wherein I encounter and grasp myself, and *wherefrom* I abstract myself. I and the other, or world, are abstractions that truly exist only in a unity by co-existence. Thus, my existence consists in existing in and *for* co-existence.

When a thing—be it something else or myself—is present to me in the way of "consciousness," I notice that it had already been present to me before in the way of existence or life. Hence, any intellectual encounter or realization is marked by the strangeness of surprise. Yet that is so not because one is surprised by the novelty of what is found, but the other way round: one is surprised by the fact that what one has found was already known somehow, that we had it in our possession before finding it, that it was something more or less déjà vu, that it was already there before being in my consciousness as something formally known. Conscious presence is thus the concentration on, or the limitation to, one particular point in [the sphere of] the said universal and performative presence.

It is solely in this fashion that one understands, first, my consciousness of something, of something that can only be explicitly realized or known now, if it already existed for me before in a pre-intellectual manner;[71] and, second, self-reflection in me, or self-consciousness, which idealism and phenomenology have failed to cast any light on. [One can gather as much] because, if A (the act reflected upon) is not B (the reflecting act), then one does not understand how B can see A, which transcends it, and is non-present to it, as much as anything else. If an act of mine, besides existing, is to be for me by way of self-consciousness, then there must be a reflective [dimension] to itself proper, it must—already by itself—see itself and exist for itself somehow. [Only] thus will act B be able to *retain* and take advantage of the dimension of self-regard that act A, by itself, was endowed with.

By means of what I have said, I do not claim to cast sufficient light on these problems, but only to show you the radical sense inspring my system [of ideas], since everything taken as *ultima ratio* [final justification] in a traditional system appears in mine as a secondary or tertiary plane and concept. At the same time, I [would like] you to grow used not to encumber your understanding of what I am saying, by supposing that I admit those established concepts and positions, for, of course, in terms of such a supposition, anything I say would be devoid of sense.

It is evident that, as long as we understand by "consciousness" what has been understood by the term during the last three centuries, we will not be able to escape idealism and its insoluble antinomies.

Phenomenology asserts that it abides by what is given and present as such. Accordingly, it asserts [for example] that I encounter the fact [describable as] the "noise of a car's horn" with evidence, but that I also encounter, by means of reflection, my *hearing* of that noise, my "consciousness" of it. In other words, it asserts that I encounter not only the noise itself, but its "presence before me" as well. I acknowledge that I have never encountered any such thing. This gives notice of the fact that the way I have chosen obligates one radically to reformulate the theme of "perception" and, therefore, that of "consciousness" [too].

If we talk about the least questionable modalities of consciousness (e.g., paying attention to something, imagining it, thinking it or thinking about it), we will soon enough discover that they always amount to taking something as [if it were] separate from its pre-existence in my life, to my manipulating or operating with it. Consciousness is, therefore, doing something with something, one of the countless things that are part and parcel of my life, such as making a chair out of wood. It is thus a reduction of my entire existing or living, whence it would follow—let me just say this by way of anticipation—that, far from being an expansion of myself whereby something would be given to me that I did not already possess, something that did not exist for me, the consciousness of something, strictly speaking, amounts to having a pre-existing and richer sphere contract to, or concentrate on, a single point; it is the abandonment of the whole *[todo]* for the sake of the specific, a withdrawal from the rest of my life which implies a motivation.

In short, my consciousness proper, my intellectual ego, my ego as the subject who thinks the world and for whom it is an object, is something that my living ego finds in its life, and which, besides, it usually takes a long time to find.

Let me summarize. My life, the primordial and absolute reality, is endowed with a performative, not an objective being. And to such performativeness belongs a constant self-presencing dimension, a dimension of reflectiveness.

Instead I could also say that my life is an absolute event happening to itself.[72]

My life amounts to the fact that I now find myself talking about philosophy to other people in this room. This is an irrevocable, absolute event, which I am unable to erase from absolute reality. But I am thus and so—the one talking, etc.—because of something and for the sake of something.[73] If I do something, I do it for the sake of my future existing, and thanks to, or because of, my past existing. In other words, I do not find myself in the given now, unless I find myself in the broader sphere of my future and my past, all of which is also an absolute event in which the now is just one abstract dimension and component.[74]

There is nothing, there has been nothing, there will be nothing which is not a part of the absolute event my life is. Neither can my life step out of itself nor does it allow anything to exist outside itself. In fine, my life is entity, a unique entity.[75] Everything else that, in some way or other, may be said to be will be in my life. And if I call anything other than my life by the name "entity," it should be understood that it is so in a secondary, derivative sense, because its entity, its existing, its reality is acceded to by virtue of forming part of my life.

Unicity is the third note of life. My life is unique or mine,[76] because it is that which exists for me.

No absolute reality corresponds to the expression "your life." "Your life" cannot exist performatively for me. You are part of my life, and only as such you have absolute reality. In fact, what I can do in my life is to live the thought of "your life"; I can think it. I can tell myself that you are, as I am, a member of an absolute reality consisting of what exists performatively for you. But all of that exists for me as an object, that is to say, it exists ideally. Ideal or objective being, which is just a species of performative being, is found amidst all that which is performatively for me.

The fact that "my life" is unique does not imply that it is the "only one." It is possible for an infinite number of unique ones to be, each and every one of them being no less unique than the next. *That is possible,* but *possible being* is not absolute being.[77]

Unicity turns my life into an ontological realm which is impervious, non-communicating, and exclusive. No one can partake of my life. No one can do what I am doing, and no one can live *[exist]* my life *[existir]*. This is an immediate consequence of performativeness. Now, my life, by virtue of its uniqueness, is altogether different from any other thing and any other life. My life is one of a kind, and this is true in such a radical sense that its uniqueness surpasses God's unicity, inasmuch as the latter is not [a determination] internal to the reality [called] God but one which is grounded in our own reasons. God would be radically unique, if He were—and only to the extent that He were—living.[78]

It is to be noted here that concepts having a performative content are occasional in character.[79] Accordingly, all possibly existing lives will be lives because, in each one of them, "life" signifies a different reality, even if all their attributes—and this is an unequalled fact—were, without exception, the same. This forces us to turn the *principium identitatis indiscernibilium* around and to affirm its opposite, namely, the *principium de discernendo identico.*[80]

# PART II

# CONCERNING
# RADICAL REALITY

# Second Lecture
## (Wednesday, April 9, 1930)*

Philosophy is something a human being does. I have already said this, and someone may perhaps judge this assertion to be a commonplace or, as people usually put it, something that goes "without saying," because it is well known. To that I would respond by means of these three observations:

1. Most things which the least learned people usually take as going without saying, because they are well known, are not, strictly speaking, "known" at all. On the contrary, having always been just before their [eyes], such things have never been noticed by them; their minds have run clear through them without having stopped [to consider] them, or taken them into account so far as their structure and significance are concerned, just as one's glance pierces through glass and air without stopping [to consider] the nature of air or glass. It happens likewise in the present case: philosophy has always been defined while leaving in the shadows the unassuming, elementary evidence in favor of [the view that], whatever philosophy's other more impressive traits may be, it is, to begin with, something a human being does. This is its most concrete condition and nature, and everything else one may say of it, if it results from one's obliviousness of that and does not derive therefrom, will be vague and utopian in character.

2. But, besides, one is so poorly acquainted with [the view in question] that, even though I have just given expression to it, you—and perhaps even myself—remain unacquainted with it. For no one can say he or she is acquainted with it, except if he or she is acquainted with what the nature of human beings and their doings is, although, however strange this may seem, there is nothing that one is less acquainted with, in the history of thought, than with [what] human beings themselves [are], as we shall soon discover.

*The first lecture was not committed to writing; it corresponds to the first few pages of the third lecture of the course which began to be imparted at [the offices of the] Revista [de Occidente]. *Ed.'s N.* : This note was composed by the author, who is referring to the course appearing earlier [in this book. Cf. supra, Part I, pp. 40 ff.]. The text of the second lecture [which appears here] was published in the [Madrid] daily *El País* on May 8, 1983 [on the eve of the centennial commemoration of the author's birth].

3. Even if such a view were well known and most familiar, the attitude of philosophers would have [nonetheless] to be such [as to require them] completely to strip themselves of anything that is their own and to act with such firm humility that they are to think only of saying what they have to say, i.e., the naked truth, rather than keep their own counsel in order just to make surprising or interesting utterances.[1]

Philosophy is something a human being does, and every human doing is done because of something and for the sake of something, a motivational void being impossible. But since the forms of human doing are so numerous, it is of course advisable to determine within which particular species philosophical doing can be accommodated. We would then observe that it belongs to that sort of conduct of ours, the starting point of which is always a question. Questions also are among the things we human beings do to ourselves. But even such interrogative or inquiring kind of doing takes up many forms, [as expressed, for example, by] Where are the keys? What's that woman's name? or At what time does the train leave? These and all questions, different though they are from each other by virtue of their quality and intensity, derive from a fundamental human condition—someone has recently argued that it is the fundamental one[2]—called "curiosity." This locution, like many others, has a twofold sense, one primary and substantive, another pejorative and disparaging, as *amateur* signifies both the one who loves something and the one who only endeavors to do it non-professionally.

The proper sense of "curiosity" springs up from its root, namely, *cura,* i.e., "care" or "pre-occupation."[3] Hence, even in everyday speech, curious human beings are understood to be care-ful individuals, that is to say, those who do what they have to do with the utmost attentiveness and extreme precision and neatness, those who do not act in an unpreoccupied fashion with that which occupies them, but behave the other way round, being preoccupied as they are with what occupies them. In old Spanish, *cuidar* [4] still meant the same thing as *curare* [in Latin], i.e. "to be pre-occupied with."[5] [Spanish] words like *procurar,*[6] *curador,*[7] and *procurador,*[8] which are in use today, preserve that sense. *Incuria* means "neglect" or "care-lessness," and *seguridad (securitas)*[9] signifies "being exempt from care" or "being free from pre-occupation." We shall have an occasion to appreciate the full significance of what underlies such etymological suggestions.

If I ask [someone], Where are the keys? it is because I am preoccupied with them, and I am so preoccupied because I am in need of them in order to do something, to be occupied. To ask a question about something is to do precisely that—to ask—in view of some other, ulterior doing. It is, then, to anticipate what we are going to do; it is to be occupied by way of anticipation or to be pre-occupied. One is confronted with a human vice whenever one engages, without sufficient motivation and to the point of frivolity, in that form of preoccupied behavior consisting in asking a question. The vice [I have in mind] amounts to feigning that one cares for something that one sincerely could not care less about; to being falsely preoccupied with things that are not going to occupy us truly; to being, therefore, incapable of genuine preoccupation.[10] And that is the meaning of expressions like "curiosity," exercising "curiousness" [i.e., nosing about], and "being curious," when used pejoratively. Someone who is "curious" [in this sense] is never at home in his or her own life, but lives off the lives of others.

We are then preoccupied with the location of the keys, a woman's name, or the train's hour of departure. But none of these questions serves to give rise to what a philosopher does. By contrast, there is a vast array of them [which are good for that purpose], having as they do the structure, what is that? (for instance, what is this light?).

Has anyone noticed the odd character of the preoccupation that such questions give expression to? When I ask, "What is this light?" is "this light" the object of my preoccupation? Obviously not: "this light" is there, before me, and I do not set myself the task of doing anything with it when I raise that question in my mind. Even more [to the point]: I am not asking [a question] about it, I am not [venting] my desire for it, I am not seeking after it; rather, what I [mean to] say is, "what *is* this light?" I wonder about the being of this light, not about the light itself. I am not in search of things, but of their being. Now, what new sort of thing is this we call the "being of the light"? On the one hand, it seems to be something intimately tied to the thing whose being it is; but, on the other hand, it is not the thing [itself], for, if we keep to the example given, [we would have to say that] the thing [referred to by the expression] "this light" serves by itself to signify what we are seeing, something that is manifest before our eyes, something that is found there by us, and which [therefore] we do not have to seek after. Apparently, the being of the light is located behind and beyond it, and it is—mark this well—concealed by it. I say that it is concealed, because [at a given point] I would not be intent at all on seeking after the being of light, if I did not have, or had not had, the light before me. I must see it if I am to feel curiosity, care, or preoccupation for its being. And that means that this light, just as it presents itself, *is* not itself. [That is to say,] it is not its being, but is, to the contrary, the harbinger of the being of the light. The light [thus] incites me to seek after its being, inasmuch as the light does not, in conjunction with its presence, surrender its being to me.[11] It seems that, in order for me to arrive at the being of the light, I must refuse what lies before me and is manifest, and endeavor to find its being, which is behind the light. I must, then, remove what I am seeing from my mind[12] so as to dis-cover what is latent.[13] Therefore, the light covers up its [own] being. That is why the event of finding being was called *à-letheúein* by the Greeks, that is to say, dis-covery, un-concealment. But *àlétheia* has been translated by the word "truth." The light I am seeing conceals or covers up its own truth.[14]

I have said that the *thing* "light" incites me to seek after the new *thing* [describable as] the "being of the light," or [as] "what the light is." Obviously, the word "thing" is being employed here with two different significations. When we speak of the "thing" called light, we use that word in a more or less proper sense: "thing" is the name we avail ourselves of, though imprecisely, to refer to anything ostensibly and non-mediately found in our surroundings. However, the "being of the light," into which the question I asked inquires and which it postulates, is not something about which we know whether or not it will be like the things found in our surroundings; it is not, therefore, something about which we know whether or not it will be, strictly speaking, a thing. In order to be able to employ the word when speaking of the "being of things," we will have to broaden, generalize, and purify its use, and make "thing" synonymous with "something," a most abstract term.[15] Obviously, [then,] the being we are in search of will be "something."[16]

This calls us to rectify our way of speaking [of these matters] and say that the light is a thing, but that its being is not. At best, it would be a quasi-thing.[17] Let us employ the word "essence" to name the quasi-thing that that which a thing is amounts to.

This results in a duplication of the world. Everyone of us lives surrounded by things, by non-mediate objects presenting themselves and making themselves manifest by themselves. Such are the minerals, the other living things, and other people, but such also are those internal objects we find in no less a non-mediate way than they, namely, our hurts and feelings, our appetites, volitions, and ideas.[18] Let us call "world" the ensemble of all things that are non-mediate entities, or which are present by themselves. But, as it turns out now, each one of them is endowed with a being or essence, and that involves a duplication of the world. The world of essences lies behind the world of things. The sphere consisting of the being of entities lies behind the entities. An entity is nothing but that which is endowed with being.[19]

If we now compare those two worlds with one another, we will [be able to] observe the following differentiating features:

1. The world comprised of things or entities is non-mediate in character; it is found there, in front of us; we do not have to wonder about it. Every question about something presupposes that the thing [under

scrutiny] already figured in our minds before [the question was raised]. By contrast, the world comprised of essences, of being, is never non-mediate in character; it always lies behind things, mediated as it is by them. It is of great importance that we come to realize and underscore that strange condition, apparently of little import, but which, when the time comes, will prove decisive, namely, that the being of essence is something not given by itself, but is rather that which a human being has to seek after and which is found, if at all, as the outcome of an effort that is, at times, most arduous. This is precisely the opposite of what is the case about things, which not only we do not have originally to seek after, but which are given by way of anticipation in respect of any of our ways of being occupied with them, and which are even given by way of anticipation in respect of our very lives. It is therefore of the greatest importance for us to note that living signifies, already and of its own, that we find ourselves, that is to say, that each and every one of us finds him- or herself, primordially and necessarily, among things, in front of them, surrounded by and submerged in them. This is so much so that it is not possible for us not to be faced with them, and that every effort of ours to do away with them is in vain. Accordingly, while the finding of being involves a great effort on a human being's part, the finding of things not only involves no effort, but every effort not to find them is, on the contrary, hopelessly doomed to failure. A human being's existence consists in existing among and with things, in finding him- or herself in the world.[20] That is why Baudelaire succeeded in giving expression to a great paradox and to an impossibility most properly so called when, upon being asked where he would like to live, he said: "Oh, anywhere else, anywhere else! . . . If only it were somewhere outside the world!"

2. [Now, if that is so,] a consequence would follow. If a human being's existence necessarily consists in existing among things, then a human being is absolutely in need of things. By contrast, being, i.e., essences are in need of us, at least and to begin with in the sense that they are in need of being sought after by us. Please note that we take notice of the being of things for the first time when we catch ourselves in the act of seeking or inquiring after it. [Accordingly,] if we ever are successful in finding it, it will be after [experiencing] a need for it. If we [now], anticipating a little, observe that the answers we obtain to our questions are, in turn, always questionable or uncertain, we will come to the result that the most certain [knowledge] we have of the being [of things] is the one we possess when we inquire after it. For instance, the science of optics would provide answers to the question, what is light? and do so successively, so long as the question continues to be raised. It seems as if we are certain that the light is endowed with being, although we

do not know of what particular sort it is. The genus "being" is, none-theless, clear to us before we come across it in a particular case. In ef-fect, we understand each other when we raise the said question, that is to say, we understand what the being of something is in general. It is by virtue of this fact that, when somebody teaches us about the being of light in particular, or when we ascertain it on our own, we recognize it as "being" or essence.

Doesn't this already indicate that being is something that lies in a question raised by a human being, that is to say, that it already consists in being a question, [which is] a human doing? Now, if no one existed with the capacity to ask, what is this or that? would then being exist? Let that stand as a glimpse, as an odd-looking surmise. But how [is it possible]? Is the being of things something that does not belong to them, but rather something which originates in man, arising as it would in the human doing [describable as] "raising a question"?[21] To say it again: let the matter stand. I would add only one thing which now seems evident to me: that things or entities are found, while being or essence is sought after. We will have an occasion to see how the two definitions are formal in character, that is to say, that neither is the at-tribute "being found" accidental (or extrinsic) to things, nor is the character "being sought after" adventitious and fortuitous to being; rather, [the case is] that, formally speaking, things consist in being found, and being in being sought after.

3. Please note that we are doing nothing but analyzing the sense belonging to the question concerning the being or essence of a thing, [the kind of] question that here will henceforth be called an "essential question." To that end, let us simply endeavor to come to terms with the meaning of the words which form part of such a question. As we do it, we may ob-serve that the expression, *what is ... ?*—found in [a question] like, what is this or that?—implies a number of things integral to its meaning. To begin with, it implies that human beings are not content with the mani-fest world surrounding them; rather, this world incites them to postu-late a world beyond, the condition of which is that of latency, lying as it does in concealment behind the former. The world of immediacy, which we encounter without searching, we encounter always and at the same time that we encounter ourselves.[22] Let me call your attention to the fact that this is so because the mental act by means of which we become aware of ourselves is not primary, inasmuch as we have to set the world aside [or] abstract from it, if we are to take special notice of our very selves,[23] as it happens when, for instance, [I say that] I am perceiving, imagining, loving or hating, willing or not willing.[24] When I am actu-ally engaged in seeing, say, this room, my seeing—and, therefore, that

which I am seeing—does not exist for me; rather, what exists is the room where I am [together with and] undifferentiated from the other objects. In order for me to become aware of myself as such (i.e., to arrive at the celebrated [state of] self-consciousness, which has served as the foundation of idealism for three centuries), I have to tear myself away from among those objects and out of the room where I found myself. Now, in order to accomplish that, I must abstract myself from the other things and suppose that this room does not truly exist, but that only I do who am seeing it. The room ceases being what it was, namely, a place where I am, and is transformed into the opposite of that, viz., a visual image in me. But, then, the room, which has turned into a visual image or perceptual state of mine, no longer is an actual room; the world is no longer the world. Now then, my act of perceiving—i.e., the one which is a mere seeing or an act and state of an ego all by itself, and which no longer consists in actually encountering a real room wherein I find myself enclosed—does not have the same significance [for us] as did the primary sort. At best, it is an element or component of the primary situation in which what was truly found was a room, a world wherein I really was. The one who is now thinking that only he or she exists really, and that the room is just an image, is the same one who was and continues really to be in the real room. That only I really exist is just a thought entertained by that human being who was, and is, existing in a real world.

For a long while we are going to be busy in the attempt to bring about this radical rectification of idealism, which, as we shall have an occasion to see, is not the same as relapsing into realism. Don't mind if this first formulation of what is decisively to be borne in mind [for that purpose] is not clear to you. The problem is to reappear once and again in one perspective or another.[25]

I only wanted, at this point, to underscore the fact that the world of immediacy is the one we find without seeking after it, [that] what we [thus] encounter we encounter in such a primordial sense that encountering the world in question does not presuppose [the performance of] a specialized sort of mental act; rather, to encounter it is one and the same thing as our existence. To live is, in effect, to encounter oneself among things and face to face with them.

Now, by means of the question, what are things? we are making it apparent that we do not rest content with that which we find, which means that such things (or the world or ensemble thereof) seem to us to suffer from a strange insufficiency. [The world of immediacy] is not enough for us. *Non sufficit*. But why?

# Third Lecture*

As I have said, philosophy is, to begin with, something a human being does[26]—for example, [what] we [are doing] now. Later I spoke a bit more precisely [and specified that,] among the countless human doings, philosophy was found to be one of those activities that always begin by posing the question, what is this or that thing? to oneself (as, for example, when one asks, what is this light?). By means of names like "essential questions" or "questions concerning being," I have referred to questions of that sort, i.e., those which inquire into—and postulate—what a thing is. They serve, in turn, to institute a most special sort of human doing. We were involved in analyzing it. [As we did,] a fact caught our eye, namely, that when we ask, say, about what this light is, we do not mean thereby to seek after the light. A blind man could ask us, "Where in the room is the light?" He would not be inquiring, then, into the being of the light, but would be seeking after the light itself. By contrast, we find the light right before us; it is manifest to us; it lies there without mediation, unquestioned, giving us no reason to seek after it. What we inquire into is something other than the light: it is its being or essence. Now then, the essences (or the being) of things are not found right before us, without mediation; rather, it seems that they are always behind things, in the state of latency, lying, resolutely, beyond them. Over against the world of things, or world of immediacy, they constitute a world beyond, which, by virtue of its inexorable nature, lies at an absolute distance from us. In other words, the being of this light is not more or less removed from us, as the streetlamp at the Puerta del Sol[27] is farther removed from us than this light. Rather, it is radically or absolutely distant from us. By the same token, the world-beyond imposes on us the task of seeking after it. It never presents itself on its own and overtly, but, by its very nature, [can only] be found at the conclusion of our effort of looking for it. It would seem that the world is a hieroglyph, and that the "world-beyond," or "world of being," is a phrase which, at the same time, signifies and conceals the world [of things].[28] But a hieroglyph would not be what it is solely by virtue of the figures we see in it; [for it to be what it is,] someone must say to us that "these figures are endowed, above and beyond their manifest form, with a latent sense." In the world, we find only figures which stand out, and which no one has told us to hold suspect of harboring a secret sense. That is why it occurred to me to ask the question as to how it is possible for

---

*Ed.'s N.: I am reproducing here the second article of the abovementioned series. [Cf. supra, n. 1.] The article resulted from a reworking of the original manuscript of this lecture.

human beings not to be content with what they encounter before themselves, with the world of immediacy, but to go after the world-beyond, or world of being, of which no ultrahuman seafarer has ever told them, of which they do not have the slightest inkling.

"Knowledge" is the name usually given to our effort to arrive at being, of which the said question marks the beginning. Accordingly, that question can also be phrased as follows: why does a human being strive to know? In the solemn first page of his *Metaphysics,* Aristotle, acting the part of Molière's doctor,[29] gave us this answer: "All men by nature desire to know."[30] We could translate Aristotle's reply into our terminology by saying that human beings seek after being by virtue of the fact that they constitutively are entities seeking after being. But we, who do not aspire to play the part of Molière's doctor, [will have to] inquire precisely into what, in the makeup of a human being, brings him to [engage in an effort to] know.

It is to be noted that Aristotle does not clearly grasp this prior question, which is precisely the one we are raising now. The proof of it is found in the fact that he adds the following to his statement: "An indication of this is the delight we take in our senses . . . and above all others [in] the sense of sight."[31] Here Aristotle is thinking of Plato, who placed the men of science, the philosophers, among the *philotheámones,* i.e., those who are fond of looking or attend spectacles.[32]

"To look" is to examine what is there with one's own eyes, while "to know" is to seek after what is not there, namely, being. To know, then, is precisely not to be content with seeing what one can see, but rather to refuse what one sees, as being insufficient, and to postulate the invisible.

By means of that remark and many others which are plentiful in his books, Aristotle makes his idea of knowledge apparent to us. According to him, it would simply amount to using or exercising a faculty possessed by a human being, just as looking consists in using [the power of] vision. We are endowed with sensibility, with memory (which serves to preserve the data derived therefrom), and with experience (in which [the contents of] memory are selected and decanted).[33] All of them are mechanisms belonging to the psyche of a human being, who, like it or not, exercises them. Knowledge would be that exercise.

In my opinion, there exists a radical confusion with which the entire history of philosophy has been weighed down, especially in the area of epistemology. When one asks why human beings occupy themselves with knowing, the forthcoming reply consists in exhibiting the intellectual mechanisms a human being sets in motion in order to know. The said mechanisms thus come to be identified with knowing. Now then, it is evident that to know a thing is not the same as to see or remember it, or, on account of it, to carry out intellectual operations properly so called, such as abstracting, comparing, or inferring. All of these are "faculties" or devices that I happen to possess, and of which I avail myself in order to know, but they are not knowing itself.

In the first place, it would be advisable to ask why it is that a human being "makes use" of such faculties. It will not be enough to say, as Aristotle did, that we employ them because we possess them, [for,] in order to make use of an instrument, it is not enough to possess it. [Consider:] our houses are full of implements which have fallen into disuse, which we do not avail ourselves of, because the service they provide does not interest us any longer. [Or again:] John may be a man who has a great talent for mathematics, but, since he is only interested in literature, he does not occupy himself with mathematics.

But, secondly, it has not been established that the intellectual devices in question are adequate [to the task], so that their functioning would yield, without further ado, a product [describable as] "knowledge" properly so called. Now, it is an indubitable fact that human beings occupy themselves with knowing; moreover, that they, apparently, are in need of knowing; and [also] that they, to that end, avail themselves of any means they happen to find (such as sensation, memory, reasoning, and quite a few others), without however becoming satisfied with any one of them in particular or with the ensemble they form. To tell the truth, human beings feel a strange eagerness to know, and yet they lack the gifts for the endeavor. [In other words,] what they lack is precisely a "nature," in Aristotle's sense of the term.[34]

Why is it, then, that human beings are moved to know, to inquire? In the lines of Aristotle I quoted above, one also finds, more by way of suggestion than actually expressed, [the point] that human nature consists too of a faculty that serves to incite them to set their other (i.e., intellectual) faculties to work. Curiosity is the faculty in question. For Aristotle, it amounts to nothing else than an urge to stick one's nose everywhere, to go from here to there in order to see everything visible. Therefore, it is, so to speak, a love of spectacles.[35]

We have already pressed the term "curiosity" just a little,[36] and that allowed us to have a glimpse of how something more serious may be contained therein, above and beyond our urge to see. Let us not return to that now. Suffice it to remark that the word in question, even if taken in its pejorative sense,[37] does not permit us at all to arrive at an explanation of the case at hand. Rather, it is the word that has to be clarified. I [can] well understand what curiosity is when I witness a man, who has been told that they are showing a good picture at a given theater, going to see it; yet I fail to understand its meaning when I am told that, because he is curious, he is endeavoring to know, that is to say, that he is seeking after the world-beyond, or world of being. According to its everyday employment, the word "curiosity" implies that, before we encounter a visible object, we are already aware of its existence, and that, in view of that fact, we set out to take a look at the object. But the things of the world of immediacy do not give us even a slight inkling of the [existence of the] world-beyond, or world of being. The world is not porous or riddled, as if it were some old decoration allowing us to [see through] and have a glimpse of what lies behind the stage. The world is a thoroughly manifest and gapless area, wherein nothing like being is to be found, or become present as a datum. Being as such does not manifest itself; it does not appear. On the contrary, it formally is that which does not manifest itself, that which does not appear, that which does not render itself present, whether as a whole or even in terms of any of its smallest parts. Being is that of which we do not have the slightest inkling. In brief, being is the absent par excellence. How [could] it [ever] be seen, and how could we [ever] feel curious about seeing it, once "curious" is taken in that sense, if being is not conspicuous or, if you will, is only conspicuous by its absence?

What, then, is being? what are essences? if we have no inkling of either prior to our being curious. In effect, the only originary datum we have concerning being as such is that human beings—you and I—raise the question of being. Originarily, being is not a thing lying there, more or less at hand, among things, as a pearl is found in a wheat granary. Originarily, being is encountered only in the question raised by a human being about it.

That is why we have to push further with the analysis of that strange human doing which amounts to raising the essential question. In conducting that analysis, we had, to begin with, endeavored to understand the simple sense that the expression, "what is?" possesses, and, [as a result,] we came to note that, in such a question, we mean to exchange a non-mediate, manifest thing—say, this light—for a latent one, namely, its being or essence. That notwithstanding, we still do not have the slightest inkling about the nature of the quasi-thing called "being" or "essence." We only know that it is not found right before us, that it is other than any thing [we may find] in the world; that, therefore, it is different from everything which is given or non-mediate; that it is something alien and concealed. But these are all negative qualifications. No matter how many times we try to come to terms with [the question component,] "what is?" or with essence, we will never arrive at a positive determination. Why?

When linguists speak of the signification of a word, they are, more or less knowingly, speaking improperly, by virtue of the simple reason that a word [alone] is nothing. There is no such thing as a word [by itself];

there is only a word in conjunction with others in a phrase. Moreover, the genuine signification of a word is the one it possesses in a given phrase. Separated from that it becomes a fragment of itself, a mere portion or outline. A word is the smallest organ of an organism called a "phrase," from which it is inseparable; it is only as a part of that whole that it acquires and yields its proper sense, as a head or an arm are not properly what they are, unless they are attached to the trunk.[38] It is at this point, however, where the linguists part company with me, for the phrase, in turn, does not exist in isolation either. The sense of a phrase is not found complete in itself. One thinks and utters a phrase in some living situation; only in it does a phrase possess its full sense. In other words, one thinks and utters a phrase because of something and for the sake of something,[39] as an organ of the organism which a given living situation is.[40]

Accordingly, there is no question that exists in isolation. Utterance, in general, and interrogation, in particular, are doings of ours. If I ask the question, "what is this light?" or wonder [about its essence], it must be that I am in need of doing so. Yet the need is not found expressed or declared in the question, remaining as it does prior to it. But is it not absurd for me to attempt to understand the question, if I have previously cut it off from the whole in terms of which it was raised?

Every attempt to cast light on [the question,] what is . . . ? will prove useless, then, unless we consider the question a means human beings are in search of in order to meet a necessity, a need. We thus have to put the question [after being] back into the living situation which gave rise to it, as if it were a piece of a jigsaw puzzle.[41]

That is why we have to push further with our analysis of that strange human doing which essential questioning is.

To ask a question is a way of speaking. But why does a human being speak? Does he also do so by . . . "nature"? In connection with speaking, an error is committed that is identical with the one into which one falls whenever one asks why it is that a human being strives to know. The answer given amounts to indicating the physiological and psychological instruments a human being utilizes when he speaks. But this [procedure] does not, in the least, serve to cast light on the question at hand. [For that purpose,] it does not matter which mechanism is employed by us in order to speak.

Speaking is one of the things we do in our lives. Here we are intent on understanding the part the former plays in the latter, its role or function. Each one's life—and I mean not his biological, but his biographical life—is an organism in which nothing is inert; everything done therein is done, willy-nilly, because of something and for the sake of something.[42]

To speak is to render oneself manifest. But the event called manifestation has a twofold sense. On the one hand, I can make my thoughts manifest to another, thoughts that remained concealed meanwhile. To speak is, in this case, to converse. I lay my ideas bare before my neighbor; I allow him to partake of my thoughts; I impart them to him. But, on the other hand, my thoughts are also [the means I have of] speaking to myself. When Homer describes Achilles, who, in his rage, had withdrawn to his warrior's tent to design his revenge all alone, [the poet] says that Achilles abided in conversation with himself. Does this mean that I render my thoughts manifest to myself? In other words, do I first think and then proceed to formulate and say to myself what I have thought? No, there is no full-fledged thought which is not speech; thought, in and of itself, is already formula, idiosyncratic speech, statement. When I speak not only do I speak to someone, but I also say something, and this act of saying something—whether directed to another or to myself—is thinking.

Now then, when I say something to someone, [it means that] I have said it to myself before or, equivalently, that I have [already] thought it. Thinking and conversing are thus [different] species of speaking, thinking being the primary or radical one of the two. It is contended that there would be no language if human beings were not social creatures, if around individual human beings their neighbors did not exist. Now, would thought exist if a human being lived by him- or herself? That is a silly thing to ask. Thought and language are inseparable functions, both equally finding their origins in our social nature. From this point of view, no essential difference obtains between them. But, in the individual human being, inner speech, or [the event of] saying something to oneself, precedes one's act of communicating it. That is why I maintain, against common opinion, that we must acknowledge that the way of speaking which thinking is has priority over the one that conversing is. The Greeks were right when they employed the locution *lógos* equivocally, assigning to it as they did the task of equally signifying "saying" and "thinking."

To speak is always to render [something] manifest, but when I converse with another I communicate to him or her what is already manifest to me. By contrast, it is on the occasion when I think or speak to myself that I originarily perform the operation of rendering [something] manifest. The thing I render manifest to myself was hidden and secret to me before [I thought of it]. If not, what would have been the purpose of wearing myself out thinking?

To think is to discover that which lies concealed; the same goes for speaking. Please note that one only speaks of what is not manifest or at hand. Cervantes' joke proves my point. He wrote that Orbaneja "inscribed 'this is a rooster'" [next to it] at the bottom of his painting.[43] Now, where is the humor in that? It is presupposed that, normally, a painting renders an object present; therefore, it is idle to add that the object, which is already there on its own or by means of its faithful representation, is this or that. In a display of great humility, Orbaneja [shows that he] is aware that one cannot find a rooster, or anything remotely like it, in his painting of a rooster. Orbaneja's rooster is absent or invisible; that is why, in a very human gesture, the painter proceeds to name it, speaks of it, or renders it manifest.

It may very well be that we could succeed in determining what speaking is by studying one of its most frequent distortions, namely, chattering.[44] The chatterbox is one who wrongly avails him- or herself of language, i.e., against the purpose intrinsic in stating [anything]; in fine, he or she is one who says what need not be said. Therefore, one who speaks properly and naturally does the opposite of what the chatterbox does. We are bored by the chatterbox, to the extent that [his or her speech] renders manifest to us things with which we are already acquainted, that were already present to us, or, if they are not present to us, that it is our desire, for lack of interest, that they should remain concealed from us. This is, then, the precise reversal of speaking, the function of which consists in uncovering for us what is a secret to us.

To speak is, for example, to narrate. A narration presents a listener with something which is absent, with something that he or she has not witnessed. It then consists always in rendering manifest something that was concealed, in making the latent apparent, in laying bare that which was covered up. Isn't that what [the Spanish verb] *decir* ["to say" or "utter"] means, in light of its etymological origins? [Consider] *deico* (as found in Latin inscriptions), *deíknumi* (in Greek), or *diçami* (in Sanskrit): [they all mean] to show, to make visible. *Díke,* or justice, originally signified to "accuse," that is to say, to reveal or uncover a crime. The same can be said of the root which is part of the negative Spanish word *indecible* [i.e., "unsayable" or "unutterable"]: it derives from *femi* and *fasco* (in Greek) and from *bha* (in Sanskrit), [all of which mean] "to shine," "to glow," "to make [something] appear."

When I am thinking, that is, when I am speaking to myself, I am obviously attempting to make something clear to myself. And my entire endeavor in such an intellectual doing amounts to laying things bare by removing their confusing covering, in order to bring them to the light of day, make them rise to the surface, or render them manifest.[45] That which is other [than the thing I am thinking about], the confusing matter that lay non-mediately in front of me before I began thinking, was not, therefore, the thing itself, the *autó èn* [the one itself], the genuine [thing]. Or equivalently put: it was not the thing in its truth. Please note that here "truth" does not signify, to begin with, an attribute of a proposition or judgment, of an utterance, but of the reality itself. One of the most radical and enduring errors committed in philosophy has been to suppose that the truth is originarily an attribute of judgment, of thinking. It is only with Scholasticism that one faintly [comes to] make out that the truth is, to begin with, an attribute of things. And that is quite plain for, if someone were to inquire into the nature of the truth of a judgment, the reply would be forthcoming to the effect that it is a character it possesses whenever what we think therein about a thing corresponds to what the thing in question is. The truth is thus transferred from the judgment to the being of the thing. The short philosophical dialogue [that once took place] at the Praetorium expresses it better: "What is truth?"[46] [Pilate said to Jesus]. Truth is *that which is*.

But this is the question: what about a thing is its being, what about it its truth? There are many values or aspects to the thing itself (say, to this light). To begin with, it is such as it appears [to be]. Yet the appearance of a thing is not the thing itself. If it were, seeing the thing would suffice, and we could dispense with the job of thinking about it. But it so happens that, when things [are considered] in terms of their non-mediate appearance, they happen not to coincide with themselves, they are not equal to what they genuinely are, with what they are in their truth. I see the stars above as persistent specks of light. [Many questions may then occur to me. For example:] Are they far or near? How big are they? What are they made of? Why do some of them move, while others do not? How do they hold themselves up there? My seeing of the stars, far from disclosing to me the truth about them, their genuine being, or what "they themselves" are, only furnishes me with one single, solitary finding, namely, that they are not as they seem to be. Behind the light I see, there is, then, the true light, which I do not see. And the truth of my judgment about it will not amount just to the coincidence [of my judgment] with the light, or simply with the thing, but with the truth of the light, or with the light in its truth. People are always oblivious to this decisive point; they are always unaware of the fact that the behavior of reality itself is essentially twofold. If by itself it were, as a matter of course, genuine in character, then every contact of ours with things would already be the possession of their truth, and the troubles and exertions involved in our thinking or knowing [them] would be superfluous. But if human beings err when they attempt to know, that is not due, primordially and solely, to some defect of theirs. How could a human being err when confronted with a univocal reality, with one that is just as it appears? An error in thinking consists in taking as true reality something which is a reality [indeed], but one which [nonetheless] is not a true or genuine reality. Concerning this matter, we must correct those modern practices which lead one to pose the problem of error exclusively in terms of the knowing subject, while leaving out of account the fact that reality is a partner in error. It is urgent, therefore, to pose that problem before we [even] begin with epistemological considerations, at the very threshold of any philosophical system, at [the level of] pure ontology.[47]

However, let us leave this matter alone. Perhaps we may return to it later in a more substantial way, at which point we may come to realize the frightful significance of [the question,] whether "a thing is in its truth or not," or the problem of the genuineness of being.

What is important to us presently is only to think that thought or speech is the locus in which things manifest their truth; that, consequently, they are not [out] there by themselves in their truth; but that, if they are to be uncovered and laid bare, so that their genuine "nature" may come through, they would require an effort on the knowing subject's part. That is why, as I pointed out,[48] one speaks only of what is concealed and secret, of what is not manifest. Every act of speaking, or utterance, is that whereby a secret not belonging to us, but to things, is revealed. If it were otherwise, our speaking and meditative doing would be altogether superfluous and meaningless.

Let this suffice in respect of speaking in general. Please note, however, that raising a question in one's mind is that way of speaking in which what one is saying reveals no secret. The question raised is precisely the expression of our ignorance. What are we saying, then, what is it that we are speaking about when we raise a question, if it turns out that, when we do so, we are not in possession of the key to any secret, if we do not make anything manifest to ourselves?

It is evident that, before we come to uncover a secret, cast light on something that lies concealed, or solve a riddle,[49] there must have been [in us] a mental state in which we simply realized that there was a secret, a riddle, a concealment. Without a mental state of that sort, the process of thinking would not be triggered [in us], we would not strive to know and speak.[50] But how would we give expression to such a situation, in which our minds are being confronted with a riddle as such?[51] We would say to ourselves: here is something about which I have to think, and, since to us thinking is presently synonymous with speaking, here is something about which we must speak. A problem or riddle is just that and nothing else, viz., something about which one has to speak.[52] Consequently, the mental state in which we realize that there is a problem or riddle is, by itself, [the condition in which] thinking or speaking is postulated, required, or demanded. Now then, is that not the sense of every question? A question is an incomplete way of speaking, for a response is solicited therein. Strictly speaking, it is nothing [but] a request; or, equivalently stated, to raise a question is to ask [someone] to speak. It is to discover, or to arrive—before oneself—at the discovery of that for which speaking is genuinely needed, namely, the uttering of a truth, the rendering of something concealed manifest. Therefore, a question is speech *in statu nascendi* [being born]. It follows that an interrogative phrase, as opposed to all the other kinds, is not self-enclosed; it does not come to an end, even when judged in terms of intonation. It is the other way round: at its conclusion, it remains open in midair; it goes in search of another phrase (namely, a reply) upon which to find support in order to continue. It is the germ of speech because it is essentially a beginning, a drive toward it. Before one speaks, it is evident that one must feel the urge to do so, an urge that already is the anticipation of speech. Therefore, it is, as it were, speaking before speaking, a *lógos* before *lógos*, a *pro-lógos*.[53] Perhaps it is not by chance that, in our writing practice, the question mark has such a strange look, its graphic representation being inconclusive, as it prolongs itself as a superfluous boundary line that never closes, remaining, as it does, loose in the wind.

In an essential question, we make a request, to wit: [that someone] declare the being of something to us. Now then, being or essence is, as we already had the occasion to see,[54] that which, constitutively, lies concealed, remote, distant, and absent; in fine, it is the mysterious or enigmatic par excellence. But our theme was the determination of how we came to take any notice of that which is absolutely concealed, of how it is that we came to speak of being, even though we lacked any data about it which would be non-mediate and straightforward in character.

# Fourth Lecture*

In brief, what is the meaning of the locution "being"[55] in the question, what is the light? It is not reasonable to believe that a simple inspection of the locution would allow us to ascertain its meaning. If taken in isolation, every word is ambiguous; it is an isolated organ. This is [also] true of a phrase: every phrase refers to an organic totality, namely, to one's living situation (which is the fictive aspect of our example). [In order to understand] a question, we have imaginatively to place ourselves in the living situation out of which the question would arise.

Suppose all lights are turned off. Let us attempt to determine what has occurred in such a situation. Before that was the case, we had not inquired

---

*Added by the Spanish editor.

into the nature of the light; or, equivalently, we had not called the light into question. The light was part and parcel of our lives; we availed ourselves of its services. It was, in our lives, what it is non-mediately, namely, that which illuminates us. Our living dealing with it originally consisted in availing ourselves of its services, just as we do with all other things in our surroundings. At nightfall, as we found ourselves in need of light, we would turn it on and thus reap for ourselves the benefits of its power to illuminate, [just as] we would turn it off when we were no longer in need of it. During the day, [we would handle our situation] analogously, by opening or closing the windows and curtains. In other words, the light was not, to us, a "thing" properly so called; [rather,] it was a utensil, i.e., something the reality of which consists in rendering a service [to us]. And since no service exists except in reference to the person taking advantage of it, [we must say that] there is no utensil at all except within the scope of someone's life.[56]

A utensil, as such, does not exist except insofar as it is being put to use; its existence or reality is reducible to its functioning, [whether] actual, past (which I remember), or posible (which I anticipate). I do not, however, occupy myself originarily with a utensil apart from its actual employment. I do not think of [the question,] what is a utensil? when I am making no use of it, when it is not [actually] a utensil. Otherwise, it would follow that my dealing with a utensil could not be reduced to my use of it as a means in my life, for I would be able to occupy myself with it outside that relationship. Moreover, outside its relationship with me, I would [thus] be able to attribute to it a reality above and beyond that which it possesses for my life, [that is to say,] therefore, a reality of its own, a reality pertaining only to it, a reality in itself. [Now,] strictly speaking, that is what the name "thing" refers to, [for] something is [taken as] a thing when I realize that it is endowed with its own existence, with a nature that belongs to it when I neither see nor am occupied with it.

Let me insist on this: one cannot think of a utensil as such without thinking of its functioning; without, therefore, thinking of the service it renders; without, therefore, thinking of the person to whom it renders its service and to whom the utensil would not render it, if that person were not in need of it. But that person would have no need of it if he or she were not needy, that is to say, if he or she were not constrained to do or make this or that. Now then, to live means to have to do or make this or that, to be in need (of doing or making this or that). A utensil, then, implicates a life of which it is an element, and, apart from which, a utensil does not exist, it is nothing. You could say to me that that is not so, for, apart from what a utensil is in a given life, it is a material thing endowed with a reality of its own, with a reality independent of any life. Yet if you reflect a little, you will come to note that for a hammer to be a *thing*—above and beyond what it is as I avail myself of it when I need it to drive nails in—presupposes that I have called into question what happens to a hammer when it is not a hammer. But now we are endeavoring precisely to ascertain how it is that a human being calls that and, in more general terms, anything into question.

It is evident that no one's life, to begin with, calls whatever surrounds it into question; on the contrary, it finds itself, to begin with, in the midst of a stock of items which make their appearance as utensils already inserted therein. Let us try to think of the lives of primitive human beings: the earth is to them the solid [ground] supporting them and allowing them to walk,[57] by contrast with water, which serves to wash, clean, and refresh them, but which does not offer them any support unless they swim. A tree is that which serves to supply them with wood, fruit, or shade. If such original instruments did not exist, human beings would not [be able to] live. In other words, if human beings did not find in their surroundings facilities of which to avail themselves as living support, the fact we call "life" would not exist. To begin with, living consists, then, in encountering oneself, in encountering necessities or needs alongside oneself, and in encountering, alongside them, a stock of facilities that befit and serve to meet them. Let it be clearly understood that the discovery of the original stock in question does not take place at a particular moment of one's life, but is identical with it. To live is already, *ab initio* [from the beginning], to be engaged in using such utensils or facilities. If [you do] not [agree], try to think of a life wherein there were, to begin with, no adequate correspondence between necessities and means. Such a life would of course be impossible, [and] it would be impossible not only to live it, but even to think of it; it would be something radically other than that which we call life.

Our situation is no different from that of the savage. Originally, we also encounter utensils; strictly speaking, we encounter many more utensils than the savage, utensils that provide us with greater facilities. It will not do to say [however] that this electric light would not exist if someone had not wondered about the nature of light, if someone had not, therefore, wondered about the light as it is in itself, not as a utensil. Who would doubt that? But, as a matter of fact, even we, who are living now, encountered the light originally as a utensil, later to find out from someone else that it was an artifact fashioned by other human beings. Accordingly, dealing with something in terms of utility always has priority; it is most probable that even a present-day human being would never have seriously wondered about the nature of light, if he had not been obliged to study physics, which is not the same as spontaneously wondering about it.[58]

To keep to our example: in order for us to ask about what the light is, it was necessary for it to have failed; therefore, in order for us to come to the realization that the light has a reality of its own (precisely the reality we are oblivious to, and which we are inquiring about), it was necessary for that utensil abnormally to have ceased rendering its service [to us].

Let us take down this important admonition: a human being does not inquire into what something *is,* unless he encounters a difficulty (that is to say, some failure, limitation, or impediment) in dealing with it.

Now imagine [a situation] opposite to the one I proposed before [for your consideration], namely, a life in which a human being would be surrounded only by facilities, in which everything—mind you, absolutely everything—would function by itself, without effort, annoyance, or failure. The world of immediacy would [then] by itself respond to our every need by corresponding adequately thereto without limitations of any kind. We would not miss anything. Upon arising, our desires would be satisfied by the surrounding [world]. Human beings would not have to wonder about anything; rather, they would always be held by what is present and non-mediate, which would fill—exactly or without remainder—the sphere of their attention.

However, in a world of that sort there would not even be anything like attention, for paying attention is a manner of effort (perhaps, the prototype of any effort). There is no attending, except where subjects have to seek after something they are lacking but need, and there is no seeking after something, if it does not lie hidden among many things we actively prescind from in order to isolate that after which we are seeking. Or to put it otherwise: attention is the twofold effort in which, in order to focus on something, we have to disregard all other things. What is paid attention to is paid attention to (i.e., favored by the central and more intense light cast by our minds), because it stands out over against a sphere [consisting of items] not attended to. Accordingly, in a world exclusively comprised of facilities, there would be no need to heed anything; rather, the mind would effortlessly coincide always with the world. And, in that case, the mind, free from effort of any kind, would not become aware of itself and would blend with the world; in other words, there would be no subject who would be conscious of itself as other than, and opposite to, the world. Now then, a reality like that would not deserve the name "life." It is essential to anything so called that one should come therein to the realization of one's existence, as well as of the fact that the nature of one's existence amounts to finding oneself among things other than oneself, the totality of which things would constitute what we call "world."

We have come to a definition of life, without having set out to do so and without assigning, for the time being, any formal character to our finding. [It is this:] life consists in encountering oneself in the midst of facilities and difficulties. This definition is so simple that I do not believe there is any risk in accepting it, inasmuch as it is given [to us] with such clear evidence. There could not be anything more trivial and hackneyed. Nonetheless, at this point, I do not [wish to] keep from you that that is to me the most important thing in philosophy, and that such a triviality is, if accurately understood, the source out of which springs the rest of the system of philosophical truths.

Life consists, therefore, of facilities and difficulties, and not just of facilities or difficulties. Now, as we had the occasion to see, human beings and their minds display different behaviors when confronted with either facilities or difficulties. A facility is what I have referred to by means of words like "instrument," "utensil," or "implement"; it is that with which one does or makes something that one has to do or make; it is something that presents itself as being suitable for the action in question. Instruments, then, are the first sort of reality about which it would be advisable to find an accurate definition. In other words, they are the sort of reality to whose attributes one must point, while endeavoring not to mix them up with other attributes that do not have to do with it ([for they would specifically belong to] the definition of, say, a carpenter's brace, a drinking glass, a bicycle, a stick, or a cane). Entities of this sort are defined, without exception, in terms of their use, and the most natural way of doing so is to feign that we are using them. Accordingly, among the attributes of instrumental realities, one would find, to begin with, their fungibility, for they are nothing unless they are being put to use. Their existence is *actual;* their being consists in rendering a certain service (e.g., the being of a hammer consists in driving nails in, so that [one must say that,] when the hammer is not being engaged in driving a nail in, the hammer *is* not).

But someone could say to me that, when the hammer is not being used to drive in nails, it *is located* in a corner of the room and that, when I am occupied with writing and not with driving in nails, my eyes discover it over there in the corner where it is found. What is the hammer I see when I see it but not put it to use? Is it not then also endowed with *being?* Yet the *being* it then possesses would be a manner-of-being different from that which it possesses insofar as it is an instrument.

To this I reply as follows: when I see the hammer, I say to myself, "my dear fellow, *there it is!*" Now, what is the meaning of this private form of expression? Someone could say it simply means that I have seen the hammer. Not at all: when I see the hammer, I do not say to myself, "I have seen the hammer," because that would be [tantamount to] my having seen and encountered my act of seeing. No, I do not see my act of seeing in that case;[59] I am but what I am to myself, and, in every case, I am to myself only what I am doing. Seeing something is no living *doing;* it is no activity of which, as such, I am aware while I am engaged in doing it, just as the digestion or the biochemical reaction taking place now in the cells of my [body] is no doing of mine. Here the everyday use of [the Spanish] language falsifies matters in part, for it gives one to understand that one has, or has not, done the digesting. But, in truth, one does not do the digesting; rather, it is one's body which does. I am not my body, for I encounter myself upon encountering my body in my life, just as I encounter the Guadarrama range or this table. Just like everything else in the world, my body is an ensemble of facilities and difficulties I find. [For example,] my body is agile (which would count as a facility), but it is sickly as well (which would count as a difficulty, or as a string of difficulties). My body is an instrument like any other, even though, of all the instruments, it is the most important one, since it is the closest and most permanent one to me; [it is the most important one] since it interposes itself between me and all the other instruments. Accordingly, one could say that my body is, in various senses, the instrument of [all] instruments. Yet, whatever comes to pass therein (say, my digestion), I do not do [myself]; on the contrary, I encounter it as one of the manifold elements forming part of my surroundings, of that which is other than I.[60] In physics, it is said that my body would not exist if there were no heavenly bodies; if that is so, one would be less off-target in saying that it is the stars which do the digesting than in saying that I do.

As you can gather, the word "do" is employed here in a twofold sense. If I say that my body, in conjunction with the stars, does the digesting, the "doing" I am talking about is one of which I take notice only externally. But if, while presently engaged in speaking, I say that speaking is what I am doing, I am taking notice of it internally and non-mediately. This doing of mine is not external to me; it is not something happening outside me, something of which I would actually possess only my thought concerning its occurrence out there; rather, when I presently engage in speaking, I am this act of speaking, and this act of speaking is myself. I do not think that I am speaking in the way I do when I think that my body is comprised of cells; rather, speaking and entertaining the thought that I am speaking are, in this nexus, one and the same thing. I am nothing but that which I am aware of doing, whether the doing in question is active or passive. I am the one who is speaking, walking, meditating, or writing; but I am also the one who is suffering, putting up with [someone's] chatter, or waiting a while for the appointed hour of the train's arrival, that is to say, the one who is "killing or marking time."[61] Instead of "doing," I could now say "being occupied with." I am the one who is occupied with this or that, and I am nothing but the swarm of my occupations. Living is being occupied with something. This term is better suited to make apparent that which is essential to my doing, since, as a matter of course, it suggests that a doing of mine is only the one of which I am aware, the one in which I am posited, the one, in fine, of which I consist, which is my being. But just as an instrument is no thing, neither am I. I am neither my body nor my soul. I am the one who lives in this world *by means of* the body and the soul which have fallen to his lot. And if my soul is not endowed, for example, with much of a will, with much of a memory, or with much talent, I would have to put up with the fact, just as I would with not having much money. Whether I like it or not, I have no choice but to live by means of this poorly endowed soul and this rheumatic body in the midst of the not very pleasant Spanish world of 1930. I am the one who has to avail himself of all that (i.e., soul, body, and world), the one who has to avail himself of all that in order to lead his own life.

Now, since it is a matter of innovating the most radical philosophical questions and of turning the most venerable of traditional concepts upside down, when I engage one of them I have no choice—to some extent—but to touch on the rest by way of anticipation. Thus, by means of ever-nearing turns or circles,[62] I will be rendering specific the system that such concepts form. A philosophical system can only be understood as a whole.

Let me now return to the [case of the] hammer I see, which served me as the occasion of saying to myself, "my dear fellow, there it is!"[63] It was [then] a question of determining the manner-of-being that the hammer would be endowed with when I am not putting it to use, but when I merely find it lying in the corner of the room. To that end, I raised the question, what is the meaning of such an expression of silent discourse with myself? I have already corrected my first and most obvious reply thereto, according to which it would merely signify that I have seen the hammer. We have learned that we always have to ask ourselves, *whenever* we speak of something, the question, what am I doing by means of it, or in its midst? Primarily, I do not realize that I am seeing a hammer; I only realize that I have found a hammer, that I have encountered it out there, that is to say, that I have recognized it [as a hammer].[64] And that was precisely what that phrase gave expression to, viz., that I have recognized a hammer. And this—to recognize it—is what I have done with it. Nothing else.

Please note, however, that a new complication arises: previously I had made use of the hammer (e.g., I employed it to drive in nails), but at this point I [come to] re-cognize it. Is it possible to re-cognize something if one has not previously taken cognizance of it? Now, strictly speaking, I had not previously taken cognizance of the hammer; my dealing with it consisted in *putting it to use*. I am not denying that my faculty of seeing, and even certain intellectual operations, necessarily play a part, as do my muscles, in my employment of the hammer. Yet none of that implicates [an act of] taking cognizance, just as turning the electric light on and off does not presuppose that one is in possession of concepts belonging to [the sciences of] optics and electricity.

Let it be clearly understood that our dealing with worldly utensils is not primarily cognitive in character. To entertain the opposite view has been the most deeply rooted shortcoming exhibited by philosophy in its entire past, and particularly by modern philosophy, by idealism.[65] Cro-Magnon man, who polished stones in order to perfect them as instruments, did not first have [for that purpose] to raise the question concerning the being of a stone; therefore, he did not occupy himself, properly speaking, with [the task of] knowing a stone. The same was true in the case of the wood out of which he would make his bows, arrows, and the stakes of his dwelling place. If his bows, arrows, and stakes were to him just instruments he would make, wood was a natural instrument he would not have to make. In effect, an instrument is anything that can be used to do or make something. Now then, wood is that which can be used to make bows, arrows, and stakes. The Spanish word *materia* ["matter"] derives from *madera,* [a Spanish locution meaning "wood,"] just as the Greek word *húle,* [which means] "matter," also signifies "wood."[66] But it so happens that the renowned category "matter" is possessed of an instrumental sense: it is that out of which something is made; it is something human beings avail themselves of in order to fashion artifacts. Later, as human beings engaged in thinking and [were] already [members of the group of the] original philosophers, they endeavored to understand the objective being of things and proceeded to interpret it as if someone more powerful than they had created the numberless and complex things out of one, two, or four primary and simpler things: [this is] matter, be it water, fire, or the so-called four elements.[67] The being of man [thus] consists in doing or making, or so it seems to me, inasmuch as I have not yet furnished the proof for it. [Understood in such terms,] human beings, when they explained the world to themselves, thought of a principle they would call the "Supreme Maker." Now, since they are *homo faber* ["man, the maker"], they would also see in God a superlative fashioner. But once their minds became subtler, they stumbled on the contradiction consisting in presupposing, on the one hand, [the existence of] an almighty God and, on the other, [that of] another independent principle (namely, matter), which, for that very reason, would be a limitation to God. Human beings then wondered who in turn fashioned matter and attempted to withdraw it [as an ultimate principle], while maintaining their explanatory scheme. They then asserted that God created the world out of nothing, therefore, out of something, out of that something I call "nothing". Nothing is the ideal wood which replaces real matter. However, do not take this assertion to be a mere phrase, [for] in Aristotle [one finds] matter to be a subsisting negation; [according to him,] it is nothing determinate, and yet it is.[68]

The same negation or nothing already makes its appearance with Anaximander's *ápeiron* [the "unlimited" or "indefinite"].[69] The reasoning [involved is] inevitable as long as the fashioning scheme is preserved, [that is to say, as long as one keeps] the idea that things are made out of something. If I place all things on one side and wonder about what they are made of, that which would remain on the other side is just the one thing which is *none of them*.

But let me say it again: human beings do not engage, to begin with, in taking cognizance of and explaining whatever surrounds them, but in dealing with it in a pre-cognitive manner, that is to say, in making use of it. This way of dealing [with what they find in the world] is intelligent, of course. If I turn on the light, that means I clearly realize that that is what I am doing, and I understand the what-for of that which I am doing and, moreover, that the light is that which illuminates [me].[70]

# PART III

# WHAT IS LIFE?

# Third Lecture*
## (Wednesday, October 29, 1930)

To take something as the object of our meditation[1] is to make our departure on the basis of the thing as it readily presents itself to us, but at the same time to realize that, at first blush, it shows itself to us in a confused, insufficient manner. In terms of the original aspect it spontaneously displays [before us], every thing is [given as] a muddle. We are in need of achieving clarity about it. To that end, we analyze it [and] establish a preliminary order in the midst of the confusion. This would already yield a second aspect of the thing in question, one which—by virtue of our analysis or meditation—would appear beneath the original aspect [exhibited by the thing]. And yet the newly emerging aspect would not prove sufficient either; [at that point,] we would again subject it to analysis and obtain a third aspect placed underneath the second. It is then that we may say we have made *progress* in our meditation. This process is to continue until we come to an aspect of the thing that, to us, would already seem to be sufficiently clear; it would arise under all the others, and that is why it would be the deepest aspect of the thing. Therefore, meditation is the path traversed by the mind as it moves from the surface and muddled aspect [of a thing] to the one [presenting itself] with clarity and depth.

Now then, the meditative path in question is marked by a feature that distinguishes it from a physical footway. In effect, we cannot proceed from one aspect to another without mentally preserving the sequence of aspects [already considered] or the itinerary of the stations [visited thus far]. In order for us to seek after a new aspect, we have to make our departure on the basis of the preceding one; however, since the latter only made its appearance because, in turn, we arrived at it on the basis of another, we must keep continually alive to the steps we have taken, or to the thread of our reasoning,[2] if we do not wish to go astray in our meditation. We may walk along a road without being concerned with what we are doing, since the path is there, apart from our traversing it and prior to our treading it, while, in the case of meditation, [to proceed] is at once to walk along a path and to bring it about. This is the reason why the mind

---

*Ed.'s N.: I take it that the missing first and second lectures of this 1930–1931 course must have been similar to those immediately preceding them in [Part II of] this edition. They were probably derived from them.

has to wrap itself up with the path it follows as it unfolds it;[3] it has to carry it—so to speak—on its own back, to keep it alive, or—to put it in other words—it has to retrace it constantly, to traverse it time and again. Otherwise, the mind would lose its way and make no progress, [with the result that] the muddle would thicken again around the mind and render it captive once more.

We will find ourselves [in these lectures] constantly in need of reproducing the milestones of the intellectual process that is being born in us. Let me remind you of them:

1. [To the question,] what is metaphysics, or philosophy proper? we replied that it is something a human being does.[4]

2. Now, when we went in search of philosophy, understood as one among the things a human being does, we again found ourselves lost in the midst of their boundless multiplicity. We then attempted to ascertain—at least—the class or sort of doing of which philosophizing would be a species. [As it turned out,] knowing is the sort of doing in question.[5]

3. [Then we asked about] what knowing is and found ourselves going astray once more in the midst of countless possible definitions of knowledge. Among them we sought [to identify] the simplest one, the one that would compromise us the least. This should have been the safest one. We set aside all the definitions of knowing which, in one way or another, amount to saying that knowledge is a human mental - state corresponding to what things are, [for] who can assure us of the existence of any such state? Furthermore, such a definition—no matter which form it adopts—would tie up the large question, what is knowledge? with one of even greater proportions, namely, what is the being of things?[6]

   Accordingly, we proceeded to reduce our answer to its minimal expression and said that knowing is what a human being does when he or she begins to pose an essential question, namely, what is this or that thing?[7]

4. In this fashion, we succeeded in establishing the scope of our problem. We had started by asking, what is philosophy? and [then] we found ourselves wondering about [the meaning of] asking a question, and [specifically of asking] the question concerning being. We answered that to ask a question was to speak or, more exactly, to begin to speak, to demand that one speak about something.[8]

5. But what would speaking be, when it is taken as something that a human being does? Why does a human being speak? Apparently, an action of this sort is so typical of us that—often enough and in not an

inconsiderable number of languages—"human being" signifies "the one who speaks." [In fact,] when the attempt was made to identify the rung immediately preceding the one occupied by a human being in [the scale of] biological evolution, the name "human being devoid of speech" was assigned to the animal that was already endowed with every gift possessed by a human being except one, namely, that which apparently is essential, for it would transform that which "is-not-yet-a-human-being" into that which "is-already-one."

What then is speaking? My answer was this: [since] one speaks only of what is not present or manifest, only about that which lies concealed, speaking would be the action of making or rendering something manifest, of bringing it out from concealment. *To say* something to someone consists in taking out into the open that which is not apparent to him or her. And yet we do not only speak to our neighbor; we also speak to ourselves. To think is to speak to oneself. If in effect human beings think, it is for the sake of making something clear to themselves, of rendering manifest to themselves that which, before, was given to them as concealed, undisclosed, veiled.[9]

Yet, in addressing a question to someone, or else to ourselves, we do not render anything manifest, we clarify nothing. On the contrary, the question conveys the fact that we are faced with a confused state of affairs, for it is precisely by means of the question that we are making a demand for clarification. Or what amounts to the same thing: we are asking that something be said about that state of affairs, that speaking or thinking begin to take charge of its clarifying, unconcealing, disclosive task. This is the reason why I said that a question is the beginning of speech.[10]

A question, therefore, always arises out of a living situation in which we find ourselves in a state of confusion, in which we are face to face with something hidden, closed upon itself, enigmatic, muddled. And the question gives expression to our eagerness to leave such a state behind us and to achieve clarity.

One may not come to a satisfactory understanding of the meaning of a question, no matter how simple it may be, unless thereby one bears in mind the living situation provoking and triggering it—[e.g.,] "the keys; which keys?" It is even less feasible when one is dealing with essential questions, such as, what is this or that thing? And even less so when one is concerned with the metaphysical question proper, to wit: What is Being? which is what one is inquiring into in all such questions.

It is evident that the situation of clarity we postulate is a function of the specific situation of confusion that brought us to postulate it. In this fashion, we come to give our question its final formulation, viz., what sort of thing (is) this most distinctive living situation that leads a human being to ask about Being in general, and not merely about the being of this or that thing? It is evident that a living situation of this kind would be the wellspring of philosophy, the one out of which philosophy would emerge.

But this would unavoidably oblige us at present to consider in all earnestness that matter upon which we have seen ourselves falling back time and again from the very beginning. I mean life, human life, in the situations of which any manner of doing—and especially every act of knowing and asking—apparently originates. Let us then pose a question that will be, for the moment, the final one to be raised: What is life? It is at this point that we have to begin giving an answer. It will be a long one and will occupy us throughout a sizable portion of this lecture course. In a way, the answer would contain the whole of metaphysics.

We shall proceed slowly until we arrive at a most exact formulation of the concept of life. We are to subject life to a forceful and radical analysis. Now, it would be suitable to have before us the very body we are to dissect, were I to propose to you, at this point, that we join forces in carrying out an analysis of life. I need you to "see," to have the immediate intuition of that to which I refer by "life." In other words, what we are going to do today is to formulate a preliminary description of life, a phenomenon of vast proportions. In such a description are already contained the precise components that would eventually form part of the exact concept of life; yet, at this point, they would not be presented as the notes constituting its formal definition, but only as mere suggestions in terms of which you may—let me say it again—first come to "see" the fact of life. It is not possible to define, conceptualize, or think of something without having first seen it.[11]

# Fifth Lecture
## (Wednesday, November 12, 1930)

I believe I have succeeded in putting you in touch with that odd reality I call life, which—strange as it may seem—has been paid so little attention. To begin with, [let me say that] we are not about to deal with a definition. In order to come to understand a definition, one is required first to see the object defined and then compare the latter—in a stepwise fashion—with the concepts that form part of the definition in question. Accordingly, you should henceforth endeavor to recreate the intuition of "life" you have formed during [our meetings] these last two days, and to do so time and again until it completely becomes a habitual possession. To this end, I suggest that you begin by thinking of any life situation whatever, possibly the one in which you find yourselves at this very moment.[12] Next, you should seek to identify the minimal set of general conditions fulfilled therein; in other words, you should prescind from anything that belongs to it concretely and exclusively. You would then see the ingredients of the situation which are responsible for its being "life" pure and simply, and not for its being of one sort or another, stand out on their own. It is clear that if our life situation were not that of participating in a university lecture, as it presently is, but that of being in attendance at a party, then the set of ingredients would be different from those which now constitute this moment of our lives. Yet it is no less clear that some of the ingredients would be common [to both situations]. Accordingly, in each of them (namely, in participating in a university lecture and in attending a party), one would find that whatever is an actual part of it would be present or evident to us, that one was occupied therein with some circumstance or other, that at every turn one would be engaged in deciding this or that and thereby in anticipating one thing or another, and so on.

We can now resume our way on the basis of the trustworthiness of the intuition of life you have already gained. Now, the first thing we are about to add to what we have already stated is something of the greatest significance. Thus far we only have tried to make sure that we have grasped which reality it is we call "life," but we have not inquired into the relationship between this and the other realities. Among the latter, we had chosen three as mere examples, namely, the chair or bench we are sitting on, the person next to us, and God. Our purpose [in doing so] was to come to see clearly the relationship between life and those realities. You realize, of course, that what is valid for the three realities in question, given the fact that they are so different from one another, would [also] be valid for the rest. We wonder, then, how such "things" are related to my life, [i.e.,] whether they are realities apart from my life or not.

In order to engage in the process of answering this question and all its sequels, it would be advisable to render our terminology more precise, to tighten it somewhat. We have seen that life is always someone's life, that it belongs to the one living it. We have also seen that the someone in question—i.e., the one living his life—only constitutes one of the two major and radical components of life, the other being the circumstance, surroundings, or world.[13] It would be advisable to find a suitable name to refer to the someone whose only function is living. Without further ado, we could call him "the one living," except that such a designation would be awkwardly abstract [for our purposes]. It is better to use the expression "human being." A human being is [thus] the one living; he or she is nothing but life. And yet [the name] "human being" must be taken in its individual sense. It is not a "human being in general" who lives; on the contrary, every life is a most individual affair. It is always a given human being who is living, a human being who is unique and irreplaceable, i.e., I. We shall then be using the terms "human being" or "I." However, the locution "I" does present us with some serious difficulties, [since] for the last three hundred years [those who have cultivated] philosophy have been concerned with the "I" [or ego], and have assigned various terminological significations to the word, as a function of the standpoint adopted [in turn] by each philosopher. This notwithstanding, when I say now that I will be employing "I" to refer to the one living his or her life, you must completely disregard all the senses given to the word throughout the history of philosophy, and keep only to its everyday, primary meaning, namely, that which it has when [each one of] us, Mr. or Ms. So and So, says *I*.

The series of surgical and orthopedic operations to which the original sense of the locution "I" has been subjected is astonishing, almost incredible. What else has not yet been tried! Descartes began by defining the ego as *pensée* [thought] or consciousness;[14] Kant would [later] restrict the scope of application of the term, but would at the same time complicate matters more by distinguishing the empirical from the transcendental ego.[15] Nonetheless, the empirical ego is not to be identified with what the locution "I" refers to in everyday speech, namely, the one living his or her life; rather, it is the ego of which Descartes spoke. [Much later we will find that,] for Husserl, the ego also is just the subject of the acts of consciousness.[16] Let me say it once more: it is incredible indeed that, for the first time in the history of philosophy, the locution "I" is simply going to be assigned its original meaning, namely, I, this Mr. or Ms. So and So who is engaged in living his or her life; who, among other things, talks to his or her neighbor, suffers from stomach acidity, plays the lottery, attends philosophy lectures at the University of Madrid, or bought a hat yesterday.

Having made this terminological observation, I now proceed to answer the question I had posed earlier,[17] namely, how is the reality I have called "life" (i.e., "my life") related to any other? We soon come to the realization that any reality other than "my life" is part of my life, in the sense that it depends on the reality which "my life" is. God himself, should he exist, would first somehow exist for me in my life.

Let us try to think of a reality that would be completely divorced from my life. What could I possibly say about it? I would not be able to say whether or not there is any such thing, or (whether or not) it is [of] one [kind] or another. And this means that in no sense would it be a reality. "Reality" is a concept I establish in my life by keeping in view that which

is lived by me; it signifies a modality [of being] or a comportment I find in
some elements belonging to my surroundings, as opposed to the modality
[of being] or the comportment exhibited by others, which I call irreal.
[For example,] in my surroundings, there are [both] horses and centaurs:
the former are real and the latter irreal.[18] The idea of reality would be devoid of sense were it not for this special manner of comportment in my
life, which is different for each one of the two species. There is then no
way of avoiding [the notion] that any reality or thing that is not my life is
either a part (or ingredient of it) or something which would have to be
made known to me in some modality of my life.

As realities go, I have my life and nothing else; conversely, any reality
would first acquire that status in my life; its primordial reality would be
whatever it is as lived by me.

I am inexorably confined within my life. To be sure, my life consists in
my stepping out into the world, in my encountering the world or circumstance, wherein there are plenty of things. But, in turn, the circumstance is
only made up of whatever is lived by me. Let it be clearly understood,
then, that in the circumstance—which is each and every person's "own"
world—there are no things which are inoperative, or that would be found
there without however having obviously been lived by a human being,
that is, by me. For example: a few days ago, I was unaware of the existence of the classroom in which we are gathered. Last week I discovered
it, and it became part of my life. I say now that this classroom did exist in
the world, even though I was unaware of its existence. But what would
such an assertion of mine mean, if it is understood exactly? It signifies
that, as I go on living, I notice that new things constantly make their appearance within my actual circumstance. This leads me to understand—
or to "sense," rather than to understand strictly speaking—that my circumstance encompasses not only the stock of things present [to] and
acting on me at this point, but also that which comprises things past, as
well as the vaguely defined stock of things future. One of the constitutive
features of that which I call "world," wherein I encounter myself, is to be
a sphere marked always by its incompleteness and its never being subject
to a final inventory. Indeed, there are no things, no things *concretely* exist,
except those which are actually lived by me; and yet it is the case that,
[even] if I ran through each and every such thing, I would still leave out of
account something else, namely, that which I have not yet seen, or the unknown, which is irreducible to the former, and that I live in no less concrete a fashion than them.[19] Please note that a life would be no life, if the
surroundings in which human beings would encounter themselves were
completely known to them and involved no possibility of novelty for
them. There you have it: our surroundings are such that they contain,

among other constitutive dimensions, that of the unknown as such. I do not know, of course, which particular things are to be found in the makeup of the area of the unknown, but I do see concretely the unknown as a whole. I would say that I see it as the non-concrete in the most concrete of fashions; it acts on me most concretely, precisely insofar as it is not concrete. Sometimes human beings would be led to commit suicide, if they believed that the world is reducible to what is already known to them, but, realizing that the circumstance contains the dimension or realm of "that which is still unknown," their hopes [serve them to] cast anchor by the land of the non-concrete, thus finding support and stability in life by means of what they hope for. There are other occasions, however, in which the unknown, precisely as unknown, produces terror in human beings, [for] they are [then] afraid of that which they do not know.

The circumstance consists of that which exists for me, and yet the unknown also exists, inasmuch as it is a dimension of the circumstance. This classroom now exists for me in a concrete fashion. But when I say[20] that it also existed previously even though I was not cognizant of the fact, I mean to restore it to the dimension of the unknown in which it was found previously, except that, now, it makes its return to it enriched with a concrete character it was not previously endowed with.

We are not yet ready—not even remotely—to make a frontal attack on the serious ontological problem palpitating behind all this. We were only in urgent need of pointing out that human beings find themselves hermetically confined within their lives. What is lived by us serves to delimit the sphere containing every reality. Or equivalently expressed: life is the absolute reality, including as it does all other realities, and being that on which all other realities depend. Let us not try at present to render precise what is meant when it is said that life includes all other realities, or determine the exclusive sense in which the latter depend on the former. Suffice it for us to be content with the clarity unavoidably resulting from saying that human beings are unable to speak of any reality which has not been lived by them. This is sufficient for us to be entitled to assert, with a modicum of intelligibility, that life is the absolute.

Without claiming here—to say it again—that I am dealing with the question fully, and simply for the purposes of instruction, let me assert that the philosophical term "absolute" can be used in two senses: first, it may refer to anything that exists independently of anything else; second, it may point to that which, in itself, is all-encompassing. Now then, the fact of my life, with and in which I encounter myself,[21] does not appear to be conditioned by any other. My life does not exist conditionally but absolutely, even to the point that any other fact or reality—note this well—already presupposes the fact of my life, in which it [would] appear to me or come to my attention. It is no objection against [the thesis of] the non-dependence of the reality of my life to argue that there is a cause to it, since to acknowledge there is such a cause, to seek after it, and [even] perhaps to find it are so many performances of my life, which [thereby] involve, *impliciter*,[22] its existence. Let it be clearly understood, then, that the fact or reality of my life is prior to—and a presupposition of—any other fact. Any other fact, no matter which, is relative to my life; in effect, it is nothing but a particular fact belonging to my life. Life, then, is absolute in both senses of the word.

It is in such terms that the problem of life suddenly assumes a significance beyond measure within the totality of our knowledge, in the system of our ideas. It may have seemed to us that, during the last few days, we had been talking about life by reason of its being a matter of great moral concern to human beings. But now we have come to suspect, even without dealing with the question in depth, that life is nothing less than the primordial reality in which any other reality finds its basis, and the one to which we would have to reduce—in one sense or another—all other realities, if we want to come to know their radical essence. This is so because in life there are living ingredients only; therefore, everything entering into it, emerging or appearing in it, or anything which is found in it, would be *primordially* endowed with a substantive living character. [In other words,] it would be "life." [And I mean] everything: *I* am nothing but life, my life; but so are this *table,* and the light, and you yourselves; even God—*to begin with*—is nothing but a living component of mine.

I realize this is difficult to understand, especially all of a sudden. In the beginning, those of you who have already studied philosophy will experience greater difficulty in understanding it [than the rest]. In effect, we are dealing here with a novel thought, which is set—more or less—against the entire philosophical past. That is why I ask of you to have a little patience and [show] a little constancy. But I ask something further of you: as I give you notice that my intent is to set forth before you a new style of metaphysics, a manner of engaging in philosophical thinking that is different—*at the most radical level*—from the one we have received, let me give you fair warning that you should (not) treat past philosophical ideas as if they were firm and incontrovertible. Doing this would hinder your comprehension. If you wish to understand what I am saying, the first requirement you should meet is to free yourselves—at least provisionally—of those old concepts and simply open yourselves to the intuition of the things themselves as I engage in presenting them to you. Later you will always find the occasion to compare my ideas—once they have been properly understood—to the traditional ones, and freely to keep that which may seem truer to you. It goes without saying that, in this very lecture course, we will, most exactingly, bring the new doctrine face to face with the classical ones concerning every fundamental problem.

Accordingly, we are now going to attempt—in a somewhat more precise manner—to develop concepts about the sort of primordial reality which life is, about its strange, peculiar, exclusive manner of being.

I have [already] stated that [my] life consists in encountering myself in the midst of my circumstance or world. Anyone who, informed by traditional notions, hears this [assertion] would take it to mean that I am a thing or substance endowed with the power to come to notice, see, think; that [I am a thing or substance that] notices, sees, thinks of other things and people that are found in my surrounding world and are substances too. The sense of the technical name "substance" is well known: according to Descartes, substance is "*[. . . quod] nulla alia re indigeat ad existendum*" ["*. . .* {that which} needs no other thing in order to exist"].[23] Color [for example] is not a substance, because its manner of being requires something else that would serve as its support or substrate. A color alone, by itself, is incapable of holding itself up in being, that is to say, it cannot be on its own, for it needs to be borne by another that would carry and sustain it. This is the reason why it is said that the manner of being of color is accidental and not substantive.

It is surprising to find, however, that in what we call life, in that reality that appears to us as primordial, nothing is endowed with a manner of being [characterizable as] either accidental or substantive.

I, the one living, Mr. So and So, do not have being or exist apart from my surroundings. In no sense am I what is usually called a thing, whether material or spiritual. I am the one living, and this means that I am the one who is in need of many of the so-called "things" in order to exist *(ad existendum)*. I am the one who is now sitting on this chair and in need of it, so as not to grow tired or fall down. If I did not have a chair [at my disposal], I would be standing and in need of what I call the "muscles of my body" to prop myself up, and of what I call the "ground," so as to have support for my body. I am the one who is reading to you [what is written on] this paper, and [thus] I am in need of the paper from which I am reading, of the ink I employed to write on it, of my eyes and glasses, and of the light illuminating me. I am the one who is reading [what is written on] this paper; in other words, I am the one who is doing something with something belonging to my surroundings. There is no moment, there could not possibly be any moment of my life that does not consist in doing something with something or, as I said the other day, in being occupied with the elements of my surroundings, with the world. The least I could do is to kill or mark time,[24] to wait in readiness to do something, and this is as good a manner of doing something, or of being occupied with the world, as any other. And what is more: "waiting in readiness" usually is an exasperating and most difficult way of being occupied. "To kill or mark time" is—in fact and not metaphorically—a living activity in which one is busy with that "thing" called time, just as—when he is making a table—a carpenter is busy with a "thing" called wood and those things known as saw, chisel, and hammer.

I am then, willy-nilly, the one who—in order to exist and be—is in need of occupying myself with, or acting upon, that which is not myself. Therefore, I do not exist, nor am I the one I am, except *by virtue of* the fact that I am with and upon my circumstance, with and upon that which surrounds me. A follower of Aristotle and Descartes himself would say that the one living is then an accident, since *ad existendum* ["in order to exist"] he is in need of the surrounding world. Quite so, but unfortunately that which is other than I and in which I find support—the so-called "things" of my circumstance or world—is devoid of being in itself, of substantive being, of being that [would be] independent of me. [For example,] the ground upon which I find support is in effect—primordially speaking—nothing but "*that* upon which I find support."[25] This light, which is now illuminating me, is not something endowed with a nature or being of its own, and independent of [the fact that] it is now illuminating me. On the contrary, it is, purely and simply, [just] this: "*that* which illuminates me, insofar as and to the extent that it is illuminating me."[26] If I asserted that that which is now illuminating me, above and beyond doing so, is *endowed with a being* independent of me and consisting, [say,] of vibrations taking place in [a medium called] aether, or in being a state of the electromagnetic field, I would have employed the term "being" in two different senses.

The *being* of light as a state of the electromagnetic field is a being that I have invented, that I have fashioned by means of my thinking and that I attribute or add to the primordial and only genuine *being* of this one light, namely, that which is exhibited by it when it is illuminating me, and which is neither a product of my thinking nor something I have wrought.[27] I come to invent the theories belonging to [the science of] optics, because I find myself illuminated by this light fixture or by the sunlight. And yet, no matter how firm such theories may be, they always remain problematic and, above all, exhibit the character of derivative reality when contrasted with the primordial, evident, and *unproblematic* reality of this light, as simply and actually engaged in illuminating me. We have thus discovered that the so-called "things" are not—originarily and truly speaking—anything of the sort, that is to say, items the manner of being of which presupposes that they are independent of me. They are not apart and by themselves, since their being consists only and exclusively in acting upon me with living evidence. I am very sorry [to say that] you are "the ones who are hearing me now," and nothing else. That is to say, by hearing me, you are now acting upon me. If you did not hear me, I would be someone other than the one I am at present, namely, the one who is addressing you verbally. But what is more: if you were some other people and nonetheless were listening to me now, I would also be other than I am, because I would sense the difference [between you and them] with some measure of clarity or other, and I would comport myself otherwise, no matter how minor the difference might be. In effect, I am the one who is saying what I am saying, because you—my listeners now—appear to me to be the same people who heard me in the past. This is the reason why I say to you what I am saying, trusting to some degree that you are ready to understand me on the basis of what I have already said.

Strictly speaking, I am then nothing but the one who is acting upon my circumstance, and [conversely] my circumstance is nothing but that which is acting upon me. Neither I nor my circumstance have a *being* apart; neither I nor my circumstance are "substances." Moreover, neither I nor my circumstance can be accidents of one another, for every accident is an accident of a substance. Accordingly, in the reality called "life," neither life nor anything therein exhibits a substantive or accidental character. Rather, those two venerable categories are of no use to us, if we desire, by means of them, to think the primordial reality life is and everything present therein.

This is the pressing and most concrete reason why we are in need of a new philosophy or conceptual system. [I do not say so] for the sake of novelty, which is always a matter of frivolity, but because of an irresistible intellectual necessity, for we are—by means of a clear and unimpeachable intuition—face to face with a new manner of reality, that is to say, one that has not been noticed heretofore, and which is not amenable to being thought about by means of traditional concepts.

Let us then recapitulate our findings. I live; my life exists; there is life, each and every one's. But if there is such a thing, then there also are this "I" who lives and the surrounding world in which one lives, my existence essentially consisting in co-existing with such a world.

# Sixth Lecture

As you look back and gather together the impressions received in these lectures, you will probably come across an experience that was undergone time and again, namely, that we often take a step which, right before our eyes, serves to draw, as it were, a curtain concealing a new landscape. The day such a landscape makes its appearance before you for the first time, you have the sense that you are not seeing it clearly. The next day, however, it seems that we are not taking a step farther, but the other way round, i.e., that we are returning to the one already taken, that we settle therein, and then, and only then, that we begin to see—clearly, with ease—what in the prior stage of our journey escaped our grasp or perplexed us. In effect, this process will take place repeatedly throughout this course, so that, soon enough, once you have become accustomed not to understand the first time around, but to succeed on the second round, you will come to regard your sense of being blind and at a loss as the unavoidable condition to be met, if you are later to have the sense of being farsighted and in charge of the situation.

Today we find ourselves in one of those "second" days, and we are to take ourselves back to the preceding one and dwell in the landscape, at which we had arrived with painstaking effort, until such time as we [can] cast a glance at it.

Now, two points were emphasized during the last lecture: one, that life is the absolute reality; another, that the manner of being of such a reality was most strange and evaded all our attempts to think of it by means of the traditional concepts of "being."[28] Neither life nor anything therein was, as such, a substance, an accident, or anything like that.

Today it is not necessary for me to insist much on the first point, since you understand it, I hope, with a degree of clarity sufficient for us to continue. No doubt the moment will come in which, since understanding what I am saying will no longer be a problem to you, it will be permissible for me to start upon the examination of the matter in depth, to discuss possible objections, to compare my thesis with the classical ones—in brief, to "prove," in all strictness, what I now am only suggesting to you. It does not escape you, I suppose, that this, and no other, has to be the method that I am [to follow]. It would be meaningless for me to begin the discussion of my own doctrine before you have understood it.

That life represents absolute reality is, I contend, sufficiently clear to us. In fact, we do not find life to be conditioned by, or dependent upon, any other [reality]. It is the other way round: to find that life is conditioned by, or dependent upon, another [reality], already presupposes that we are engaged in living, that we find life in life, and that—from the [standpoint of] life—we note the conditions to which it is subject, etc. This will do concerning the first signification of the absolute as that which is independent. But, above and beyond that, we see, with complete evidence, that it is not possible for us to think of any reality which is not included in the reality of our lives, inasmuch as that is the only one we possess, and it is therein that any other reality will have to appear, arise, or be made manifest to us. Thus, for Christianity, God is the most independent reality we can conceive in respect of our lives, and yet, even if it may seem contradictory [to think so], the said God turns out to be dependent on our lives in virtue of a most far-reaching theological reason. In effect, when we say of God that he is a reality independent of us, we are saying that he *transcends* our lives altogether, or, equivalently, that we cannot say anything at all about such a reality, or about its manner of being, or even, in all strictness, about whether it exists.

If nothing in theology but God's transcendence or absolute independence in respect of us were asserted, it would be tantamount to saying that there is no such reality. That is why, in theology, one does not limit oneself to saying that God is a being altogether independent of and concealed from us, but it is added that God, as the one who is independent of us, in turn reveals himself to us. A God who would not bestow his revelation on human beings would not be God, [for] even to that point is revelation a necessary attribute of the idea of God. Now then, revelation is God's entry into a human being, into the life of a human being. God is real to the extent that he reveals himself, and he has no other reality than that which he has pleased to disclose to us in his revelation.

There is no way out, then. These [past few] days we glanced at life out of sheer curiosity, and, lo, we now find that we can no longer leave it behind. When one takes a look at life, one inevitably discovers that *there is* nothing but life, that we are imprisoned therein. But since only *my own* is life, that is, life [as that] which belongs to each and every one of us, a human being finds him- or herself to be absolutely immersed in the exclusive and hermetically sealed sphere of his or her life. Let us not be distressed by this, however, for our prison is not confining, being as it is coextensive with the universe. The error committed throughout our entire philosophical past, the error I am attempting to correct, does not consist in reducing the dimensions and wealth of what there is, of reality. Indeed, we are in possession of no less than the universe, and yet, in the past, one neglected to add the qualification "living" to the [term] universe. It is not that my life is in the universe, but that the universe is in "my life," inasmuch as the universe is not, except because I live it.[29] Life consists in my being at the universe; it consists, therefore, of three things: myself, my being-at, and the universe.[30] Consequently, life is the whole and the universe a part. At this point, however, it would not be advisable to employ, except in passing and by way of mischievous anticipation, a word as vague and compromising as "universe." Let us be content with using locutions like circumstance, surroundings, living sphere, or, at best, "world."

When one realizes that life is the primordial reality in which every other reality has its foundation and makes its appearance, one finds oneself obliged to form a precise idea not only of what that reality contains but, as well, of its manner of being real. I have devoted two lectures to [presenting] a preliminary description of the essential characters or ingredients of life, and that led me to say that to live is to be aware that one is existing, to encounter oneself occupied with the surrounding world, to decide at every moment what we are going to do next, etc.[31] All such notes are part and parcel of the reality called "my life." But let me now inquire into the meaning of the real being attributed to life and to every one of its ingredients.

Generally speaking, it is ill-advised solemnly to inform the listener or reader that the subject one is about to deal with is of the greatest importance. Doing so would upset his or her mind and deprive him or her of the coolness and serenity [needed] to understand the question with ease. But in this case it would be unforgivable not to remark that the matter at hand is decisive and of the greatest significance. In effect, the question involved is the reduction—it is nothing less than that—of every known modality of being or concept of reality to another which is altogether novel. The fact that this novel and radical modality of reality has not been discovered until now is due precisely to its having been covered up or hidden by other, more obvious concepts of reality. That is why, if one wishes to take a look at such a modality, one must be ready not to rest content with those concepts, i.e., to take them for granted and as being beyond discussion. I take the liberty, then, to demand of you the greatest possible attention and patience both today and in subsequent meetings. Undoubtedly we are now going through the most difficult moment in the whole course, but, once it is over, I promise you the most suggestive perspectives and landscapes.

A human being first encounters a reality; it is later that he or she thinks about it, that is to say, strives to form a concept of it. The task of thinking, then, is always a reaction to a reality already present [to us]. Or to put it equivalently: to think is to interpret reality.

As you can gather, intellectual progress as a whole is dependent on our taking care always to compare our interpretations or concepts with the realities [they are about]. To this end, it is essential for us never to mistake the given interpretation or concept for the reality itself, even in the case in which the former seemed to us to be on target or evident.

You are now going to observe in yourselves an inclination that is quite difficult to resist, namely, that of feeling at home with received concepts, as if they were the reality itself.

Let each one of you attempt to take note of what your life genuinely is and contains righ now. [If you did that,] you could say, for example, [the following]: I am sitting on a bench or a chair in this room; I am surrounded by other pieces of furniture and other people; I am illuminated by electric light fixtures, etc., [as well as] I am reading or hearing these lines, [and so on].

Now let us try to think of the manner of reality belonging to each one of the elements that are presently constitutive of my life, of their manner of existing.

The first interpretation to come to my mind—and which is as well the first one, historically speaking, to have been proposed in philosophy—amounts to saying that the room in which I am exists independently of me, that is to say, that it exists in and by itself. This is what I call the "corporeal or material world." I give the name "substance" to that which exists in and by itself, to that which sustains itself in being. The corporeal world, e.g., this room, is a material substance.

Soon enough you will realize that this is not a neat transcription, a plain interpretation of the reality this room is originarily endowed with in my life, since it involves much, by way of addition, which is not present to me, and neglects to underscore precisely that which now it is as a plain presence. In effect, this room is, first and foremost, the enclosed place where I now am, [which is] therefore inseparable from me, just as I am inseparable from it. How could I claim to think of its existence accurately when I say that it consists in being independently of me? Such an interpretation is already a construction,[32] that is to say, a hypothetical theory, the basis for which is that I remember having been in it on other occasions, and that I find it now to be the same as I remember it. In view of this, I entertain the supposition that, while I am not in it, the room continues to exist just as it does when I am in it. This thought—mark this well—is unintelligible, unless I feign that, while I am actually absent therefrom, I leave behind a double or ghostly copy of myself in the room that continues to live it. This abiding character, exhibited by the room or the material world when it is regarded in and by itself, is not, then, a plain and adequate interpretation of its manner of existing, but a hypothesis about it. Or equivalently put: it is a second-order interpretation. Now then, every second-order interpretation presupposes the reality properly so called from which one departs in order to make additions or entertain suppositions or hypotheses. Or to say it otherwise: this room, or the material world, when it is regarded as substance, presupposes the room as prior and more radical, insofar as it is being lived now by me. But, insofar as it is being lived by me, the room is what it is *for me*.[33] Its way of existing, far from being in and by itself, is, purely and exclusively, its existing for me.

What I have just remarked about this room could likewise be said of the pieces of furniture in it, the electric lamps therein, etc. We usually refer to all such elements of our lives by means of the term "thing." One also thinks of this room and the material world as "things." The word "thing" signifies, then, a certain manner of being, to wit: independent, substantial, or substantive being—the sheer manner of being exhibited by something when it is in itself, when it sustains itself. We are used to saying of a "thing" that it "is [out] there," an expression by means of which we signify that: (1) it is not in us, as an image would be, or as if it depended on us in some sense or other; (2) it exists in and of itself; and (3) its manner of existing is static. The being of a substance consists in statically being what it is. This is the reason why we say that it is [out] there, that it is in itself.

We think that the world is a large "thing," and that there is nothing in it, or outside it, that does not seem to us to possess, in the final analysis, a substantive manner of being, or the character of a "thing." What obviously is no "thing" (e.g., a color or a motion) does not seem to us to be endowed with genuine "being," and we are always motivated thereby to search after some actual "thing" to serve as its support.[34] That is why we say that *there is no* color in and by itself, but rather that color is always the color *of* a thing, and that motion is the moving [behavior] of a thing. I even think of myself as a "thing": when my analysis leads me to the realization that there is something in me—i.e., the most characteristic and important something about me—which is devoid of corporeal traits, I invent a way of being a "thing"—i.e., being unextended and imponderable—which is dispossessed of the attributes of matter, but which is nonetheless endowed with the essential traits of a thing, namely, subsistence apart from everything else and a static existence. This is what I call soul or spirit.

There you have the concept of being, [or] of perennial reality, in the history of philosophy, [a notion] undoubtedly borrowed from the pre-philosophical interpretation human beings found as soon as it occurred to them to think of being. This is, I would then say, ontology in its original form. Why it is that human beings encounter that idea of being first and rest content with it is a matter which, of course, will occupy us some day. It is not probable for such an early and persistent understanding to be a product of chance. What at this point I must underscore is that, to my surprise, it has endured without interruption throughout our philosophical development. [This has been so] because the differences between philosophical systems amounted always to a preference of one over another object (say, of matter or spirit, of finite or infinite mind, etc.) as substantive being, while taking being or reality to mean static subsistence was never formally cast in doubt, as we shall have an occasion to see in detail.

And yet it is undeniable that such a manner of being, regarded as prototypical and fundamental, is simply a supposition and a construction we have made concerning a different manner of being or reality, which is the one we truly encounter and to which, that notwithstanding, we pay no heed when we fashion our interpretation [thereof].

When I say that this electric lamp is a "thing," I have already ignored what the lamp primordially was [for me], for I have already added hypothetical attributes to its originary being. In effect, this lamp, to begin with, is just that which is presently illuminating me.[35] Its being is nothing else than its performance of the function of illuminating me, just as this chair is "that which allows me to sit down" and the earth "that which serves to prop me up," "that which offers resistance to my feet," "that on which I sow and from which I reap the harvest," "that which I avail myself of to keep the dead," etc. The being of anything of the sort originarily consists only in rendering a positive or negative service in my life and for my sake. Now, that the earth, above and beyond propping me up, permitting me to walk, and allowing me to reap the harvest, be endowed, *as well,* with a different [manner of] being or existing of its own, one that does not consist in rendering me a service, is something that cannot evidently occur to me, except after the earth originarily displayed for me its sheer serviceability as its being.[36]

We have, then, that the originary being, the primary reality of anything that forms part of my circumstance, consists in either rendering me a service or getting in my way, in being therefore a facility or a difficulty for my life. To begin with, it is not to me a thing lying there by itself without any reference to me at all, and which would later turn out to be something useful or harmful to me. Let me remind you that my circumstance consists only of that which exists for me; only that forms part of my life, and only that which forms part of my life exists, so that "existing for me" and "existing absolutely" are, to begin with, synonymous expressions. Thus, what we are now trying to ascertain is the nature of [that way of existing describable as] existing for me. And I contend that, primordially speaking, it amounts to concretely facilitating my life or rendering it difficult. But this signifies that it does not *exist for me, except insofar as it is in fact acting* on me, that is to say, insofar as it is functioning. A chair is a chair because I am sitting on it. When I see it as part of the landscape while failing to put it to some use, that is to say, when it is not actually functioning, I say of it that it is that which did or will render me a service. Originarily, I never regard it apart [*"abstraigo"*] from the service it renders me. But [imagine] I came to the realization that a chair on which I am not sitting presently, and which would render me a service later or tomorrow, is endowed as well with a form of being irreducible to its serviceability, namely, that which is proper to what is called a *thing*, i.e., a being in and by itself. This would presuppose—*mark this well, for it is decisive*—that I have called into question what happens to a chair when it is not a chair, that is, when I put it to no use. But this[37] new way I have of being occupied with a chair, which is different from my sitting on it, is also a way of doing something with it, namely, to inquire into its being, therefore, to philosophize.

Now, this way of being occupied with things, not taken as utensils or obstacles but in respect of their being, this sort of occupation which already is formally intellectual in character, is nothing but a modality of my life, a manner of living of mine. My sitting on a chair is as much a manner of living of mine as is wondering about what the chair is when I put it to no use. Placed in this new relationship with me, the chair is endowed, as well, with a manner of existence that is also in the nature of a service, and which is also dependent on me, to wit: the chair no longer serves as a seat for my body, and yet it certainly exists as a problem for my intellect. It is a problem for me, that is to say, it is a difficulty for me. Nothing has changed, then. Accordingly, the being of that which lies in my surroundings still amounts to its being referred to me, to its living action on me. It is not, it does not exist, except insofar as it acts and functions. Its being is not static but dynamic, not substantive but active. The chair does not exist by itself, while acting on me now and then; rather, it exists only as long as it acts and in conformity with its action.

What we must grow accustomed to seeing and understanding is this: a being requiring no prior, static substance behind its action, but amounting to sheer self-performance, i.e., not substantive, but *performative being*.

Yet, unless one inquires into the sort of being or reality I myself am endowed with, one cannot grasp well [the point] that the so-called "things," or the elements of my circumstance, originarily are sheer actions [being effected] on me insofar as I live, or that they are nothing but facilities or difficulties. In fact, those items inaccurately called "things" have been defined, in reference to myself, as actions [effected] on me. Now, if *I* happened to be a "thing" or substance, no innovation would have been introduced here. We would still be under [the rule of] a quasi-idealism, in terms of which the "things" of the world only are, in effect, in relation to the subject thinking of them, a subject, however, that would be a substance bearing them within itself as its states or modalities. I have certainly not rested my case by saying that things—in terms of their living and, therefore, primordial reality—constitutively refer to me, that they exist only insofar as they exist for me, formulae which, without exception, belong to the most orthodox form of idealism. On the contrary, I have specified that their way of referring to me and existing for me is tantamount to their *acting* on me. When the time comes, I will have the occasion to explain—for the benefit of anyone unable to understand it today—why it is that the small variation between a mere "being for me" and "acting on me" radically surpasses any form of idealism.[38]

Let us now turn to what is urgent, [namely, the question,] what sort of reality is mine, what sort of existence do I possess in my life? Each one of you could say of yourself: I am someone who is being illuminated by this light, who is feeling this pain, who is sitting on this armchair, who is hearing and thinking this, who finds him- or herself in the middle of this room [and so on]. But each one of you is not all of that disconnectedly and by sheer chance; rather, each one of you is all of that *because* each one of you wanted to come to the university this afternoon, and wanted to do so *because,* or *in view of the fact* that, each one of you was and is—as well, and prior to all that—someone who wants to learn about philosophy. Moreover, that each one of you was and is someone who wants to learn about philosophy is so, in turn, *because,* or *in view of the fact*[39] that, each one of you has decided that your life as a whole, as it presents itself to you today by way of anticipation, should be, more or less, the life of an intellectual. To be accurate at this juncture, I would have to speak only about myself, since each of us sees—non-mediately and fully—only his or her life. Each one of us only knows about his or her neighbor's life and, therefore, envisions it only indirectly. But we are dealing here with life as lived, and not with life insofar as one is more or less cognizant of it.

Someone could say to me it is quite true that many of those things "I" presently am I am *in view of,* or *because of,* the fact that I have decided to be an intellectual, but that I feel physical pain or pleasure, at the moment, is not *because* or in view of that. It is possible and even very likely that, in effect, the pain someone may perhaps feel did not exist because of his or her decision to be an intellectual, and yet, in other cases, he or she certainly would feel pain or pleasure because of that, as it happens, for example, [in connection with] all illnesses that the person in question knew he or she was very probably going to suffer from, if he or she devoted him- or herself to the given profession. Along with its advantages, every profession brings disadvantages, proper to the field, to both spirit and body. But that is the least of it. Let us say it is not so. However, I am not just someone who has decided to be an intellectual; I am something much more elementary, something which, being so familiar, one is oblivious of, namely, a human being who has decided to continue to live. I would say that this modest and elementary occupation is responsible for inevitably bringing, as a consequence, the pains and illnesses proper to our kind. Now then, to continue to live is as much a [matter of] decision—of a most elementary sort too—as is the pursuit of a doctorate in philosophy. Just as it is always possible to give up one's studies and, *in view of that,* to fail to attend classes in metaphysics, it is possible [too] simply to give up living. Let us never forget the fundamental point that life is a reality having, as an essential constituent, the capacity for self-annihilation. It is devoid of the power of radical self-creation, but it certainly possesses the power of radical self-destruction or self-extinction. Death is a possibility always available to the existence or reality that a human being is; it is, in principle, as much of a possibility as turning right or left is as one later comes to leave [the room] through that door.

Feeling well or poorly, sitting down, being illuminated, occupying myself with philosophical subjects—that is [the sort of thing] my life is now comprised of. In fact, *I* am none other than the one to whom all of that is happening and the one who does all that. *I* am nothing more ([for] if, literally speaking, I were something more, the something more in question would consist of elements of the same type). Underneath or behind that, *I* am neither a corporeal nor a material *substance.* Of course, if I am someone who is sitting down, I [must] have taken a seat by means of my body, but that does not mean that I am my body. With equal justification, it could be concluded that I am this armchair, because, in order to take a seat, I am in need not only of my body, but, as well, of something [else] on which to sit. But that is not so: the armchair and my body are those elements of the world which render a living result possible, namely, to be seated, which result indeed I am. To "be seated" is not primarily a "physical" fact, not even a "spatial" one in the geometric sense of the word. It is an event in my life.[40] From the standpoint of my life, it is not the same to be sitting or standing, if I am tired and weak. [Such "things"] are, then, livingly different, each state being endowed with its own quality, prior to and apart from being different from each other as purely physical locations. By virtue of the fact that [the given states] are two [distinct] purely living realities, it is possible for me—once they are—to start thinking of them and of a world composed of bodies (and of my own as being one of them), to study their spatial positions, and to differentiate one position [from another].

In other words, we again encounter the same thing as before:[41] when theoretical or scientific thinking is the modality of living in which we are engaged, we occupy ourselves, in a new way, with our originary surroundings, which act on us in a new way too, namely, not as simple or primordial facilities or difficulties, but as "objects" of cognition. It is then that the armchair, which consists in being that upon which I am sitting, appears as a "thing" by and in itself, independently of me, and as constituted by its spatial shape and size, its physico-chemical and metaphysical matter, etc.

Please note, however, that this "new being" of the armchair, like that of "standing" or "sitting," [is to be characterized as follows]:

1. It exists and is what it is only as a function of my life, which is now theoretical, intellectual, scientific life.

2. Its "being independent of me," therefore, is just a way of depending on my action; in other words, something is what it is when I act theoretically on it. In my theoretical action or life, I adopt a disinterested attitude in which I would have no stake in my life, and that is why I go in search of and find a manner of being independent of me and without a vested interest in me. This is the paradox of knowledge.

3. As you may note, the "new being" in question is not, however, in opposition to the primordial one; on the contrary, it is just one of its particularizations. There is only that with which I occupy myself. But with each *thing* I can occupy myself in two ways: [in the case of the chair, for example,] by sitting on it (i.e., by putting it to use) or by thinking of it.

But let us return to our subject. I am nothing underneath or behind my being someone who is sitting, reading, intellectually occupied with this or that, bearing up during an illness, suffering from pain, showing enthusiasm over a painting or a woman, getting a business ready, sacrificing myself for my children, sunbathing without a care in the world, etc. Now then, none of that is [the same as] being a "thing" or substance; rather, it amounts to acting by means of the things of the world, to dealing with them, to handling them actively or reactively. My reality, then, is also purely dynamic, functional, performative. If things are not, except insofar as they act on me, and if they are just such a performative manner of acting, "I" also am just insofar as I act on and by means of things. If their existing is their being for me, then, conversely, my existing is just my being for, in, and with things. Take the acting circumstance away, and you have taken the self or I ["*yo*"] away; take the self away, upon whom the circumstance acts, and you have taken away the circumstance. Here one can make out what the radical overcoming of idealism will be [like].[42] Livingly, the "world" does not exist, if "I" do not exist; yet, if I am to exist, quite simply so must the world in which "I" live. Hence, the fundamental principle of Cartesianism, which is the source of every form of idealism, is false. [I mean Descartes's] *cogito, ergo sum,* or "I think, therefore I am."[43] As we will have an occasion to see, the truth is otherwise: I think, therefore the world and I *are.* However, the evidence in support of this cannot become available to us as yet, since we still have not inquired into the nature of "thinking."[44]

# Seventh Lecture

Let us continue with our attempt to take into account the odd manner of being which the reality called "life" (and everything therein) exhibits. We have emancipated ourselves from [holding] a substantialist interpretation and have substituted for it the idea of *reality as performativeness*. Reality would [accordingly] amount, purely and simply, to the action effected by the circumstance on me and to my action on the circumstance. The armchair [for example] is that which serves me for the purpose of sitting down, and I am the one who puts the armchair to [that] use.

We are now to take notice of the fact that the action which something (say, an armchair) consists in is always twofold, or one [so to speak] that is raised to the second power. I mean that the armchair consists not only in acting on me, but, as well, that the armchair's acting on me is already dependent on my action on it. Or to put it more clearly: the being of the armchair [to keep to my example] consists in serving as the means for me to sit down. But the armchair could not be endowed with that manner of being, unless I were someone who is in need of sitting down and wants to do so. [Consider] another instance, that of solid matter, say, this table which consists in resisting the pressure I am exerting; it is evident, however, that that could not be the case, unless I, before the fact and on my own, were someone pushing [against] and exerting pressure [on it]. It is only because I am pushing [against it] that the table *is* resistant. Therefore, please note that the action on me which solid matter amounts to presupposes my prior action on it; it contains that action within itself, i.e., it includes or implicates it. But the converse is true as well: if matter did not resist me, I would not be "someone [engaged in] pushing," and [the action of] pushing would not be among the attributes—a most unassuming, yet evident one—constituting me. Accordingly, my action on the table presupposes—as something prior—the table's action on me; my action includes and implicates it. One is dealing here with a reciprocal implication, which is the reason why I said above that action is always twofold. A human being and the world are, to such a point and so unfathomably, linked to, and affected by, each other. This formidable reciprocal implication and the capacity of linkage between the two is precisely what I call "life."

When human beings speak of their very own "existence," it means that they find themselves at that which is other than they, that is to say, that they are at the world; therefore, that they are nothing but their being at, and with, the things that are other than they (e.g., pieces of furniture, houses, animals, people, money, pleasures, pains, all of which are—let me say it again—things other than I). Now, I hope, a more accurate and more technical sense will be available to you as pertaining to the words with which I began my description of life, words which, then, may have been taken as a novelist's vague suggestion, namely, that living consists in being occupied with the things of the world.[45] At this point, we [can] appreciate that this sentence has a content that is as precise as it is significant. It would be idle for one to strive and attempt to live without being occupied with the things of the world. From top to bottom, one's life is filled with this sort of occupation, and that is all there is in it. Even when the mystic "withdraws" from the world into him- or herself [and] loses interest in the surroundings, he or she continues to be occupied with the world. [And this is true,] first of all, because everything in life is action, and "withdrawing" from the things [of the world] is as much a way of being occupied with them as any other, i.e., something one is to do, and do again, constantly. But, secondly, [it is true because] he or she would be "withdrawing" from the world in order to occupy him- or herself with God, who, livingly speaking, is intramundane or belongs to the world.

If it were meaningful for us to avail ourselves of an old category which is precisely the one we have given up, it would be fitting to say at this juncture that I and the world are consubstantial. In so doing, we would be emphasizing that we find ourselves forced, for the purpose of determining anything about myself and the world, to extract it by means of an analysis of the mutual action or reciprocity between the world and me, an analysis that would become, each time, more precise and detailed.

In the prior lecture, I pointed out to you that a human being is his or her life.[46] That is the reason why "I"—whether I am speaking of myself or of any one of you—am now the one who is sitting in this university classroom, etc. All of that befalls me, and the circumstance is as described, *because of* or *in view of* the fact that I had decided to be a professor of philosophy or pursue a doctorate in the field or become an accomplished intellectual. This qualification is of the greatest importance. Not only are my circumstance and myself at present what they are *because* I have decided to be a philosopher and in view of that I have come here, but, [as well,] once I have stepped in this classroom, what for me has existence about it is dependent on that decision. Imagine an eight-year old boy, who is obliged to stay and take a seat here, lending an ear to what he does not understand or care about. The elements of the classroom which would exist for him would be different from those of which it is comprised for us. The bench, which for us is "that on which we are sitting," would be for him "that which is tormenting him," not a bench at all, etc. And all of that [would be so] because his [self] or "I" would not be constituted by the decision to philosophize [as is the case with us]; that is to say, because his action on his circumstance or world would be different from ours. He could say [of himself]: I am someone now being tormented by this bench, by the words I have to lend an ear to, by this prison. All the elements of the world which are presently facilities and conveniences for us would become difficulties and inconveniences [for him]. His actual life and self would be completely other than ours, simply because the one thing *in view of* which he is motivated, and for the sake of which he lives, is different [from ours].

This leads us to the realization that my present or actual life—and, therefore, my self now, my actual and present self—is what it is in virtue of my future self, my future life, and not the other way around. If you now are thankful for being seated, the reason is that it facilitates your listening to me attentively and without annoyance, inasmuch as you not only made the decision to learn philosophy or to increase your knowledge of it, but you also, time and again, reiterate that decision or continue to relive it at every moment. In other words, you do not now limit yourselves to living your life of the moment, but—*at the same time, at the very selfsame time of the clock*—you are living in your future. But we can obviously go further and say that your future as philosophers is livingly prior to your present as listeners. This is what one would give expression to, in everyday parlance, by saying that you *are hearing* [me] *because* you aspire to philosophize. "Because" [serves here to] indicate that what I would call *cause*—without taking the word seriously at this point—is prior to the *effect*. In our lives, it turns out that the cause of our now is our future, [which is] therefore prior [to the now]. Life begins by being future; it is only because we live ourselves in future [terms] that the present circumstance arises, and does so endowed with its concrete characteristics, whether convenient or not. Now we [can] understand why it is that every self must have its exclusive circumstance, as well as appreciate, with greater clarity, the sheer performative or operative being thereof. If I lived myself in future terms according to a different style (i.e., not as a philosopher, but, say, as an industrialist), by that very fact the present moment would be altered. My future, then, amounts to the pressure exerted on my circumstance, to which the latter responds by constituting itself as it is. To the pressure exerted by my future, the world responds in effect [by providing me] with a series of facilities and a series of difficulties. In opposition to my wanting to be a philosopher, the world sets up particular obstacles—for instance, by not endowing me with sufficient talent for the work; by presenting me with a sickly body incapable of focusing its [powers of] attention for an extended period; by being responsible for my being born in Spain, where the tradition in those studies has disappeared, etc. Yet the world also goes my way by providing me with particular facilities—for instance, by endowing me with a strong will; by supplying me with sufficient means and thus rendering me able to devote my short periods of health entirely to my studies; by my being well acquainted, since childhood, with various languages, etc. But suppose that my future were of a different sort (say, that *I* had decided to be a bullfighter), and you would find that, by that very fact, the value of the world's responses would change, [for] what would I do [for example] with my knowledge of German when confronted by a bull?

Thus, were I again to raise the question as to what the "self" is who is living, I would no longer say that it is just, or even chiefly, what *I*, as a matter of fact, am presently doing with, or suffering from, the things of the world. Rather, I would say that I am the one who is to be a philosopher, the one who has to be a philosopher. In other words, I would start by defining the self as future, as "the one who is to be."

In order for you to understand what follows with stark clarity, it is necessary that I point out, once and for all, that, when I say that my future self consists in my having to be a philosopher, I am only simplifying matters by means of the example. In fact and in reality, such a thing is but a component of my "self." By virtue of reasons, the postponement of the consideration of which is advisable at the present time, [one would have to say that] that is a most important factor among those which constitute me, but [also] that it is not, by any means at all, the only one. [For] I am the one who as well has to support my family; the one who has to be a Spaniard; in short, the one who has to continue living. Moreover, I am, or have to be, each and every one of those characters by modulating them in the most individual of fashions, something that words, because of their ever-generic nature, are incapable of conveying. In reality, then, my future "self" is comprised of a very substantial number of characters or ingredients in conjunction. And what is more: some of them are unknown to me; that is to say, I have not clearly thought of the fact that they constitute me. And still others I try not to admit to myself; I evade acknowledging them; I endeavor to conceal them from my own eyes. We shall have an occasion to appreciate how it is not just a matter of "unbecoming" ways that I find in myself, but, rather, something running much more deeply and which is common to all human beings. We shall have an occasion to appreciate how it is that, in life, there is a natural tendency to avoid raising, in a serious and thoroughgoing fashion, the question as to who I am in future terms.

Having made this observation, let me continue. I am not just the one who is now living in a certain way. Rather, what I actually am has its foundation in the fact that I am, priorly, the one living, in future terms, in that certain way. Since I am thus and so in future terms, I am [thus and so] presently. My present does not exist except by virtue of my future, under the pressure exerted by my future. Now then, this means that, in the *now* forming part of the time measured by the clock, I am at once my future and my present. How this is possible is a matter of consequence that, for the time being, I am leaving untouched. As will become apparent, there are two different sorts of time, namely, living time, the real and primordial kind, and the time appertaining to "things," to the world of substances, the one measured by the clocks.[47]

To begin with, the only thing important for us to understand well is, in effect, that I now *am* the one who is here, etc., *because,* at the same time (as measured by the clock), I am the one who *has to be* a philosopher. But already please note the odd lack of harmony [here]. Some of you, perhaps nearly all of you, might be able to say [this]: in effect, I am under the impression that I am the one who has to be a philosopher; I find in my present something like the inevitability of having to be a philosopher; in other words, if I now imagine that I did not achieve that [goal], my future life would now appear to me as a failure or, equivalently, as if the "self" I have to be had not come into being, as if it had been cancelled out.

I contend, then, that I *now* am [both] *future* and *present* in conjunction. My *future* exerts pressure on the now, and my present life arises by virtue of the pressure [so] exerted on the circumstance. It is ill-advised, then, to conceive of such a *future,* of my "having to be," as if it referred to a later time, as measured by the clock, which I now think of or imagine. It is not the case that I think of my future from [the vantage point of] my present. It is not a question of thinking, but of something prior to thinking. Conceive of it the other way round: from [the standpoint of] my future I live my present, and all of that as lodged in the *now*. But did I not say that my actual surroundings are what they are *because of,* or *in view of,* the fact that I have to be a philosopher? Therefore, from [the standpoint of] my having to be a philosopher, I live what is now surrounding me; therefore, I also presently live my having to be a philosopher.

It is thus impossible to separate our living present from our living future. The latter is an actual part of every present. What is more: it renders it possible; it is the dynamic-ontic pressure constituting it. It is not that you are going to be, or think that you are going to be, philosophers at some appointed time in the future; but, rather, that you already are philosophers in that future manner of "having to be" which is, at once, present.

We have at our disposal two words that serve us admirably to give expression to that "future self," to my "having to be." They are "anticipation" and "project." In the phenomenon I call "my life," I encounter myself as being not merely lodged in the given surroundings; I also find, as we had the occasion of seeing,[48] that my-being-lodged therein is active in character. I encounter myself occupied with the given surroundings, and my being occupied, or what I *do,* with my surroundings, I *do* because I have to be a philosopher, that is to say, because I am something by way of *anticipation.* What I actually do and my present surroundings arise from what I am by way of anticipation. My life, then, is anticipating itself constantly and essentially. Life is anticipation. When I, of a sudden, livingly awaken and come to realize that I live, I encounter myself, as a matter of course, obliged to carry out, in the world, the character I am by way of anticipation. And everything I do (i.e., my present) I do in order to carry out the project I am. To live is to project oneself, in the twofold sense of the word, to wit: as a program [of being] and as the act of projecting the program in question upon the world. I am, first and foremost, a certain program of life.

Let us now [attempt to] see, with some care, what is being advanced upon saying, by means of all those synonymous expressions, that "I am the one who has to be," that I am anticipation, project, or program.

Let me remark, first and foremost, that here we again come across that which has so often blocked our way, namely, that we take the locutions we employ to name the primordial ingredients of life in the intellectual sense they have come to acquire. When I say that "I am a project," I am not referring to the fact that my mind sometimes deliberately sets about to think of the future and to construct, at pleasure, a program to live by. I am not a program I have thought about; if at all, I am the one who is now thinking of his future; I may now be the one engaged in thinking or projecting, but not that which is being thought about [or projected]. Therefore, please do not take a future self to be one engaged in thinking about what is going to be the case, say, in a year's time. None of that [is true]. Let me reiterate it once more: every act of thinking is a particular doing of my life in which I intellectually occupy myself with it; my life is thus prior to, different from, and independent of my thought. The only thing that indeed is a primordial ingredient of my life is what I called "evidence," i.e., life's altogether preintellectual act of self-attendance or self-realization.[49] This is life's presence to itself—[for example,] the way a toothache is present to myself, which has nothing whatsoever to do with the fact that I, above and beyond feeling it, would perceive, imagine, or think about my toothache.

Thus, I would likewise say that I encounter myself being the project I am before I wonder which project I am. What is more: none of us has ever succeeded in thinking through the project each one of us is. That is why at Delphi the commandment, *"Know thyself!"* was inscribed as a utopian imperative and, so to speak, as a summit hardly reachable [by us].[50]

Ordinarily it is the elapsing of life which ongoingly discloses for us the *project* we are. Let it be clearly understood that what we are is active in our lives, and that, moreover, we come to realize it by way of "presence," which is a dimension inseparable from everything living. It is not, then, something transcendent and mysterious, and yet it is not something intellectually known either. The miser realizes that he or she is miserly, but it is not for that reason that he or she knows him- or herself to be a miser, and defines and judges him- or herself in such terms.

There is, however, a rather simple procedure permitting us—each one on his or her own—to catch a glimpse of who each of us is and who it is that the self of each one of us has to be. The procedure in question[51] consists in placing ourselves imaginatively in a different set of circumstances and taking note of which ones among them would annihilate or cancel out our selves. If, for example, we imagine a social situation that would have gone further than Bolshevism (i.e., one in which every intellectual occupation would have been absolutely prohibited, and where every book and every form of dialogue concerning scientific and, generally speaking, spiritual matters would have been suppressed), some among us would feel as if, in such a life, what appears to us as our genuine life had been excised along one of its essential dimensions. Somewhat hastily each one of us would say: "I could not live that way." But that would be a mistake, [since] we would indeed be capable of living [in that situation], inasmuch as other elements of the self we have to be would come to be realized even in that set of circumstances.[52] But it is true that the life we would live [therein] would appear to us as constantly checking, negating, or excising an inalienable part of our selves, namely, our intellectual lives, our being engaged in the occupation of philosopher. The rest of our lives, if led [under such conditions], would only serve the purpose of pointing out to us that we were not living our lives integrally, that every day, every hour negated the being which is ours as intellectuals. Therefore, it would be living against the grain and contrary to our genuine lives; it would be [tantamount to] the constant failure and annihilation thereof. Under such circumstances, living, for us, would mean the undoing of our lives, or proceeding in opposition to them. If our project of being intellectuals were just a matter of whim, or even a reflective resolution born in our will, that would not occur. With a greater or lesser degree of vexation, we would renounce our [project of] being intellectuals, but underneath that renunciation our lives and selves would remain intact. But, unfortunately, it is not possible to prescind from the ingredients of our actual self, from the program of life we inexorably are, without undergoing a real mutilation. Let it be clearly understood that, just as in fact my circumstance [may] perhaps oblige me to prescind from being the one [self] I am, so can I in fact—by an act of sheer will—prescind therefrom, and yet I do not cease being my self by prescinding from a part of it. [On the contrary,] I continue to be that self. The *self* one has

to be is indestructible; that is why the only thing one [thus succeeds in] excising is the realization thereof; [in fact,] upon excising it, one takes note,
all the more strongly, of the inexorable reality of the self one has to be. As
a project, it abides and constantly turns against one's present life to level
an accusation against it and to exact torment from it, because of the crime
our present life has committed in negating, in prescinding from, it.

As you can see, we are gradually rendering specific the makeup[53] of the
two termini which, by implicating [each other], constitute our lives, namely,
the circumstance or world and the self. The former amounts to the system
of facilities and difficulties encountered by the living self, and the latter to
the life project or program that has to be realized within the circumstance. I
may want not to live, that is to say, [I may want not] to realize the self I have
to be, but, even though I may avoid its realization, that does not imply that
I cease thereby from inexorably being the project I am. But that means that
my existence, my reality, has two components, to wit: my life as project and
my life as actual realization, my having to be "thus and so" and my actual
being "this or that." As a project, I am a possibility; as lodged in the circumstance (i.e., as present), I am a realization. Let it be clearly understood that
that possibility I am is not the possibility of a mere thought; it is not just a
possibility thought about, but a real one as well; it is a modality and component of living reality; it is an existing or living possibility.[54]

Similar to [the case of] "having to be" a philosopher is that of "having
to love a person and be loved by him or her." *(Amor, ch'a nullo amato
amar perdona.)*[55]

Now we can clearly see the various layers of meaning which are
crammed together and, so to speak, fused with one another in the formula, "I am the one I have to be." Here they are, one by one:

1. It means that I am a definite project; that I am, therefore, something
   "prior" to and independent of the *events* of my life, that is to say, of
   the circumstance, since the latter is tantamount to the worldly response given to the projective pressure I exert on it.

2. It means that, intrinsically, the project in question necessarily points
   towards its realization.

3. It means—and here lies the paramount sense of the expression—that
   my being qua project is incorrigible, that I cannot modify it at pleasure, that it exists beyond the sphere of operation of my will.

These three senses, then, represent, as it were, three powers of being
oneself arranged in ascending order, three senses which can be formulated
as follows: (1) I am the one who has not yet realized myself, that is to say,

I am a mere project; (2) I am the one aspiring or striving to realize myself, that is to say, I am projection; (3) I am the one who inexorably requires to realize myself, even if it be impossible to do so, that is to say, I am . . . vocation. For the first time, we run into this idea with which we will be long occupied. At the most radical level of my very self, I am "vocation," that is to say, I am the one called to be this or that. What is that call calling me to, what does it invoke and convoke me to? To a certain life path; therefore, to a certain conduct in the world, to a certain shape and line of existence. It does not call me to an extramundane existence, but to one of the infinite, imaginable ways of co-existing with things. Even when my vocation is religious in character, that is to say, when I am called not to be preoccupied with the world, to conduct myself in accordance with and in view of the ultramundane, of the "other life" and the "other world," I am really being called to lead a kind of life in this world and in this life. A religious vocation does not consist in my living, as a matter of course, the blessed life or the life beyond, but rather in my living, to begin with, this life which is not blessed in the least, in my doing so in this "vale of tears" as such. In heaven, there is no religious vocation, the reason therefor being that it is, as much as any other, an intramundane vocation. To live by denying this world, by denying its pomps and vanities, is as much [a way of] living in the world as it is to do so by wholly taking delight and morose delectation in such pomps and vanities. Every vocation is intramundane; it calls us to this world because we are a project, obviously, of life, that is to say, of co-existing with the surroundings.

Ordinarily, by "vocation" one understands the sense of being called, for life, to the practice of a trade or profession, that is to say, to one of the typical occupations which are already available in society—a vocation to be an artist, a teacher, a soldier, a merchant, a monk, etc. But this is, of course, an imprecise way of employing the term "vocation." First of all, the names of trades are used to signify various life-occupation types. "Type" and "typical" signify "kind" and "generic" [respectively]. Now then, no one senses that he or she has a vocation to be a teacher or an artist or a soldier generically, but to be so in the most individual and concrete of ways. It may very well happen that that most individual way of being, say, a soldier, presents itself identically in many human beings. I do not take the expression "most individual" to mean "exclusive" or "incomparable," but rather to signify something totally concrete, not something vague, generic, or lacking its full complement of determination. However, having a vocation for a given trade or profession, which the *self* is in part, is never anything that is adequately conveyed by the general names of the trades or professions, [for] there are innumerable different ways of being a teacher, a physician, an intellectual, a friar, etc.

But it is not only for that reason that the vocation my *self* is cannot be adequately expressed by the names of the trades or professions and, in general, by those signifying life types (e.g., a dandy, a bohemian, a *jouisseur* [or sensualist], an adventurer, a Don Juan, a "bourgeois," etc.), but also because my life (and, therefore, the project I am) consists of various living dimensions, of occupations, of activities not covered by the notion of trade or profession or by that of life type. I am my vocation not only to do philosophy, but as well, for example, to take walks in the country, to enjoy gourmet meals, to converse with my friends (and not just with any one of them, but with those whose condition is most specific); but I am likewise my vocation to fall in love not just with any woman, but with one whose qualities are very special, indeed so much so that perchance she may not exist.

In brief, a vocation anticipates a life in its entirety, with each of its sides, facets, and dimensions, while it fails to anticipate, of course, only whatever finds its source in the circumstance. It anticipates as a whole the one I have to be, but it does not anticipate the one I, in collision with the circumstance, would later turn out to be. That is the reason why "I" am *not* my circumstance, but precisely that which is other than my circumstance.[56] That is the reason why my life is essentially tragic, i.e., because it is a contradiction, which means that it consists in my having to realize my vocation, the vocation I am, in that which is not me, in the world, in the counter-self. It is in this sense that one can say that life is alienation and essential betrayal, [for] to live is to encounter oneself delivered into the hands of the enemy, of the world.

Vocation, then, is one's sense of being called to be that most individual, unique entity which, in effect, one is.[57] Every vocation, strictly speaking, is a vocation to be *me ipsimum,* my very *self.*

# Eighth Lecture

In the last few lectures, my intention had been only to [help] you concentrate on the sort of reality which, during this course, I will be referring to by means of the word "life." To that end, we conducted a preliminary analysis of it, and thereby we were able, as well, to gain a lot of ground, which will already be at our disposal when the need arises. We [thus] came to see how it is that life consists in my co-existing with the surrounding world or circumstance. [However,] my co-existing with what lies in my surroundings did not amount to my finding myself alongside things, and to things being found alongside myself, in an inert fashion. Rather, livingly and originarily, things are sheer facilities and difficulties arising before me, because I am, as a matter of course, the definite pressure I exert on [my] particular surroundings. As I said, I am the one who has to be this or that; I am the vocation of my existence, or, to put it otherwise, I radically consist of a need to realize a certain life program or project in the world. To the active project I am, the surroundings respond by adopting a special countenance, which is partly favorable and partly unfavorable.

We have come to form a preliminary idea of living reality, an idea presenting it as a modality of being radically different from all the others which, thus far, have been given expression in philosophy. In effect, life appeared to be, in our eyes, something uncharacterizable as substance, whether corporeal or spiritual.[58] I contended that I am neither body nor spirit; rather, I encounter myself with my body and with my spirit, just as I encounter myself with the earth, the animals, and my fellow human beings.[59] I am a life *task* or program, something, therefore, which is in no wise similar to a living *substance*. If anything, the latter would *already be* this or that, and not that which amounts to just having to be. Likewise, the elements of the world in which I have to be, that is to say, in which I have to carry out the program I am, are not originarily endowed with a substantive character. This chair, primarily speaking, is not a "thing" properly so called; [instead,] it is a service being rendered to me by the surrounding world, a service that allows me, when it is suitable to me, to take a seat. That which is primordially endowed with no form of being other than that of "something on which I am sitting" will later become a theoretical problem for me, to wit: what about the chair when I make no use of it? or, to put it otherwise, what *is* the chair when it is not "something on which I am sitting," but, rather, when it is "something I am thinking about ontologically," that is, when I wonder about its *being?*

I and the world are *for* each other. The being of my self and the world is not substantive in character. Neither my self nor the world abides separately, in and by itself. Rather, the being of my self refers to the world: to live is to be, or to exist, at the world. And conversely: the world, originarily and formally, is that which makes up the surroundings *for* the one who is living.

It is important to me that one thing be clear in your minds about all that, namely, the intuition of our life as a reality that amounts to a task. Life is not something given to us ready-made; rather, we have to fashion it.[60] Its reality, then, is not that of a thing, but instead that of a task.

Now then, if this is so, every ingredient—and even every detail—of life would consist, necessarily and exclusively, in being, in part, a function of the task in question. Or to say it otherwise: if life as a whole is a task, then anything found therein will be a task element and nothing else. It will thus be a "means" for the task, or an obstacle thereto, or a defect of, and a failure at, the task.

By this assertion, I only want to refresh your memory—after a month's break[61]—about what had been discussed in the last few lectures. Having achieved that [goal], let us move in a different direction.

Why is it that we have devoted several hours to trying to understand the meaning of the locution "life"? Let us attempt to recall the stations we have traversed along the way.

Philosophy is something a human being does. It is a doing belonging to the species "knowledge." It is a form of "knowledge" which marks its beginning by raising an essential question, or the question about the *being* of things.[62] The being of a thing is other than the thing. A thing *is there,* but its *being* is not. Since it *is* not *there,* one has to go in search of it, knowledge being the search [involved]. The question both announces and initiates a search.

The elementary definition of knowledge usually sounds like this: to know is to go in search of the truth, and, when in full, it is to possess the truth. But saying that is just rehearsing again the scene that took place in the Praetorium,[63] since, as used [here], "truth" means an intellectual state, the content of which would coincide with what things *are,* with *being.* There is, then, no way of defining knowledge without making the ghostly idea of being, of the being of things, part of the definition, an idea that is part of every essential question, [the form of which is]: what *is* this or that?

As I then pointed out,[64] the being of the light does not, by itself, make its appearance before me as the light does, that is to say, by means of visual perception. *Being* makes its appearance before me by means of a locution, i.e., the *is* found in the question. If we want to ascertain what *being* is, we cannot focus on our perceptions; rather, what we need to do is to begin with the humble task of understanding the meaning of the locution *is.* But a locution only yields the fulness of its sense [when it is regarded] as a constituent of a phrase,[65] and yet a phrase is nothing else than a living action performed by a human being, so that no one is able to understand it accurately, unless it is taken to be a constituent of the living situation responsible for its emergence. The question, what is this?, considered as a question, is an act by means of which a subject postulates something he or she is lacking. The question is thus devoid of genuine sense, if one abstracts from the prior situation in which the subject feels he or she is lacking something.

When one raises a question, one is attempting to bring oneself to completion, or to remedy a lack of something one suffers from. Usually the pair "question/reply" is regarded as a self-sufficient whole. But that is false. A reply, as such, is something secondary that implicates a prior element, namely, a question; and yet it would be an error to believe that the question comes first, [for] a question, in turn, is a reaction to a prior situation without which it would be unintelligible. That prior living situation is called "ignorance."

Therefore, I said that, in order to understand the meaning of the locution *being*, we had to reconstruct the living situation from which arises the question a human being poses about being.[66] But there is, of course, no way of reconstructing the peculiar living situation ignorance is, unless we come to an agreement about the nature of life, which is the ultimate matter every particular living situation is obviously made of. Herein lies the how and why of our having to come to engage in the effort to render what life is specific.

This occupation we have devoted ourselves to has not, then, been born of a whim; rather, we were forced to practice it because of the two major and inseparable philosophical problems, namely, the problem of knowledge and that of being.

In my opinion, to claim that works like Nicolai Hartmann's *Metaphysics of Knowledge*[67] are representative of today's sensibility to philosophical problems truly is a [display of] scandalous superficiality. In such works, it is still held that the problem of knowledge has been posed when one has asserted that knowledge is the apprehension of *being*, then to proceed, without further ado, to analyze the consequences of that definition. In effect, neither the fact that human beings strive to apprehend being nor the *being* apprehended [by them] raises any questions for Hartmann. For him what does is only the relationship between them, viz., how it is that a subject is capable of grasping an object. One may be led to despair of philosophical progress when one notes Hartmann's composure in employing the three terms in question (namely, being, entity, and object)[68] as if they were equivalent, and in turning them indistinctly into the content of knowledge, i.e., into that which one apprehends in knowing.

No, this is not the case. In my opinion, the problem of knowledge runs much more deeply. In other words, I would say it is something that arises much earlier and something the problematic character of which is much greater. I do not admit, without further ado, that something deserving the name of *being* exists, nor do I presume, without further ado, that I know what that name stands for. Besides, I marvel at the fact, and wonder why it is, that a human being has to seek after *being* and has to apprehend it, while Hartmann takes it as something that is just found there. In my opinion, then, the problem of knowledge does not originally arise with the relationship between its two termini, namely, the act of "apprehending" and "being," but already with each one of them. It does arise, therefore, at a deeper level than it does for Hartmann and, in general, in the history of philosophy.

The fundamental error committed by Hartmann—and, as well, by so many other philosophers, in fact, strictly speaking, by nearly all of them—simply derives from failing to note the radical difference obtaining between the concept "being," on the one hand, and that of "entity," object, or thing, on the other. The light is a "thing" that I just find there, before me. My seeing the light is not the same as my knowing it; rather, it amounts to its being before me. By contrast, to know the light consists in knowing its *being* or essence, which is not something just found there; it is not, therefore, in the thing; it is not simply identical with it. If by virtue of the fact that the thing [called] light is endowed with the being one is trying to apprehend [in the science of] optics, I assert that it is an "entity," I must take great care not to confuse the "entity" in question with its "being," since they are altogether different from each other. The "entity" [called] light illuminates me and is seen by me, but its "being" or *essence* does not illuminate me and is not seen by me; [in fact, it is something that] I may never come to know in full.

One should have come earlier to the realization that it is implicitly absurd to say, if one is to speak exactly, that "we know things" or, to use Hartmann's terminology, that we apprehend them. For me to apprehend this table would mean to have it within me, but that is impossible, because the table is spatially extended while my mind is not.[69] But, moreover, it would be something superfluous, [for] what would I profit from having this table in my apprehension [of it], if I already had it out there? No, it is not the thing that is apprehended in knowledge, but its being or essence. But, if so, one is forced to inquire into the nature of *being,* which, unlike things, is not there. [To engage in] such an inquiry is tantamount to genuinely and radically posing the problem of cognition.[70]

I have said that, in my opinion, it is quite inapt to believe that one succeeds in formulating the problem of knowledge when one subjects to analysis the intellectual mechanisms, be they psychological or logical, employed by one engaged in knowing.[71] Psychology taken as a whole, or logic taken as a whole, or both of them taken in conjunction, are insufficient to provide one with the most elementary definition of knowledge. It is asserted that, when one engages in knowing, one is seeking after the truth, and that knowledge in full would be tantamount to the complete possession of the truth. But to do that—as I brought it to mind then—is just to rehearse once more the scene that took place at the Praetorium,[72] because, traditionally, "truth" refers to an intellectual state, the content of which would coincide with what things are.[73] Let me reiterate it: there is thus no way of defining knowledge which would fail to include the ghostly idea of being, of the being of things, in the definition.[74] Now then, neither psychology nor logic casts the least amount of light which would allow one to ascertain the nature of the being of things, the grasping of which knowledge apparently amounts to.

It is evident that the problem of knowledge is not posed with any [degree of] radicalness, unless one calls into question precisely what traditionally has been considered its elementary definition, to wit: the search after, or the apprehension of, the truth, that is, the being of things. Instead of taking these words as a satisfactory answer and resting our case with them, they should serve to awaken the greatest disquiet in us. Once such a definition has been advanced, it is not legitimate for one to go, without further ado, in search of the being [of things] here or there (say, in psychology, logic, or elsewhere), [since] this [procedure] would presuppose that, without further ado, one admits the existence of something which would deserve the name "being," and that, without further ado, one presumes to know what "being" is about. It presupposes, as well, that one does not find it surprising or problematic that the being [of things], which apparently is found [just] there, has also to be sought after by us, instead of being found by us without search of any kind. For it is the case that, properly speaking, one does not have to seek after things; rather, they are there, as a matter of course, exerting their pressure on one's existence, whether by causing offense or delight. Not only is it true that one does not have to engage in the effort of searching for them, but also that one cannot get rid of them. To live is just that: to be inescapbly besieged by them. This is so much so that one need not go in search of them. [However,] what may come to pass, at a given moment, is that we require something that is beyond our reach. Yet, if we sense our need for it, it must be that we had already had it, that we relied on its being available to us, and that now, due to sheer chance, we are lacking it. The absence of a thing, then, comes after its presence; we miss it now because we had it in our possession before. Our being bereft of it is accidental in character; it may be that we will come to have it again soon.

However, nothing of the sort happens to us concerning the being of things. I find the light in my surroundings, as something making its appearance by itself, at its own risk, about me. That is why I say it is there. Yet what the light is, the "being of the light," is not found there, in my surroundings; it is not where the light is, but is always located beyond the there [of the light], characterized as it is by its essential absence and transcendence. If one wishes to get to being, one must unavoidably set oneself in motion, leaving behind every "there" and traveling to the "beyond";[75] one must go, necessarily and always, in search of it.

Now then, the fact that the being of the light is marked by its absence bears no resemblance at all to the fact that, perhaps, one may accidentally lack the thing called "light." We are not now bereft of being because we had it in our possession before, as we are in the case of a watch or other utensil we used to employ, but which someone has taken away from us. No, we would have never [come to be] in possession of it, unless we first had set out in search of it. For a shade or glimpse of being to exist, it is necessary that a human being go in search of it first. But obviously one cannot go in search of it, unless one senses that one is lacking it. Being is, to begin with, a lack, or to say it formally: being is an absolute lack or absence, not just an accidental one. While things are characterized by their being there, by their surrounding us and exerting their pressure on us, their being is precisely that which is not found there at all, in the active way of not being found there, to which privation, or the fact that "one is lacking something," amounts.

Let us now return to the traditional definition of knowledge as the search for the being of things. Isn't its deplorable frivolity apparent [to us] at this point? It refers to being as if it were just one of the things found there; consequently, it takes the cognitive manner of seeking as if it were the same as any other. In comformity with that, there would be no difference between searching for being and searching for a key one has lost. But it is even less than that: when we see someone searching for a key, his endeavor seems comprehensible to us,[76] since, as a matter of course, we bring its sense to completion, inasmuch as the sense in question, as [in] any other living act, is always dramatic in nature. The dramatic character [exhibited by] one's searching for a key may be minimal, and yet it undoubtedly exists and is comprised of all the components of a drama. The effort involved in the pursuit appears to us, as a matter of course, motivated by a blow of fate, signifying as it does that something has been lost which someone was precisely in need of. We regard the action of searching for a key as arising, in a completely intelligible fashion, as a result of its being needed now when it happens to be lacking. But, in that definition of knowledge, the motive that would lead one to go in search of being is not apparent. The definition in question does not give expression to the reason why one is in need of being, and this is especially true, if one keeps in mind what I have said, namely, that being is that which does not [already] exist *[hay]*, that which is not [just] found there. Would it not be frivolous to wear oneself out, for no reason at all, in searching for something that does not even exist *[hay]*?

In fact, nothing is more common than this frivolous manner of engaging in knowing. The great majority of scientists—and here I am not referring to those who are not of the genuine kind—find themselves involved in research activities, without ever having felt any original need moving them to do so.[77] They work in physics or philology because, when they came to life, they found the professions of physicist or philologist [already] established, and they took them up as they could have done with any other. Like it or not, one has to do something in life, which is intolerant of the absence of all doing. Being bored—one of the most anxiety-provoking tasks—would come to the fore when one sidesteps all others. It is the dreadful task of marking or killing time,[78] of sustaining—by sheer effort of will—an empty life, which is the most burdensome of all, one that collapses upon every single minute it lasts. Many human beings do science, I contend, just to "do something." But it is evident that they themselves would not have invented the sort of human occupation found embodied nowadays in regulated and endowed [research] institutes, professorships, and social posts. The first person to have done physics did not do it [just] to "do something," but by virtue of an inner and most concrete sort of need.

(Please note that, in almost every philosophy of the past, knowledge makes its appearance as if through a trapdoor, without any account being rendered of its existence in the universe. Nobody inquires into its provenance or its roots; only the problems affecting its functioning—once it exists—are subject to study, but not that of the origin or foundation of its existence. It is in this fashion that this major problem—as well as all others, of course—arises in midair, rootless, absent all generative earth, and belonging nowhere. Now then, I believe that philosophy is of very little import, unless it consists, first and foremost, in ascertaining the foundation and root responsible for the existence of something, unless it does not amount to resting content with taking up what exists already in order to study the way it functions.)

This need, which is the root of knowledge, must be laid bare by means of a definition of the latter [which is advanced] with a claim to meaningfulness. The effort by means of which one goes in search of being emerges from, and feeds on, our ignorance, which is one of the radical dimensions of our lives. Ignorance is the most genuine presupposition of knowledge. Only an entity ignorant by nature is capable of setting itself in motion by engaging in the operation of knowing.

Yet not just anything would qualify as ignorant. Neither a stone nor God is ignorant; that is why, strictly speaking, neither one nor the other engages in knowing. One is dealing here with a human privilege, both glorious and formidable.

What does it mean to be ignorant?[79] Evidently, it is something other than just not knowing. I do not know how many hairs belong to the white hare which, at this very moment, is running along a given Arctic parallel. And yet I am not ignorant of that fact; the ignorance in question does not form part of myself, is not a component of my actual being. With as much right one could say that a stone is ignorant. But no, my real, constitutive ignorance is more than just not knowing; it is not knowing something I am in need of knowing. Consequently, only an entity that is needy by nature, that is to say, one whose makeup suffers from lacking something, can truly be ignorant [of it].[80] Here lies the reason why God does not engage in knowing either: [he does not] because he is not ignorant, and he is not ignorant because he lacks absolutely nothing, least of all the knowledge of something. If God is perfect, he is in no need of knowing anything. Knowledge is superfluous to him. The possession of a given piece of knowledge must have a justification. Only one in need of knowledge may engage in knowing, and only one is in need of it who, by means of it, would fill in some gap, lack, or absence in his or her makeup.

Now then, to know, properly speaking, is to know what a thing is. The proper object of knowing is being. To speak of ignorance, then, is to speak of the fact that someone is in dire need, like it or not, of ascertaining the being of things. And this is precisely the human condition.

That is why it would be idle—let me reiterate it once more—to continue any further with this sort of considerations, unless one understands the only thing one has at one's disposal about being, namely, the word "being." It comes up in certain questions raised by human beings when they are engaged in interrogative speech, which is a reaction to a given living state, as is the case with any manner of speech. In order to understand a question, we had previously[81] agreed to place it within the living situation that provoked it, because it is only therein that it acquires its exact sense.

To live is to encounter oneself immersed, without knowing how, in the surrounding world, which is comprised of things, namely: minerals, animals, and people.[82] To begin with, life is one's dealing with things, be it pleasant or unpleasant. Now, the primordial form one's dealing with the surrounding world takes is not "contemplative" in character; it does not consist in one's thinking of things and about them. It is evident that, for me to be able to think of things and to "contemplate them," they must have already been previously in a non-"contemplative" relationship with me. Before I started thinking of the earth,[83] I had found myself supported by its solidity and walking on it, pleasurably going downhill and arduously uphill. And the same thing is the case about the light: before reflecting on it and transforming it into an "object" for my intellect's consideration, I had been illuminated by it and, if the light in question is artificial, I would have turned it on and off. The primordial form of dealing with things consists in using them, taking advantage of them, or avoiding them. Only because, previously, I had already done all those things with the earth and the light, only because they were found, as a matter of course, in my life, is it that I can later, above and beyond making use of them, engage in thinking of them. "Thinking of things" is but a special way of dealing with them; but, as is obvious, it is a secondary manner of doing so and [thus] presupposes another [i.e., the primordial one]. The fundamental error—the "intellectualist" error[84]—committed in Greece and modern Europe is tantamount to presupposing the opposite and to regarding one's intellectual manner of relating to things as one's primordial form of dealing with them and, therefore, as one's primordial way of living. Descartes thus dared to define a human being, that is, the one living or "self," as *une chose qui pense d'autres choses* ["a thing that thinks of other things"].[85] That's done it! As if living were just being engaged in thinking of things! What about stumbling on them?

Descartes believed that we live or exist because we think, and insofar as we think, while failing to notice that thinking, as a matter of course, presents itself as a reactive effort into which we are obliged by our pre-intellectual existence. To tell the truth, I do not exist because I think, but, on the contrary, I think because I exist, because life creates harsh, inexorable problems for me.[86]

[Suppose] the reader were in need of arriving in a distant city before long. As is his custom, he would get into his car and depart [for his destination]. The reader [however] is no mechanic. His way of dealing with a car is limited to handling it, starting it, driving it, accelerating it, braking it. [But say that,] suddenly, the car were, on its own, to come to a full stop on some deserted Spanish highway. The thing called "car" [would] have failed to function in its usual way. Because it [would] have failed, and because the reader [would nonetheless] be in need of using it, while the thing in question refused to render him or her its ordinary service, [would] he or she raise the question, what is the motor of a car? If the reader [only] knew, he or she could fix its defect or lack.

Here lies the origin of every question concerning the being of things, namely, our noticing their inadequacy, defect, or lack within the economy of life. If all things were obedient to us, if there were nothing lacking in our lives, we would not stop to think about the being of anything.

But there it is: human life is by nature deficient, needy, wanting. The proof of it is sound. One does not have to go on a special journey intent on collecting the empirical defects from which life may suffer. It will suffice to carry out a radical consideration. If the reader were immortal and his or her car came to a full stop on the highway, he or she would not care less, because he or she would have an eternity to live. It would be the same to him or her, whether he or she would arrive in the city of his or her destination one day or another, because the [passing of the] days makes no difference to one who is sempiternal. He or she would have time enough to be everywhere and [in attendance] at everything. Things and places would also be indifferent to him or her. A personage of that sort would be in need of no car, and, since he or she would be in no need of it, he or she would not own one. God goes on foot because he has time enough to be anywhere. Even if it takes him a century to go from one thing to the next, God never finds things to be far removed from himself. "Being far removed" or "being close by" are [determinations] existing only for someone who measures and counts, but only someone whose days are numbered counts.[87]

We are our lives, and our lives consist in finding ourselves having to sustain ourselves in the midst of things, of the wide and complex surrounding world. We have to decide, at every moment, what we are going to do, that is, what we are going to be next. If we were eternal, that would not distress us; making one decision or another would then be the same to us. Even if we came to the wrong decision, we would always have time enough to rectify it. But the trouble is that our moments are numbered and that, therefore, each one of them is irreplaceable. We cannot make a mistake with impunity; our lives—or an indispensable part thereof—are at stake in that. A human being has to be on target in his or her life and at every moment thereof. That is why every human being's existence may not amount—as it did with the Olympians—to sliding, indifferently and elegantly, from one thing to another, from occupation to occupation, in conformity with what every day would happen, by chance, to bring along. Assured of the fact that they would never die, the Olympians could risk doing that, since [to them] today would be as good as tomorrow, one thing as good as another. But a human being is in a hurry. Life is flowing [by]; life is haste; hence the essential desperation caused by lying in wait, [by] the stillness of things. The amount of time that is available to things, and which they allow themselves, is greater than ours.

For that reason, submerged as we are among the countless things of which our surrounding world is comprised, and swimming in their midst as if in an ocean, we are in need of complementing the paucity of our time, its dearth and inexorable limitation, by anticipating the things themselves. [And we do so] by means of an image or schema in terms of which their definitive texture would become manifest to us. We are not satisfied with this light that is illuminating us, and which yesterday did [too]. We are in need of being certain as to whether or not it will [also] do that tomorrow, to which end we must know how one stands about the abiding light, or, equivalently, we are in need of discovering the essence or being of the light.

This brings us to realize what the originary meaning of the being or essence of a thing is, to wit: just the image thereof that provides us with living security about it. As long as we lack that image or idea of each thing and of the totality of things, we feel at a loss, absolutely insecure. Because it is haste, life is by nature insecure.[88] Let the reader imagine a life altogether secure, and he or she will be confronted with something like a square circle. That is the reason why we are inexorably in need of knowing. I said before that knowing is, properly speaking, to know the being of something.[89] Now we [are able to] understand the meaning of the assertion: to know is to know *what* [we can] livingly abide by. To us "being" signifies security, clarity about how to abide by each thing and the swarm or world [things constitute].

A consequence follows immediately from what I have just said: being is endowed with sense only in regard to a subject who, like a human being, is in need of it. And what is more: it is exclusively a radical need of human beings. God is capable of directly dealing with things, which are infinite both in number and in the ways they have of behaving. Each and every one of them is present to him, [and this is true of] those existing today, as well as [of] those which will exist any future day. He is infinite, as they are; the sphere of his existence coincides with the sphere comprised of things. He is in no need, then, of going in search of the being of things, which lies behind them. When in the catechism we are assured that God is everywhere, the assertion in question only serves to symbolize the peculiar condition of divine existence, responsible as such a condition is for making divine existence so different from, and opposite to, what we understand by "human life." God, who is everywhere, lies still. Every single thing is before him; he deals with it face to face; everything is present to him, but no present causes fear. No matter which peculiar present it may be, if it is ours, then we already are at it; [hence] it is no problem. The terrible, by definition, is the future, wherein we do not find ourselves yet. An entity's relationship with the world would not be one of dependency but of parity, if the entity in question were such that it would be at each and every part of the world, and if [all] such parts were present to it. The present is never more powerful than we are; otherwise we would have succumbed, and it would not be our present. But, in the lives of human beings, the surroundings are more powerful than the human being [involved], precisely because one of its component parts, namely, the future, is not there. But the future is infinite not only temporally and quantitatively, but also qualitatively. It is the indefinite—mysterious, shapeless, imminent. That is the reason why a human being is in need of reducing the infinitude or [un]limitedness of the world in which he encounters himself living to the finite and limited dimension of his life. In other words, he has to fashion a finite foreshortening of infinity. He has to know today, say, what the stars are abidingly. The foreshortening in question is being, that is, the being of something, what it "is abidingly," as projected onto a mind which lasts only a while. The renowned [notion of] being would accordingly possess a purely intrahuman, domestic character. Apart from human beings, there is no such thing as being (though perhaps, perhaps—let us tread with care—one may have to take animals into account as quasi–human beings). That is why being is not there; rather, for it to come into existence, a human being has to go in search of it. Being is born precisely in this search.

Consider the sense in which ignorance is a radical attribute of human beings. It amounts to the insecurity of which our lives consist, as a sort of bitter matter. It is [our] not knowing what to abide by. Knowledge does not have a frivolous origin. It is not the simple employment of [our] intellectual mechanisms, nor is it something that begins to function because of curiosity or an eagerness to look, as Aristotle[90] appears to [have] assume[d].[91]

The greatest error committed in the entire philosophical tradition up to Kant has been to presume that things, by themselves, on their own, are endowed with being.[92] Being was thus transformed into a fanciful "super-thing," and philosophy became a wandering procession in search of it throughout the expanses of the universe, bereft as it was of orientation and fixed trajectory [to do so]. But that is no way [of trying] to find anything, much less some vague "super-thing." Confronted with a problem, what one must do first is to locate it, i.e., to determine where in the universe it takes root.[93] Only thus, under the guidance of the root and settlement thereof, can one approach it in some methodical way. It is no good to say that "what I am looking for is somewhere; let us go find it." Problems located nowhere are pseudo-problems. Genuine problems always take root in some definite location. It is self-evident that there is no problem that is not a human being's. Therefore, every problem must arise in one or another dimension of human life.

Tradition overwhelms us with an avalanche of accumulated questions, in which avalanche the substantial questions are mixed up with the fictive. That is why it is urgent for us to conduct a radical inquiry into them, that is to say, a rigorous examination of their rootedness in life, [an examination] that would allow us to eliminate all those questions that are bereft of it. [This is in keeping with] a general imperative of sobriety. One must shake the world in order to reduce it, for the moment, to what is inevitable about it.

Things by themselves are not endowed with being. Being emerges as a need human beings feel when they are confronted with things. What need? It is this (let me insist on it): a human being is nothing but life. To live is to encounter ourselves shipwrecked among things. There is no choice [for us] but to hold on to them. However, they are in flux, uncertain, fortuitous.

There is no way [for us] to be in our depth in the restless element of things. Hence, our relationship with things is constitutively insecure. By contrast, if a bullet shot from a rifle were endowed with "spirit," it would regard its existence as an assured trajectory. Everything about its course is predetermined by physical necessity. At no point would it have to resolve what it is going to do; therefore, what it is going to be next. Or to put it otherwise: its existence—its trajectory—is given to it ready-made; it constitutes no problem for itself. The bullet's "spirit" would simply function as an onlooker that would regard its flight through the air from outside, without playing any role in it. The bullet's existence is, by the same token, bereft of the character proper to living. To live is to find ourselves obliged to decide, at every moment, what we are going to do; therefore, what we are going to be in the near future. Life is not given to us ready-made; rather, each one of us has to fashion it for him- or herself. [Accordingly,] a human being's spirit is not, primordially speaking, an onlooker who would regard his or her existence; it is [instead] the author of his or her existence. A human being has to decide it from one moment to the next. If the things surrounding us forced themselves on us absolutely at every moment, they would be the ones deciding about us, and our case would be like the bullet's. But the fact is that the things found in our surroundings present themselves, in respect of us, as uncertain. [Consider:] Will the sun rise tomorrow? Will I be suffering from angina pectoris this afternoon? Will stocks be devalued in the market? In conformity with its primordial essence, life is interrogation; or, equivalently, it is insecurity; or again, it is our being incapable of resting content with things—with whatever is found there now—and, as well, our being forced to anticipate what things will be like. But such "future things," or the "things lying in the future," are no longer the things that are surrounding us and that are presenting themselves on their own. The future of things has to be imagined or constructed by human beings. To that end, a human being has to review everything he or she remembers about them, what things were up to now, and has to make an effort to extract, from that "experience," an image or schema of their abiding behavior, of what they are always, and not just at this or another moment. It is thus that human beings construct a "permanent, immutable thing"—in short, the being of things—behind the actual things of the moment. As soon as a human being thinks that he or she has found it, he or she knows already what to abide by about things, and they cease being insecure, uncertain, in flux. The world is [then] an ocean no more, and life no shipwreck any longer. Under the sole of his or her feet, a human being would [at that moment] touch solid ground, and the universe would become an architectural whole endowed with cardinal points and cosmic orderliness. It is at that point that a human being would be capable of arriving at a decision with a modicum of security. It is at that point that his or her decisions would make sense to him or her, and that his or her life would be an orderly march, instead of sinking into chaos.

The idea that the being of things is something constructed by human beings because they are in need of it, and, consequently, that there is no sense in talking of *being* abstracted from human life, does not at all imply a relapse into idealism and, least of all, into the worst form it has taken, namely, anthropological idealism.[94] For I am not asserting here that things, that "realities," are constructed by the mind.[95] Quite the contrary, since things inexorably exert their pressure on us, before we come to think of them, we are obliged to go in search of their being and to discover or construct it. This light [for example] is not one of "my representations or ideas," but the other way around: because it is not one of my representations or ideas, but an absolute reality illuminating me, I strive to construct its being, "idea," or "notion" in [the science of] optics.

Life primordially consists in my encountering myself submerged in the midst of things, and, as long as it is just that, it amounts to my being absolutely at a loss. Life is being at a loss. But, for that very reason, it obliges us, willy-nilly, to engage in an effort to find our bearings in the chaos [we encounter ourselves in], so as to save ourselves from being at a loss. This effort is knowledge, by means of which an outline of orderliness, a cosmos, is drawn out from chaos. Such an outline of the universe is the system of our ideas or convictions in force.[96] We live, willy-nilly, by means of convictions and on convictions. The person who is, in theoretical terms, the most skeptical, exists by resting on a base consisting of beliefs concerning what things are. Life is absolute conviction. In living terms, the most extreme form of intellectual doubt is the absolute conviction that everything is doubtful.[97] That something, or everything, is doubtful is no less a belief in a being than another which would exhibit a more positive aspect.

Now one is in the position of understanding why it is that the intellect sets itself to work. It does not do so simply because one is in possession of it; it does so, as the arms of the castaways do, in order to keep one afloat; thinking is a swimming motion one engages in so as to be saved from being at a loss in chaos. Should one wish to insist on this comparison, one could say that being is a raft the castaway constructs for himself with what he finds in his surroundings.

The being of a thing, then, is neither a thing nor a super-thing; it is an intellectual schema, the content of which would give expression to, or disclose to us, what a thing is. And "what a thing is" is always tantamount to the role the thing plays in life, to its significance within life.

Inasmuch as a concept or thought is the doing of a human being, a most living effort [on his or her part], it was really strange to find that its result or content is altogether extraneous to life, a pure vision of the being of things having nothing to do with our lives. It is evident that we cannot speak of, or mean, anything, unless it is somehow found in, or appears within, the sphere of our lives. Everything, absolutely everything, is, to begin with, something we come across in our living. Therefore, its primordial and radical nature is nothing but that of an ingredient or element of our existence. One possesses just one thing about anything one claims to be found "beyond" our lives, namely, that it "is found beyond our lives," which is a determination that something would exhibit within life. This is the terrible thing about life: we cannot step out of it, for everything is in it. To leave it behind is impossible. There is no entry or exit to life. No one is in attendance at his or her own birth or death; no one has lived them.

In virtue of an extravagant paradox, life—which is always my own, the one actually lived by each one [of us]—has no beginning or end, and yet it is not infinite. Without knowing how, each one of us already encounters him- or herself in it, and no one encounters him- or herself outside it.[98]

Now you are in the position to understand why it is that I regard as superficial to formulate the problem of knowledge in the usual fashion, i.e., by reducing it to the question of how the intellectual subject or consciousness is capable of grasping being, as if consciousness and being preexisted apart from each other, and the only thing involved were—as in sleights of hand—to effect the passage from being to consciousness or vice versa. No, that is not so: [both] the cognitive act of apprehension and the being apprehended thereby emerge as the radical edges of something prior, namely, life. Here lies, by way of a preliminary sketch, the reason why all metaphysical problems are rooted in the study of life, in living reason.[99]

PART IV

# GLIMPSES OF THE
# HISTORY OF PHILOSOPHY

# Ninth Lecture*

When we say of two given apples that they are equal to each other, we have attributed the component of equality to their being.[1] Now then, it is evident that, when taken in isolation and by itself, each of the two apples does not possess or contain the character, note, or component of equality with the other. For apple *A* to be equal to apple *B*, not only is the existence of apple *B* necessary, but so is, as well, that of a subject who would compare the apples in terms of size. Now, to compare them in terms of size is to wonder how the two apples are related to each other in such a respect. Only in view of this question and in its wake (and, I would say, as a result of its impact) does the equality of the two apples arise in them. For equality to exist, it has been necessary, then, for someone to compare the apples, but to compare them is to do something with them. Nonetheless, what arises or results from the comparison, namely, the equality of the apples, belongs to and derives from them. Whether or not they are equal to each other does not depend on the subject who would compare them.

Shall we [then] say that the equality of the apples is purely subjective? The subject has laid on them his or her question, comparison, and measurement, but he or she has not dictated what the answer would be; he or she has not generated it; rather, it has been imposed on him or her *by* the apples.

The millenial history of the theory of knowledge and, even more generally, of philosophy is nothing but the history of the various formulae that have been tried out [in the attempt] to reduce to an equation the two terms or factors that play a role in the problem of knowledge, to wit: subject and object; or, to put it otherwise, to determine what pertains, in knowledge, to the subject engaged in knowing and what to that which is being known.

In the initial stages of the work of philosophy, knowledge was interpreted as if the object contributed almost everything to it. It was believed that knowing amounted to the coming of the thing into the mind.

*Added by the Spanish editor. *Ed.'s N.:* Of this lecture only the fragment transcribed here is extant. It is alluded to and complemented in the body of the next lecture. [Cf. *infra,* pp. 159ff.] I [have decided to] group all the remaining lectures separately under the heading, "Glimpses of the History of Philosophy," because the author himself, in the last one, characterizes them in that fashion. [Cf. *infra,* p. 169.]

According to Democritus, [for example,] every single thing would emit *eídola*[2] around itself, i.e., small self-replicas, phantoms or "images" of itself, which would come into the mind as if they owned the place. As you [may] note, this implies that knowing is an odd way of mentally taking hold of, or grasping, a thing as it is [out] there.

Yet it was soon realized that knowing a thing in terms of its most exclusive singularity is neither possible nor actual; one can only know what was called the "universal." [To be sure,] perception takes hold of, or grasps, things, but it does not [come to] know them, for the simple reason that a singular thing contains a set of ingredients that come and go, without however modifying another group of its ingredients—apparently of greater importance—which is permanent. This is what was called the essence of the thing, its being proper. And what constitutes the being of a thing, by contrast with the thing itself, is universal and necessary in character.

# Tenth Lecture*

In the preceding lectures, I believe I have fulfilled my promise to you,[3] which was to tackle—most energetically but with the greatest restraint— a fundamental metaphysical problem, namely, the problem of knowledge, [and to do so] by showing you how it is possible to formulate it in a more radical way than it has been heretofore and [point out] the sense of its solution. But, properly speaking, I did not work out that formulation; in other words, I did not prove its necessity and that of the solution I suggested for it. In brief, what I did not do was to deal with it in depth and formally. But if I did not do that, the reason was not only that I did not intend to do so, but [also] that I intended to do the opposite. To have dealt [with it] in depth would have led us, of necessity, to display the extensive series of metaphysical questions in its entirety and, in consequence, to stray, at least temporarily, in the midst of the forest [it constitutes]. Now then, as you may remember,[4] my purpose was to offer you—free of every complication and with the utmost simplicity—the complete outline of a major metaphysical problem from its first growth to its [final] fruit, so that an instance as easily surveyable as this would serve as an introduction to our study of metaphysics.

If we now desired, in retrospect, to specify the most salient features exhibited by what has been discovered, we would find the following three:

*Added by the Spanish editor.

1. That it is not possible to formulate the problem of knowledge without thereby formulating the problem of being, the beginning and the end of every metaphysical system.

2. That the being of things is not something that pertains to them when they are taken in isolation and by themselves, and that, therefore, it is not a thing at all, not [even] a super-thing [beyond. In other words,] that being is that which supervenes on things when and because a human being wonders about it.

3. A third feature, which is less important than the prior two but is perhaps more paradoxical in nature, amounts to the fact that, in the problem of knowledge, no essential role is played by the question of which are the so-called intellectual faculties of a human being. Or to put it otherwise: that a human being does not occupy him- or herself with knowing *because* he or she has such faculties or any others he or she would be endowed with before possessing the former, but because he or she has no choice but to occupy him- or herself with knowing, since a human being as such is a reality called "life," "our life." And this amounts to the fact that the self each one of us is finds itself having to exist among things, but in such a way that one must interpret them as well as oneself, in order to hold oneself up in regard to, and conduct oneself toward, them; that is to say, one must know what to abide by concerning everything. The being of a thing is the plan by means of which one abides by it. "Concept" is usually the name employed to refer to the formula of the being of a thing. The concept in question is our knowledge of the thing. This is the reason why scientific knowledge consists of the concepts we form, not of things.

Now then, if we take hold of the concept of a thing and proceed to analyze its content without pre-judgments, what could we expect to find in it? The thing itself, or something pertaining to it, and of which it would consist when taken in isolation and without any reference to a human being at all, i.e., to the life of the human being wherein the thing qua thing is found? [For example,] is the thing [called] sun, or something of it, part of the astronomical concept of the sun? When we analyze it, we are surprised to discover that the concept of the sun contains nothing but the formula of certain measurements we can carry out. This may astonish us, but it is undeniable. The being of a thing, which the concept makes manifest, does not contain the thing, but precisely the relationship the thing in question bears to us and, therefore, its way of functioning within the economy of our life.

The effort it takes for us even merely to understand this thesis, let alone to accept it after understanding it, makes me suspect that, by virtue of one or another cause, there is in us a primary inclination to admit the opposite one, i.e., the thesis according to which the being of a thing is [identical with] the thing, or is found in it, or pertains to it when it is taken by itself. This native tendency would have become consolidated in a tradition and a millenial habit of mind against which it is quite difficult for us to react.

This is the reason why I believe that directing a quick look at the historical process of philosophy from the point of view relevant to our thesis would serve to bring the preceding limited attempt to its completion. In the short film we are about to run for our benefit, we are only interested in answering this question: what have the philosophers of the past believed the being of things consists in? But even when it has been thus curtailed, our curiosity comes to be ambiguously formulated, since, in order concretely to answer that question, one would [have] to try [to present] the entire history of metaphysics. That is why it is advisable to specify what we are now exclusively concerned with. If Thales held that things consist of water,[5] and Heraclitus of fire,[6] and Democritus of atoms,[7] it is certain that they represent different philosophies, and such differences are of great importance to the history of metaphysics. But it is no less certain that those three philosophies coincided in regarding the being of things as equivalent to a *thing,* be it water, fire, or atoms. For the purposes of our subject, then, the three philosophies in question amount to an identical doctrine, at least in light of the general attitude corresponding to them, since the distance separating things from their being is, in the three of them, approximately the same.

Our interest would lie only in underscoring the major changes undergone by metaphysics in its way of interpreting the relationship between things and their being. For it could possibly be the case—[and, if it were,] it would be of exceeding elucidative value—that philosophy made its beginning on the basis of the belief that the being of things resided in them and was more or less identical with them, and [further] that the evolution [of metaphysics] amounted to the ongoing establishment of a distance between being and things, [a development] which, in some fashion, would have resulted in the fact that being would progressively become less [like] things and contain less of them. If this was the case, then the immense process of the history of philosophy would be equivalent to the progressive purification of the idea of being, that is to say, to our gradually becoming clearly aware of the fact that being as such, in all its purity, cannot be mistaken for the things of which it is predicated. For this reason—i.e., because what we say of a thing is quite different from it—it makes sense to say it of the thing, since, as we had the occasion to note,[8] the act of saying consists in rendering something manifest or clarifying it, in making something patent [and], therefore, in making it happen that what was not already there about a thing be there.

Let us be satisfied now with underscoring a few typical stages of that process. To this end, the quickest and easiest route [to follow] would consist in asking—by cutting through the history of philosophy at various moments along its path—what human beings believed they had to do—at each one of those moments—in order to come to the possession of being (or, what amounts to the same thing, in order to know).

At the beginning of philosophy, knowledge was interpreted as if the object contributed everything to it. The subject did nothing; it was simply acted upon; its role was a passive one. It was believed, without further ado, that knowing was equivalent to a thing's proceeding from its reality, or from being in itself, to being in the mind. But since this [view] would imply that a thing leaves its place and reality in the world in order to come to form part of thought, it was necessary to look for an explanation that would render comprehensible the contradiction which, to begin with, the problem of knowledge actually amounts to, namely, that a thing known qua thing lies outside my mind, while the thing qua known lies within it. Such ubiquity, [i.e., the fact that a thing] is at once within and without, is [precisely] the question.

Here is how some have answered it: each thing would emit, in every direction, small replicas of itself (i.e., *eídola,* phantoms, images, or simulacra of the thing[9]), and it is these which enter the mind. The thing, then, actually and really proceeds into the mind, even though it is only its duplicate, or *eídolon,* that does so. It could be said that there is, among the real actions performed by the thing, one that consists in producing copies of itself. To know would be to allow those copies in; it is, therefore, to copy, although, at this early stage, even the labor of copying is the responsibility of the thing.

If for the purposes that interest us now, we fix the character of this interpretation of knowledge by means of a few decisive features, we would come to the following results:

1. It would presuppose [the view]—as a matter of course, even to the point of leaving it unquestioned—that the content of knowledge (i.e., the being of a thing) is identical with the thing. Now then, since perception (say, touch or sight) is the mental act by means of which things are given to us, it is understandable that [the proponents of this interpretation] generalized [it] and regarded every form of knowing as a kind of touching or seeing.

2. Accordingly, the cognitive function would amount to pure reception and strict passivity.

3. Knowledge would be a copy.

These three notes, [characteristic of] the most naïve and primitive interpretation of knowledge, are going, of course, to be rendered complex and subtle during the subsequent evolution [of philosophy]. However, the surprising thing [about them] is precisely the opposite, namely, the strict tenacity of their persistence and the enormous and longstanding effort that has been required to overcome and dislodge one note after the other.

For the moment, let me focus on the complication they immediately underwent. At the same time that this idea of knowledge was being held, it was noted—as indeed it could not have been helped—that knowledge cannot rest its case with the duplication of the thing such as it is given [out] there. This is so, in the first place, because one obviously comes to the realization that the totality of the ingredients which a thing one sees consists of breaks down into two groups of very different significance. One of them comprises all characters, modalities, or notes that appear and disappear in the thing, which supervene on it and dissipate. The other includes precisely everything about a thing that seems to remain the same through those variations. This means that a thing, as a matter of course, is already divided, as it were, into two things, to wit: one permanent, another variable. Now then, knowledge is interested, above all, in the permanent portion [of the thing]. But if this is so, then knowledge would not be mere reception. It is well and good to affirm that [in knowing] I would allow a thing in and that, absent this, without such passivity, there would be no knowledge. And yet, once a thing has been allowed in, I would have [nonetheless] to do something that already is active in character, namely, I would have to separate the permanent from the mutable in the thing. This realization would gradually intensify until Aristotle came to formulate it as a doctrine, to which we are so accustomed that we fail to take note, in full, of how odd it should look [to us]. It is the doctrine according to which a thing consists of two beings, one essential, another accidental.[10] Both are present in the thing; they belong to it; they blend with it; and yet they are separate and distinct within it. Such a duality demands [that a difference in] rank [exist] between those two [forms of] being, so that essential being would have priority over accidental being. The former is the principal [form of] being, the *kûríos ón,* the one endowed with ultimate significance to knowledge, which is thus required to be essential knowledge, or knowledge of the essence in the thing, or better yet, knowledge of what is essential *in* the thing.

Now, this was the attitude and tendency characteristic of one of the two teams [of thinkers] which, during the first three centuries of the history of philosophy (therefore, between 600 and 300 B.C.), collaborated in the creation of science. The [members of the] other team, the Ionian school, were also of the belief that things possess being by themselves, and that knowledge is reception and copy, though it represents a special modality, so far as what it seeks as the being of things is concerned. [The members of] this team were not primarily interested in what is permanent about things, but, in a way, in what is variable about them. And what is more, they were of the opinion that what is constitutive of a thing, taken as a whole and in its entirety, is not its being permanent, but its arising and perishing. Or to put it otherwise: the Ionians departed from the conviction that the most evident aspect of things consists—to speak with precision—not in their being (at the present moment, obviously), but rather in their not-having-been earlier and in their ceasing-to-be later. Hence, the question about the being of things turns, for the Ionians, into another, namely, whence are things coming and whither are they going? Or what amounts to the same thing: the question about the being of things becomes a question about the origin and genesis thereof. When Thales asserted that things are water, he meant thereby that what is not water presently was water originally and will be water upon its being consumed. The being of things is, then, that out of which they come and that toward which they advance or [to which they] return. But this implies, of course, that [the Ionians] acknowledged, for example, that the earth, which presently does not appear to be water, truly is water beneath its appearances; that it is a modification of water. The latter persists in *being* through all the apparent alterations it undergoes. Following a different path, we end up, accordingly, with a duality similar to the one we [encountered] previously: the thing [was taken as] breaking down, in one case, into its essential and its accidental being, and, in another, into that which it is originarily—or its latent principle—and that which it is as its modification or appearance. Nonetheless, for the members of either team, the being of things is always a thing. Just as its essential being is a part of the thing, so is originary being ultimately a thing—say, water. The difference lies in the fact that, for [the members of] the second team, knowledge amounts to the reduction of many and various things to one thing or a few—e.g., water or fire—or, else, hot and cold, etc.

In order to summarize the entire complication of this first stage [in the evolution of philosophy], let us advert only to the fact that, in it, a separation and division occur within the thing, even though being and the thing itself merge. [And this means that] the thing is incapable of coinciding with its being.

Along with the complication that arises in connection with [the matter of] a thing and its being, seethes another about knowledge conceived as the reception of a thing into the mind. Much too crude was the idea that, for a human being to perceive a thing, it was enough to admit an *eídolon* or miniature [replica] thereof to the mind. This is equivalent to thinking of the mind as a large box wherein, just by entering, the external is transformed into sensation and thought. Soon enough, one comes to the realization that the entry of the external into the internal [sphere] must amount to a more radical process. My sensation, my thought, is myself sensing and thinking. The entering of a thing into myself must then consist in its being transformed into myself, or in my being transformed into the thing, in my becoming the thing. This already serves to complicate simple reception. At the very least, it requires that the subject be capable of becoming like the thing, of transforming itself into it. [For instance,] Empedocles would contend that that is possible only if I was already, before the fact, somewhat [like] things; that is to say, if, when a thing reaches me, it finds a prior affinity [for itself] in me: [for example,] the earth [must] find earth in me, and water, water. In light of this, knowledge would be a particular case of the action of like upon like, *hómoion tó hómoio*.[11]

In its extremely primitive form, Empedocles' theory anticipated and betokened the subtlest developments of the theory of knowledge, because, mind you, it seems to involve—in an unclear way—the realization that I cannot know the being of a thing unless it is already in me. Now then, this is to foresee, after a fashion, that knowledge always requires something a priori. But let us not dwell on this point.

Aristotle—who believed, like the most primitive [of thinkers], that knowledge is, first of all, sense-perception (and, therefore, reception)—would, however, come to terms with [the notion that] "things come to form part of myself" in a more refined way. It is not that things enter [into myself], or that they send duplicates of themselves to the mind, or that the elements of things—earth, fire, air, and water—pre-exist in me, as Empedocles would have had it. Rather, things have the power, even at a distance, to produce in me modifications that are in conformity with them. The soul takes on the form *[eîdos]* of the thing;[12] it becomes like the thing, but it does so, of course, after the way[13] in which that most special thing called "mind" is capable of becoming like, or transforming itself into, other things. Many centuries later St. Thomas [Aquinas] will formulate quite well this Aristotelian idea by asserting that *cognitum [. . .] est in cognoscente per modum cognoscentis*[14] [the known . . . is in the knower after the fashion of the knower]. To be sure, it is the *modus cognoscentis* [the fashion of the knower] that one should clarify, and yet neither St. Thomas nor Aristotle did so. But we are presently interested exclusively in pointing out how the subject, whether one likes it or not, is in the process of gaining ground, even in those interpretations of knowledge according to which it is sheer reception and copy, and in which, therefore, the object is assigned the dominant role and the subject is believed to have nothing or very little to contribute.

Let us jump to the second stage, which, chronologically speaking, is prior to Aristotle. Plato is its representative.

Plato analyzed the things that are out there, and sought in them something that would be equivalent to their being. But *being* is not [just] anything for Plato; for him it is that which is permanent, immutable, [self] identical. Being cannot amount to something that is not, ceases to be, [and] places itself in opposition to itself. This sheet of paper, for example, is affected by non-being. If I say it is white, and I attribute to it the [manner of] being we call "being-whiteness," I discover that it is not altogether [identical with] whiteness, but is also blueish and, therefore, non-white. But, furthermore, this sheet of paper came into being one day and will perish another; therefore, it was not earlier, and it will cease to be later. Considerations of this sort—the validity of which we are not presently concerned with putting to the test—led Plato to making the most paradoxical, astonishing, daring, and fruitful of discoveries, namely, that things, taken by themselves, are devoid of being. Since, moreover, Plato was incapable of thinking of them without [appealing to] something like being, having failed sufficiently to purify the idea of being, he found himself obliged to distinguish between two modalities of being that come through in his terminology. Things he will simply call "beings" *(tà ónta);* by contrast, he will employ the name, *óntôs ón* (i.e., that which is like being [or the really real]) to refer to that which truly constitutes being.[15] Therefore, things are not like being; they are not, in truth, endowed with being.

Now, Plato was faced with [the twofold fact] that, on the one hand, there is, in a thing, no group of ingredients, or essence, deserving to be taken as its being (as his disciple Aristotle came to believe once again), and that, on the other, no thing exists to which all others would be reduced as their originary being (as the Ionians had claimed). In brief, he was confronted with the fact that in the world of things there is no such thing as being, which must be sought after outside the world, in the ultramundane realm [consisting of] what he called the Ideas. The Ideas constitute the being of things, and yet the former have no intercourse with the latter.

Is it possible [to have] a more radical division between things and their being? I am surprised that no one has taken notice of this side of Platonism, apart from everything else it may imply: that no one has taken notice of the separation—qua sheer separation as such—between things and their being. And no one has taken notice of it, of course, because, just as Plato was obliged to think of things as well-nigh being, even though he saw—with perfect clarity—that things by themselves are devoid of being, so similarly, when he sought after [their] being outside the world, he thought he had found it in those quasi-things he called Ideas. It was impossible to expect that Plato would think of his own discovery with all the precision [it required]. Since, after all, being still amounted for him to those quasi-things he called Ideas, no one has taken notice of the fact that that was an expedient, and that what was substantial about his philosophical enterprise was to make the decision to bring about the separation in question, marked as it was by genius.

In my opinion, this is one of the major intellectual feats completed in the history of thought. Having been readied by Parmenides,[16] as you know, it represents one of the most radically liberating acts performed by a human being. And this is so because, as we have seen in prior lectures, it is characteristic of human beings not to be satisfied with things, existing as they are among things and being obliged, whether they like it or not, to have it out with them; rather, they are in need of inquiring into the being of things, if they are to deal with things (or, equivalently, if they are to live). An animal moves among things no less than a human being, but, unlike the latter, it seems to be satisfied with them; it does not seek to guide the steps it takes in its existence by means of the being of things, but by way of the things themselves. Now then, obliged as they are as such to seek after the being of things, those human beings who continue to believe to have found it in them have not yet sufficiently distanced themselves from things, so as to be able to become clearly aware of themselves.[17] They are still prisoners, then, of the animal attachment to things.

Hence, the enormous significance—the symbolic significance—that the reversal of perspectives brought about by Plato possesses. This man, in his search for what things are, was so little taken by them, so free of prejudice [in their favor] and of servility to them, that he turned his back on things, denied them being, and directed his glance in a direction opposite to that where they lie. To Plato, being is not [out] there, where things are,[18] that is to say, in the world, but, rather, "over there," outside the world—in a "place beyond the heavens."[19]

And yet, this is the right place to point to the stubborn drag of our initial prejudice, which leads us to confuse a thing with its being. The following terminological remark may serve to clarify what I mean.

We call something an "entity" when we refer to it insofar as it is endowed with being. "Entity" means "that which is." Now then, [consider this case]:[20] I presently find this light in front of me; I do not think of it, but, as I read, I let it illuminate me. My actual relationship with it consists in my availing myself of it by letting it illuminate me. To the extent that my dealings with it are limited to this, that light is not an entity. It acquires the character of an entity when I ask whether or not it is, and, [if it is,] what it is. This does not mean that the light in question would suddenly acquire a character not its own. The example I adduced the other day,[21] involving as it did two apples equal to each other, easily permits us to understand well the possible meaning [of saying] that this light would acquire the character of entity only when I ask whether or not it is, and, [if it is,] what it is. The equality of apple A with apple B does not exist in apple A, unless [1] apple B exists, and [2] someone compares the two apples. Apple A's being equal to [apple] B is, as I pointed out [then], the way it has of responding to our comparison; it is, so to speak, its reaction to our action of comparing it [to the other].

Similarly, this light acquires the character of an entity when I occupy myself with its being. How could it have been endowed with that character earlier, since it had not run into my question and had not [had the opportunity of] responding, as an entity, to [the event of] running into it? Yet this does not mean that the character in question, i.e., its response, is not its own. The hardness of the table is the way the table has of reacting to its being hit by my hand. Without the pressure exerted *by my* hand, there is no hardness *belonging to* the table.

After having clarified this point, I do not think that the following terminological distinction will present any difficulty to you. When I do nothing with this light except allowing myself to be illuminated by it, the light is a thing and not an entity. But it is an entity when I start to think of its being. In view of this, we can say that an entity is a thing when I occupy myself with its being, or insofar as it is referred to its being.

We can then formulate [this thesis as]:

$$\text{Thing} + \text{Being} = \text{Entity}$$

When we wonder about what a given thing is, we no doubt wonder about what that entity is. We are [then] preoccupied with that entity or thing in respect of, or with regard to, its being. And yet questions about the being of this or another thing are scientific, not philosophical questions. I am in need of learning what the sun is and what the moon is, what tuberculosis is, what gold is, and, perhaps, what unemployment is, or what Spain is. It is thus that, in succession, a human being—whether in his or her individual life or in the sequence of generations—finds him- or herself in need of inquiring into each of the things found [out] there in respect of its being. But this series of particular questions about the being of diverse things gives rise to a novel question, which is different from all of them. And [this is to ask,] what is the being of things? in general, which is the specifically philosophical question.

That question, however, does not point, to begin with, to its own peculiar character. It presents itself as being of the same sort, and endowed with the same sense, as the other questions; it only makes it apparent that it is not about any particular or determinate thing, but about all and any of them. That is why it is [tantamount to] taking it as sufficient, in order to be faithful to itself, to prescind from determinations. However, this proves insufficient, and it gives rise to an extended series of misunderstandings. That series of misunderstandings of the very question posed by philosophy is the history of philosophy. But, of course, such misunderstandings do not amount to sheer error. They have been necessary, so that, through them and by means of their mutual correction, the sense of the philosophical question may gradually come to attain purity and become distinct and clear.[22]

Now, what do such misunderstandings amount to, in the final analysis? One can reduce them to two: (1) that, when one wonders about what the being of things is, and not about what the being of this or that thing is, one may believe one is still asking about an entity, about the being of a thing, even if the thing is of an abstract, indeterminate sort; and (2) that, in wondering about what the being of things is, one may believe to be asking about things as a whole. In neither case does one leave [the realm of] things; one would be after another entity, another being, be it an abstract entity or entity as a whole.[23] For this reason, the answers usually advanced by philosophers to the questions they had raised were tantamount to proposing a thing, whether fire, number, strife, Idea, thought, matter, spirit, *natura sive Deus* [nature or God], or the ego. In the case of Aristotle, the answer [set forth] was twofold, and his metaphysical system suffered the confusion [resulting] from that twofoldness. To the question, what is the being of things? he first replied by pointing out the ingredients of abstract being, of being qua being, and later [by saying] that God is the entity serving as the foundation of all other entities.[24]

In terms of our formula, we may give expression to this general error as follows:

$$\boxed{\text{being} = \text{entity} = \text{thing}}$$

We see this very clearly in Plato. In answering the question, what are things? it is not possible, in a more decisive fashion, to separate oneself from them, to turn one's back on them, and to acknowledge that they are not [identical with] their being, than to say,[25] [with Plato,] that they are precisely in need of the being they are devoid of. Courageously, he abandoned the world in search of missing being; therefore, he left all things behind, but, once he had transcended the world and found that what he called Ideas is genuine being, he could not have thought of being, i.e., of the Ideas, except, in turn, as entities, as things, although [he took them to be] transcendent entities and super-things.

# Eleventh Lecture*

We have seen how Plato, in search of the being of things, discovered that they are devoid of it, that things are characterized precisely by the paradoxical condition that their own being—the being they would have in and of themselves—would be tantamount to their *not being* by themselves,[26] to *not being*.

In effect, the being we attribute to a thing—to this sheet of paper, for example—comprises the totality of expressions running like these: this sheet of paper "*is* white, *is* square, it exists or *is* existent." Of a human being we say, likewise, that he or she "is courageous, is just, is a sculptor, or is a physician." We always, then, find the being of a thing in predication, and predication consists in attributing this or that manner of being to a thing.

Now then, if we formally accept that which we are used to doing informally, or by virtue of a mere habit lacking a clear awareness of itself, and assert that things are endowed with being by themselves, we would get lost in the midst of the most obvious contradictions. [This is so] because, in fact, if [one affirms that] this sheet of paper is endowed with, or contains, the [property of] being-white on its own, what is meant thereby would be that "this sheet of paper" and "whiteness" are one and the same thing. But this sheet of paper is also somewhat blueish, or chickpea [in color]; therefore, it is non-white [too]. It is, then, [both] whiteness and non-whiteness. We could say the same thing of its being-square, because it is square, though only approximately. Its square [shape] is somewhat rectangular or non-square; its angles are not exactly right, etc. Similarly, a just human being, as it turns out, would be Justice, and yet it is a fact that no human being is identical with justice, but also and at the same time, more or less identical with injustice. Therefore,

---

*Added by the Spanish editor.

being-human and being-justice are not the same thing: the thing "human being" and being-just are fundamentally different and apart [from each other].

A thing is not, then, the being-thus-and-so-ness (e.g., whiteness, squareness, justice) we predicate of it. And the first reason by virtue of which we realize it is nothing of the sort may be formulated as follows: every thing presents itself endowed with, or containing, both a being-thus-and-so and its opposite.[27]

Yet, even if we just took the being-white of a thing into consideration, we would advert to the fact that, at a given point in time, it ceases being thus and so; and that, generally speaking, [even] its more enduring predicate, namely, its merely-being-existent, turns into its opposite, [for] the thing perishes. This leads us to a second reason not to mistake a thing for its being, inasmuch as being is not, in itself, compatible with change, with variation, therefore, with the negation of itself. Ultimately, one may only predicate the [property of] being-white of something that is thus and so always, eternally, and invariably. This obliged Plato to search for being outside [the realm of] things, in *something* exhibiting the characters of [self-]identity, permanence, invariability, etc.

But this topic also presents another aspect and gives rise to another question. If no thing contains, [say,] the genuine [property of] being-white (that is to say, pure and absolute whiteness), therefore, if nothing in the world is, strictly speaking, whiteness, or squareness, or justice, from whence have we derived our awareness of them?

It will not do to say that there are things that are a little white, more or less white, or almost white, and that it is in such things that we learn what whiteness is. [And it will not do] because that which is nearly-all-whiteness is not whiteness. That which is nearly-all-whiteness is far from teaching us, or disclosing for us, what whiteness is. What happens is the opposite: for me to be able to see that small measure of whiteness, that quasi-whiteness, I must precisely know, beforehand, genuine, pure, and complete whiteness; once I know it, I am capable of finding, by comparing, [for example,] snow, milk, and swan-down with it, some resemblance between such things and whiteness. One becomes more clearly aware of this by adducing the example of the straight line or [that of] justice. Who has [ever] seen a straight line with his or her own eyes, who has [ever] found [full] justice in a human being? Only the foreknowledge of the straight line, or of justice, would allow us to acknowledge the quasi-straightness of the edge of an object, or the quasi-justice of a given human being.

This makes us come to the realization that not only do things lack the being we hastily attribute to them, but also that they do not prove sufficient even for our [arriving at the] discovery of that being by means of them. There must be another source, a source other than things, from which to derive our cognizance of genuine being, if later we are to be able to have some inkling of it in them. Accordingly, neither are things by themselves endowed with a being of their own nor do they supply us with a knowledge thereof.

The paradox is remarkable, as you may note. It turns upside down every one of the most settled habitual ways of interpreting being and knowledge that are preserved, in its first stage, by philosophy.

We already saw the other day[28] how Plato became committed to searching for being outside [the realm of] things, outside this world. If he did free himself from [the error of] confusing things with [their] being, he did not, [however,] free himself, as the good Greek he was, from the belief that being must ultimately amount to a substrate, in short, to an entity, therefore, to something which, no matter how pure and subtle it may have become, would still preserve a certain likeness to what we, in general, call a thing. But, naturally, the thing in question is impossible, because, on the one hand, it would have to behave precisely in a way opposite to that of all actual things ([for] while these change, arise, perish, and contradict themselves, the thing that truly is, the *óntos ón*, would be eternal, self-identical, invariable), and, on the other hand, it would have to preserve the character of "being [out] there in front of the subject," "[of being] posited in themselves," which is exhibited by things.

It is evident that one cannot encounter entities as impossible as these. They are a mere postulate, which, in this case, despite its impossibility, is marked by genius because of its audacity. [Those entities] are the Platonic *Ideas*.

Several have been the efforts of philologists and historians of philosophy to cast light on what such *Ideas* were, when they are regarded as entities. At its ultimate level of exactitude, Plato's ontology will always remain something enigmatic or undecipherable, for, in all likelihood, it was so for Plato himself.

Here you have a good example of the possible fruitfulness of the method by means of which we began to gain access to the glimpses of the history of philosophy we are enjoying. The method in question did not amount to dwelling long on specifying what the philosophers [had to] say to us about their way of interpreting being and its relationship with things, but, rather, to engaging the philosophers directly and asking them about what they believed a human being has to do in order to know, that is to say, to take possession of the being of things. Thus, by flanking them and [reaching them] through an unforeseen breach, we may perhaps get from them a greater degree of clarity about their conception of being than they themselves had.

In Plato's case, the fruitfulness of our tactical approach is unquestionable. Let us attempt to see this point.

What must a human being do, according to Plato, in order to know the being of things? Since the human being in question would have come to realize that the being of things is not in them, he or she could not expect to discover it by means of a mental act in which he or she would deal directly with them. To know is not [an act of] reception; it is not an act of perceiving; therefore, the work of cognition does not amount to a thing's being translated to the mind. Please note how the entire naïve and "passivist" interpretation proper to the first stage [of the history of philosophy] is radically overcome in this second stage.

But, [if so,] what does the operation of knowing amount to, then? The being of things—which, as we had the occasion to see,[29] lies outside them—is, [for example, their] being-whiteness, [their] being-squareness, and [their] being-justice. Now then, human beings do not learn about such genuine whiteness, such pure squareness, or such full justice from the things surrounding them. On the contrary, things will only serve to mislead us concerning such genuine entities and make us get lost amid their inexhaustible diversity and number, in [terms of] the *à peu près* [approximate] and "more or less" character they abidingly exhibit. Human beings must learn to have nothing to do with things and remain by themelves, if they want to find entities of that sort. And they would find them within themselves, not in things. Plato gave extravagant expression to this paradoxical discovery in his dialogue called *Meno,* wherein he presented a slave boy, the humblest of human cases, finding all the truths of geometry within himself.

In other words, I encounter genuine whiteness and genuine justice when I come to an agreement with myself about them, when I awaken the notions thereof in my own depths. Therefore, those notions were already found in me *before* I had the occasion of seeing things and human beings; or, availing myself of a technical term to be used in later centuries in philosophy, [I would say that] they were in me *a priori.*

In effect, every strict truth or discovery of being is characterized by a strange condition, namely, that, when we think of it, even for the first time, it is our impression we already knew it from before; that to discover it now is just to come to the realization that we already knew it, though without having realized the fact. This is so in the case of every self-evident proposition. Common folk regard this strange and fundamental knowledge as a truism, one that consists in knowing that which we always knew already beforehand; that which is taken to be known as a matter of course; the knowledge that is never a novelty and already has a well-aged look when it first appears.

Please note that, by contrast, the truths we arrive at by means of the senses are always novel, always unforeseen, and that they always convey what has just occurred at the moment. Looking, hearing, touching are a perpetual surprise. Something that was not in me before makes suddenly its entry into me—by means of my eyes, ears, [sense of] touch. It is understandable that, during the first stage [of the history of philosophy] when it was believed that *being* was identical with things, knowledge was interpreted as reception and as the entry of the other into myself.

But our knowing what we already knew beforehand, though without having realized the fact, cannot be [an act of] reception. It is simply a matter of our taking possession of that which was already ours. It is then the opposite of having something come in from without: it is an emergence from my very depths; it is an ascending from the most profound to the most superficial level of myself; therefore, it is, in a way, a coming out from within to the surface of myself.

Now then, everyday speech, which contains every science in outline, also comprises a psychology. And the spontaneous psychology contained in language refers to the event consisting in my coming now to the realization of that which I already had and was by the name of remembrance or recollection. "Remember" is the term that Plato would choose to clarify what human beings do in order to know. Is it possible to find anything more opposed to reception, or perception, than that? Accordingly, he would formally tell us in the *Meno* that "seeking and learning are in fact nothing but recollection."[30]

Let us then sum up. When I endeavor to find out, [say,] whether someone is just, I must, first of all, determine what justice is. But this I cannot learn either from that or any other person. I must have nothing to do with the data reaching me from without and withdraw into myself; I must enter into and abide in myself *[ensimismarme]*[31] and, in my sole company *(auté kath'haute hè psukhé)*,[32] discover in me the concept of justice. To know, then, is to enter into and abide in myself: this is what a human being must do in order to know.

Once I have done this, once I am in possession [of the knowledge] of being-justice, I [may] turn without and can [on that basis] decide which human beings are just, and in what measure; or, again, [in light of my knowledge of being-whiteness or being-squareness, I can decide] which things are white, which bodies square [and in what measure]. Things are knowable, therefore, by virtue of the fact that I bring to bear on them the notions of being-thus-ness or being-so-ness, which they are not endowed with by themselves. In this sense, it is I who endow or supply them with the being they are devoid of; [accordingly,] the operation of knowing acquires the character of an activity or constructive work on the subject's part.[33]

Bodies, for example, would not be of any particular size, they would not be in the shape of cubes or pyramids or spheres, unless I applied geometry to them, unless I translated or transformed them into geometrical shapes and measures. But geometry is what I contribute; it derives from me; it is the work resulting from my interior labor, from my entering into and abiding in myself. It is on its basis that I construct the bodies—which the senses place before me—in terms of shapes, distances, and measurements; I do geometry, that is to say, I measure the earth,[34] I construct the world by means of spatial specifications.

The second stage of the history of philosophy and its opposite (i.e., the first one) serve to identify for us the two perpetual antagonists, whose unending combat uninterruptedly gives life to the clods of that history. [We have, on the one hand,] knowledge as passivity and reception, therefore, as perception; accordingly, as the work belonging primarily to the senses: this is sensationalism and empiricism. But [we have, on the other hand,] knowledge as activity, as that which is superadded to things, as construction, as the contribution human beings make out of their prior, innate, connate fund of ideas: this is idealism, innatism, apriorism.

Alongside the contraposition in the interpretation of knowledge there is another in the interpretation of being: the sensationalist, the empiricist will always be of the belief that being and things are identical, or, at most (as we will have an occasion to see),[35] that if things are not identical with being, then there is no being at all. ([This is the thesis of] skepticism, positivism, phenomenalism.)

By contrast, the idealist or innatist is always of the belief that things are not identical with being, which belongs to another realm; and, moreover, that a human being plays precisely a certain role in the universe, namely, that of being someone who, when occupied in knowing, joins the realm of things devoid of being to that of being devoid of things.

In idealism,[36] however, there remains, when all is said and done, a trace of sensationalism and empiricism, a fact to which I alluded the other day.[37]

Knowledge is knowledge about things, and it cannot be anything else. Things are the problem, and knowledge cannot amount, in the final analysis, to anything but to a solution of the problem that things, whether we like it or not, pose to us. Naturally, Plato made his departure on this basis, and yet, in his efforts to solve the problem posed by things, he found himself obliged to search for genuine being apart and separately from them. Now, he searched for being as if it were thing-like or an entity. As a Greek, he kept to his fundamental conviction, of which he himself was not aware and against [the dangers of which] he took no precautions, i.e., the conviction according to which, in the end, being—whatever it may turn out to be—exhibits the character of pre-existing our knowledge of it,

[of pre-existing] its being possessed by [us] in the mind. To put it otherwise: for the Greeks, being—in whatever sense and form—consists in
being already, in being in itself; therefore, so far as the mind is concerned,
[it amounts to] being [out] there, outside the mind. Therefore, the moment is inevitable in which being, external as it is, would have to make its
entry into the mind.

Now then, Plato introduced a corrective to such inclinations of his
people with regard to things, but [he was able to do so] because—and
only to the extent that—they are not identical with being. Marvelously,
he made the discovery that to know is neither [an act of] reception nor a
perceiving nor the work of the senses; but, rather, that it is to enter into
and to abide in oneself, to find being in oneself. All of this, up to this
point, is marvelous. But in defining knowledge as recollection, as remembrance, he could not but wonder how he would be capable of joining to
himself, [for example,] the notion of justice and that of square[ness],
which he was then remembering. Remembrance serves only to translate
us to a prior act, which is no longer one of remembrance, but one by
which we establish unmediated, primordial contact with what presently
is only being remembered. In short, remembrance refers us to a prior perception. Now, by "perception" we specifically understand the contact
which, by means of the senses, we make with things. This sensory [act of]
brushing against sense-perceptual things is characteristic of our lives. But
justice is not of this world; therefore, our perception thereof is no act of
this life and thus cannot be sensory in character. Therefore,[38] recollection,
our perception of it, is not an act of this life, and thus cannot be sensory
in character. Recollection, then, presupposes that we would possess a
manner of existence quite different from this one, in which the subject
would find him- or herself in a world devoid of sense-perceptual things,
and, consequently, where he or she would be deprived of a body and reduced to its purest selfhood, which would directly deal with the Ideas,
pure entities too, unchanging and eternal. The a priori condition of
knowledge—i.e., that we, as it turns out, are already acquainted beforehand with what things are prior to our seeing them, because we are already acquainted with pure being—requires that there be an a priori condition of existence, namely, the pre-existence of our soul and of another
world in which the soul would exist. It is in that world in which the soul
would pre-exist that pure beings are found. This is how Plato reconciled
his discovery that being is not [out] there (that is, in things, in this world)
with the Greek conception that being consists in being [out] there, con-
fronting the mind. The "there" where the Ideas are found is a different
"there": it is a "beyond"; it is another world.

Platonism effects a duplication of the world.[39] Human beings would [accordingly] become entities participating in both worlds: they would "be there" (by means of their pure selfhood, by means of their reason) and "be here" (by means of their senses). Hence, the major influence it was able to exert on Christianity, which is also a dualist interpretation of the universe. Without Platonism, it would have been difficult for Christianity to speak of "this and the other life." The Jews knew none but this one.

Following in the footsteps of Plato, every [form of] idealism, whatever its modulation, would continue to place human beings in that strange situation, in division and inner dissension. It does so [by having them] apportioned to two worlds—the one here, the other beyond—and moving from one to the other. They would establish their abode in two settings, as a sort of metaphysical Cartesian devil[40] that would ascend and descend from one to the other. In short, a human being would be taken as a sort of amphibian. Now, this image is not mine but belongs to Plotinus himself,[41] [who asserted that "{s}ouls, then, become, one might say, amphibious, compelled to live by turns the life there, and the life here . . ."].[42]

APPENDIX

# IDEAS AND BELIEFS

# Chapter One

# Believing and Thinking

∽

I

*We Have Ideas, But We Find Ourselves Placed in Our Beliefs.*
*To "Think About Things" and "To Count on Them."*

When one is intent on understanding a human being, a human being's life, one strives above all to ascertain which are his or her ideas. From the moment the Europeans came to believe that they were endowed with a "historical sense," that became the most elementary requirement to be satisfied. How would it be possible for a person's ideas and the ideas of his or her times not to exert an influence on his or her existence? This is evident—agreed, but it is also quite ambiguous. In my judgment, being insufficiently clear about what one is searching for when one inquires into the ideas of a human being—or of an era—becomes an obstacle in securing a clear understanding of his or her life, of his or her history.

By means of the expression, "a human being's ideas," we may be referring to very different things—for example, to the thoughts that occur to him or her about this or that, or to those that occur to his or her neighbor and which are being repeated and adopted by the human being in question. These thoughts may be endowed with the most diverse degrees of truth. They may even be "scientific truths." Such differences are, however, of little, if indeed they are of any, import, when they are seen in the light of the much more radical question I am now posing, because, whether they are ordinary thoughts or strict "scientific theories," they are, without exception, occurrences arising in a human being, be they original with him or her, or the result of being breathed into him or her by his or her neighbors. But this obviously implies that the said human being was already there before the particular idea occurred to, or was adopted by, him or her. In one fashion or another, an idea arises within a life that existed prior to it. Now then, there is no human life that does not, as a matter of course, consist of certain basic beliefs and which is, so to speak, riding on them. To live is to be in need of having it out with something—with the world and with oneself. But the world and the "self" that a human being encounters appear to him or her under the guise of an interpretation, of "ideas" about the world and the self.

Here we run into another layer of a human being's ideas, and yet how different are these "ideas" from those occurring to, or being adopted by, him or her. The basic "ideas" that I call "beliefs"—we will have an occasion of seeing why—do not arise at an appointed time *within* our lives; we do not arrive at them by means of particular acts of thinking; they are not, in short, thoughts we have; they are not our occurrences, not even of the sort that is loftier in character because of their logical perfection and to which we refer by the name "reasonings." Quite the contrary: the ideas that truly are "beliefs" form the container of our lives, and, because of that, they do not exhibit the character of being particular contents within our lives. It is possible to say that they are not ideas we have, but, rather, ideas we are. What is more: precisely because they are our most radical beliefs, we mistake them for reality itself—they are our world and our being; they lose, therefore, the character of ideas, of being thoughts of ours that could very well have failed to have occurred to us.

Once one has come to realize that there is a difference between those two strata of ideas, the role it plays in our lives clearly appears [to us] without further ado (and so does, to begin with, the enormous difference in functional rank [between them]). Of ideas-occurrences—and let it be clearly understood that I am including among them the strictest ideas of science—we may say that they are produced, supported, debated, [and] disseminated by us; that we fight in their defense; and even that we are capable of dying for them. What we cannot do is live *off* them. We have fashioned them, and, for that reason, they already presuppose our lives, which are established on the basis of ideas-beliefs that are not produced by us; that, generally speaking, we do not even formulate to ourselves; and that, of course, we do not debate or disseminate or offer any support for. With beliefs, we *do,* properly speaking, nothing at all, but we simply find ourselves *placed* in them. And this is precisely what never happens to us—if we speak with care—in the case of our occurrences. Everyday Spanish has accurately coined the expression, "to find onself placed in a belief" *[estar en la creencia].* In effect, we find ourselves placed in a belief, and we possess an occurrence and give it our support. But a belief possesses us and gives us its support.

Accordingly, there are ideas we come *upon* (this is the reason why I call them occurrences) and ideas *in* which we find ourselves placed, ideas that seemingly are already there before we occupy ourselves with thinking.[1]

Once we have seen this point, it is surprising to see the term "ideas" employed to refer to both. The fact that the name is the same is the only thing hindering [us] from distinguishing the two things, the dissimilarity between which would stand out so clearly before us just by simply using the two terms "beliefs" and "occurrences" in opposition to each other. The incongruous behavior consisting in assigning the same name to two things so different from each other is not, however, a matter of chance or of distraction. It derives from a deeper incongruity, namely, from confusing two radically diverse problems demanding two ways of thinking and naming which are no less dissimilar from each other.

But let us set this aspect of the topic aside; it is too abstruse. It will suffice for us to remark that "idea" is a psychological term, and that psychology, like every particular science, only possesses a subordinate jurisdiction. The truth of its concepts is relative to the special point of view serving to constitute that science, and its validity would hold within the horizon that the point of view in question produces and delimits. Thus, when in psychology it is said that something is an "idea," it is not being claimed that the most decisive point, or what is most real about it, has been conveyed. Life's is the only point of view that is not particular and relative, for the simple reason that all others are given within life and are mere specifications of that point of view. Now then, as a living phenomenon, a belief does not resemble an occurrence at all: its function in the organism of our existence is altogether different from, and in a way contrary to, that of the latter. In comparison with this, how important could the fact be that, from a psychological standpoint, both are "ideas," and not feelings, volitions, etc.?[2]

It is advisable, then, to confine the term "ideas" to designate everything that, in our lives, arises as a result of our intellectual engagement. But beliefs present themselves to us exhibiting the opposite character. We do not arrive at them after an effort to understand; on the contrary, they already are at work in our depths when we set out to think about something. That is why we do not usually formulate them, but rest content with alluding to them, as we usually do with everything that for us is reality itself. By contrast, theories, even the most truthful ones, exist only as long as they are being thought about. Hence, they are in need of being formulated.

Without further ado, this serves to disclose the fact that any thing we set out to think about has for us, for that very reason, a problematic reality, and that, when it is compared with our genuine beliefs, it occupies a secondary place in our lives. We do not think about are beliefs, now or later; our relationship with them amounts to something much more efficacious, [for] it consists in counting on them, always, without interruption.

The contraposition between thinking of something and counting on it seems to me of exceptional importance, if we are to cast some light, at last, on the structure of human life. Intelluallism, which, almost uninterruptedly, has exercised absolute rule over the entire past [history] of philosophy, has made it impossible for the respective values of both terms to become patent to us and has even been responsible for the inversion thereof. Allow me to explain.

Let the reader analyze any of his or her behaviors, even one that appears to be of the utmost simplicity. [Say that] the reader is [presently] at home and decides, for one motive or another, to go out into the street. What about his or her entire behavior would properly exhibit the character of being-thought-about, even if one takes the expression in its broadest sense, that is, as [signifying] the clear, actual consciousness of something? [Suppose that] the reader has become aware of his or her motives, of the resolution he or she has adopted, of the execution of the movements by means of which he or she has walked [toward] the door, opened it, and gone downstairs. All of that [would play a role] in the most favorable of cases. Thus, even then, no matter how hard the reader were to search his or her consciousness, he or she would not be able to identify any thought therein which would point out the existence of the street. Not even for a moment would the reader have called the existence or non-existence of the street into question. Why? No one would deny that the existence of the street is of some significance, if one is to decide to go out into the street. Strictly speaking, it is the most significant thing of all, the presupposition of everything else. Nonetheless, the reader would have failed precisely to call so significant a topic into question; he would not have *thought* about it, whether to deny it or to affirm it or to cast doubt on it. Does this mean that the existence or non-existence of the street would have played no role in his or her behavior? Obviously not. The proof of that would be found [the moment in which], having come to the door of his or her house, he or she were to find that the street had vanished, that the ground had come to an end at the threshold of his or her home, or that an abyss had opened up before him or her. Then a most clear and violent surprise would overtake the reader's consciousness. About what? About the non-existence of the street. But hadn't we agreed that the reader had not thought before about its existence, that he or she had not called it into question? Such a surprise would serve to make manifest the extent to which the existence of the street had played a role in the [reader's] prior state, that is to say, the extent to which the reader had *counted on* the street, even though he or she had not been thinking of it, and precisely because he or she had not been thinking of it.

A psychologist would say to us that we are dealing here with a habitual thought, and that this is the reason why we are not aware of it. Or the psychologist would appeal to the hypothesis of the subconscious mind, etc. All of that, which is highly questionable, turns out to be beside the point altogether, so far as our topic is concerned. A factor would always remain which plays a decisive role in our behavior, inasmuch as it was its basic presupposition, a factor that was not *thought* by us with a clear, distinct manner of consciousness. It was in us, though not consciously, but [only] as a latent implication of our consciousness or thought. Thus, I employ the designation, "counting on something," to refer to its way of playing a role in our lives without our thinking of it. Such is the way proper to our actual beliefs.

As I have already said,[3] intellectualism reverses the value of the terms. The sense of my charge has now become clear. In fact, intellectualism tended to regard that which is most conscious as the most efficient factor in our lives. At this point, we see that the opposite is true. Maximal effectiveness in our behavior belongs to the latent implications of our intellectual activity, to everything on which we count and which, because we count so much on it, we do not think about.

Can you already gather the sense of the great error committed by someone who seeks to clarify the life of human beings, or of an era, in terms of their system of ideas, that is to say, in terms of their particular thoughts, instead of digging deeper, until the stratum of their more or less unexpressed beliefs, of the things one counts on, is reached? To do this, to establish the inventory of things one counts on, would truly be to construct history, to cast light on [human] life from its foundations.

II

*The Befuddlement of Our Times. We Believe in Reason,*
*Not in Its Ideas. Science Almost Poetry.*

Let me summarize: when we attempt to determine which are the ideas of a human being or those of an era, we usually confuse two radically different things, namely, their beliefs and their occurrences or "thoughts." Strictly speaking, only the latter should be called "ideas."

Beliefs constitute the basis of our lives, the ground upon which the latter come to pass, because the former place before us what for us is reality itself. Our entire behavior, even that which is intellectual in nature, depends on which system is formed by our genuine beliefs. In them, "we live, and move, and have our being."[4] By the same token, we are not usually expressly aware of them, we do not think of them; rather, they act latently, as the implications of everything we expressly do or think. When we truly believe in something, we have no "idea" of it; rather, we simply "count on it."

By contrast, the ideas, i.e., the thoughts we entertain about things, be they original or borrowed, are not endowed with the value of reality in our lives. They act therein precisely as our thoughts and just as our thoughts. This means that our entire "intellectual life" is secondary in comparison with our real or genuine life, signifying to the latter only a virtual or imaginary dimension. One may then wonder about what the meaning of the truth of the ideas, of theories, is. My reply is that the truth or falsity of an idea is a matter of "domestic policy" within the imaginary world of our ideas. An idea is true when it corresponds to our idea of reality. But *our idea of reality* is not our *reality,* which consists of everything we in fact count on as we live. Now then, we haven't got the slightest idea about most things which we in fact count on. If we had an idea of any such thing, as a result of a special effort to reflect on ourselves, it would make no difference because, as an idea, it would be no reality to us. On the contrary, it would be a reality to us insofar as it is not just an idea to us, but an infra-intellectual belief.

Perhaps there is no other topic about which to achieve clarity that would matter most to our era than that of learning what to abide by concerning the role and place corresponding to everything intellectual in our lives. There are eras of a sort that is characterized by great befuddlement. Ours belongs in it. But each one of them is befuddled somewhat differently and for a different reason. In the final analysis, our great befuddlement today lives on the fact that human beings are beginning to be at a loss in dealing with ideas, after several centuries marked by abundant intellectual creation and a maximal degree of attention devoted to it. Human beings already have the presentiment that they were wrong in regarding the ideas the way they did, that their role was different from the one attributed to them during these centuries, and yet they still do not know what their genuine function is.

That is why it is of great importance to learn, above all, how altogether neatly to separate our "intellectual life"—which, of course, is no life— from living life, from real life, from the life we are. Once this is done, and done well, it will be possible to raise the two remaining questions, namely: [(1)] How do ideas and beliefs mutually interact? [(2)] From whence do beliefs derive, and how are they formed?

In the prior section,[5] I asserted that employing the name "ideas" equally to refer to beliefs and occurrences led one into error. Now I would add that the same harm would be produced if one spoke, without introducing distinctions, of beliefs, convictions, etc., when one is dealing with ideas. It is, in fact, a mistake to use the word "belief" to refer to the adherence provoked in our minds by an intellectual combination, no matter which. Let us consider the extreme case, namely, the most strict example of scientific thought, therefore, one which is based on evidence. Well, even in that case, it is not possible to speak of belief in earnest. What is evident, no matter how evident it is, is no reality to us; we do not believe in it. Our minds cannot avoid acknowledging it as true; their adherence to it is automatic, mechanical. But let us be clear about it. The adherence in question, our acknowledgment of the truth, means nothing but that, when we set out to think of a topic, we will not allow in ourselves any thought diferent from, or opposite to, the one that seems evident to us. But there you have it: our mental adherence [to something] is conditioned by the fact that we set out to think of it, that we will to think. This is enough to make apparent the constitutive irreality of our "intellectual life." Let me reiterate that it is unavoidable for us to adhere to a given [i.e., evident] thought; yet, inasmuch as it is up to us to think it or not, our adherence [thereto], which is so unavoidable and would impose itself on us as the most imperious reality would, turns into something that depends on our will. But, by that very fact, it is no longer a reality to us, because reality is precisely that which we count on, whether we like it or not. Reality is a counter-will, what we do not posit; it is, rather, that which we run into.

Above and beyond this, a human being is clearly aware of the fact that his or her intellect is only set in motion concerning questionable matters, that the truth of the ideas feeds on their questionability. That is the reason why the truth in question is tantamount to the proof that we are seeking to provide for it. Ideas are in need of criticism as lungs are of oxygen, and they support and affirm themselves by finding support in other ideas which, in turn, ride on others to form a whole or system. They set up, then, a world apart from the real one, a world comprised exclusively of ideas that human beings knowingly fashion and are responsible for, so that the firmness of the firmest of ideas is reduced to the solidity with which they bear being referred to all other ideas. Nothing less, but also nothing more. What one is unable to do is to have an idea contrasted [with reality], as if it were a coin, by having it strike reality directly, as if it were a touchstone. The highest truth belongs to that which is [self-]evident, but the value of [self-]evidence proper is, in turn, a mere theory, idea, and intellectual combination.

Between us and our ideas, then, there is always an unbridgeable divide, namely, that which separates the real from the imaginary. By contrast, we are inseparably joined with our beliefs. That is the reason why it is possible to say that we are our beliefs. We enjoy a greater or lesser measure of independence with regard to our conceptions. No matter

how great the influence they exert on our lives may be, we can always
suspend our conceptions, disconnect ourselves from our theories. What
is more, to behave in conformity with what we think, that is, to take it
completely in earnest, in fact always requires of us a special effort. But
this makes it manifest that we do not believe in it, that we have a presentiment that trusting in our ideas, even to the point of entrusting our
behavior to them by treating them as if they were beliefs, is an essential
risk. Otherwise we would not value our being "consistent with our
ideas" as something especially heroic.

It cannot be denied, however, that it is normal for us to govern our behavior in conformity with many "scientific truths." Without considering it
something heroic, we get vaccinated, we engage in practices, and employ
instruments which, strictly speaking, seem dangerous to us, but for which
science provides the only warranty. The explanation [for this] is very simple and serves, incidentally, to cast some light—for the reader's benefit—
on some difficulties he or she will have stumbled upon since the beginning
of this essay. It is just a question of merely reminding him or her that one
of the most important beliefs found among those belonging to today's
human beings is their belief in "reason," in the intellect. Let us not specify
at this point the modifications undergone by that belief in the last few
years. Whichever they were, it is beyond dispute that the essential component of that belief abides, that is to say, that human beings still count on
the efficacy of their intellect as one of the realities existing and forming
part of their lives. But please have the presence of mind [necessary] to note
that it is one thing to have faith in the intellect and another to believe in
certain ideas fashioned by the intellect. None of these ideas is believed in
straightforwardly. Our belief is a belief in the *thing* called the intellect, just
in general, but a faith like that is not an idea *about* the intellect. Compare
the precise nature of that faith in the intellect with the imprecise character
of the idea almost everybody has about the intellect. Besides, inasmuch as
the intellect unceasingly corrects the conceptions it produces and substi-
tutes today's truth for yesterday's, were our faith in the intellect to consist
in straightforwardly believing in ideas, the changes undergone by them
would have brought along the loss of our faith in the intellect. But what
happens is altogether the opposite. Our faith in reason has borne undis-
turbed the most scandalous changes about the theories it has produced,
including the profound changes about its theoretical account of what reason itself is. To be sure, such changes have affected the shape of that faith,
and yet it has continued, unruffled, to act in one shape or another.

Here we have a splendid example of what, above all, should be of
interest to history the moment it truly resolves to be a science, i.e., the science of the human. Instead of occupying itself only with developing the

"history"—that is, with cataloguing the succession—of the ideas about reason from Descartes to the present, it would endeavor to define, with precision, what sort of faith in reason was actually operative in each era and which consequences it had for life. For it is evident that the plot of the drama of life is one thing, if one finds oneself placed *in the belief* that an omnipotent and benevolent God exists, and another, if one finds oneself placed in the opposite belief.[6] Likewise, there is a difference, though a smaller one now, between the life of someone who believes in reason's absolute capacity to uncover reality, as was the case at the end of the seventeenth century in France, and that of someone who, like the positivists of 1860, believes that reason is, by nature, relative.

A study like that would permit us to see clearly the modification undergone by our faith in reason during the last twenty years,[7] and it would cast unexpected light on almost every odd thing taking place in our times.

But just now the only matter I considered pressing was to make the reader aware of the nature of our relationship with the ideas, with the intellectual world. That relationship is not one in which we would have faith in them: the things proposed to us by our thoughts, by our theories, are not reality for us, but precisely and exclusively ideas.

Yet the reader will not be able adequately to understand what something is for us when it is just an idea and not a reality, unless I invite him or her to pay attention to his or her attitude toward what are called "fantasies" or "images." Now, poetry is the world of fantasy or imagination. Well, I am not about to take a step back away from that; on the contrary, this is the goal I wanted to reach. To understand adequately what ideas are for us, what their primary role is in life, we must have the courage to bring science to the vicinity of poetry to an extent much greater than anyone has dared to up to this point. To anyone who wishes to understand me correctly after all I have stated, I would say that science is much closer to poetry than to reality, that its function in the organism of life bears a great resemblance to that of art. To be sure, in comparison with a novel, science seems to be reality itself. Yet one becomes aware of how similar science is to a novel, to a fantasy, to a mental construction, to an imaginary edifice, when one compares it with genuine reality.

## III

*Doubt and Belief. A "Sea of Doubts." The Place of the Ideas.*

Deep down, a human being is credulous in character. Or what amounts to the same thing: the most profound stratum of our lives, the one supporting and bearing all others, consists of beliefs.[8] These constitute the *terra firma* upon which we strive. (Incidentally, let me say that this metaphor finds its origins in one of the most elementary beliefs we possess, one in the absence of which we perhaps would not be able to live, namely, the belief that the ground is firm, in spite of the earthquakes that sometimes take place on the surface of some of its regions. Imagine that tomorrow, for one reason or another, such a belief were to disappear. To specify the major lineaments of the radical change such a disappearance would bring about in the shape of human life would be an excellent exercise by means of which to be introduced into historical thought.)

Yet enormous gaps of doubt, scuttles as it were, open up in the midst of the basic area comprising our beliefs. This is the moment to assert that the doubt—that is, genuine doubt, which is not simply methodical or intellectual in nature[9]—is a modality of belief and belongs therewith in the same stratum of the architecture of life. One also finds oneself *placed* in the doubt, except that, in this case, [the condition of] being placed would exhibit a terrible character. One finds oneself placed in the doubt as one would upon an abyss, that is to say, falling. It is thus the negation of stability. One suddenly senses that the firmness of the ground gives way under the sole of one's feet, and one has the feeling of falling, of falling into the void, without being able to manage on one's own, without being able to do anything to affirm oneself, to live. It amounts, so to speak, to dying in the midst of life, as if one were in attendance at the annihilation of one's own existence. Nonetheless, the doubt preserves one of the characters exhibited by belief, namely, that of being something in which one finds oneself placed. In other words, it is not something one fashions or posits. It is not an idea one may or may not think about, or that one could support, subject to criticism, or formulate, but an idea one absolutely is. Do not deem it a paradox but, in my opinion, it is very difficult to describe genuine doubt except by saying that one believes in it.

If this were not so, if we doubted our doubt, the doubt would be harmless. The terrible thing about it is that it acts in our lives exactly in the same way as a belief would, and that it belongs in the same stratum [of life] as a belief. The difference between faith and the doubt does not consist, then, in our believing. The doubt is not a "not believing," as opposed to a believing, nor is it a "believing it is not the case that," as opposed to a "believing that it is." The distinguishing element lies in that which is believed in. Faith believes that God exists or that he doesn't. It *situates* us, then, in a reality, whether positive or "negative," but one that is unequivocal in character. This is the reason why, when we find ourselves placed in it, we have the sense of being placed on something stable.

To entertain the presumption that the doubt does not make us confront a reality is what impedes our understanding of the role played by the doubt in our lives. But this error derives, in turn, from being unaware of the believing dimension of the doubt. It would be very convenient for us if doubting something were sufficient for what we doubt to disappear before us. But no such thing occurs; rather, the doubt casts us into the realm of the doubtful and makes us be face to face with a reality as real as the one based upon a belief, but a reality that is ambiguous, two-headed, unstable, a reality in respect of which we do not know what to abide by or do. The doubt, in short, consists in our being placed on what is unstable as such: it is our life at the moment of an earthquake, a permanent and definitive earthquake.

On this point, as on many others concerning human life, we obtain greater clarity from everyday language than from scientific thought. Strange as it may seem, thinkers have always completely ignored the radical reality in question; they have turned their back on it. By contrast, human beings who are not thinkers, more attentive as they are to decisive matters, have cast keen glances at their own existence and left, in the vernacular, the sediment resulting from their glimpses. We are too forgetful of the fact that language already is thought, doctrine. When we avail ourselves of it as an instrumernt [to form] more complex combinations of ideas, we do not take seriously the primary set of ideas that it gives expression to, that it [itself] is. When, by chance, we are oblivious of what we ourselves want to convey by means of the pre-established turns of phrase of our tongue and heed what they say to us on their own, we are surprised by their keenness, by their perceptive uncovering of reality.

All everyday expressions concerning doubt serve to convey to us that, [when a human being] is doubting, he or she feels him- or herself to be immersed in a non-solid, non-firm medium. The doubtful is a liquid reality where a human being cannot hold him- or herself up; as a result, he or she falls. Hence, [the phrase], "to find oneself in a sea of doubts." This is *what lies in contraposition* to the element of belief, namely, *terra firma*.[10] Moreover, it would convey to us, if we insist on the same image, that the doubt is like a fluctuation, like the movement to and fro of the waves. The world of the doubtful is decidedly a seascape that awakens presumptions of shipwreck in a human being. When described as a fluctuation, the doubt brings us to the realization of how much it is [like] a belief. It is so much [like] it that it is tantamount to the superfetation of believing. One doubts because one finds oneself placed in two opposite beliefs, which collide with one another and hurl us from one to the other, leaving us without ground under the soles of our feet. The [component] *two* is quite evident in the *dou* of the doubt.[11]

When a human being senses that he or she is falling into those abysses opening up in the firm tract of land consisting of his or her beliefs, he or she reacts in an energetic fashion by striving to "shed his or her doubts." But what is he or she to do? The doubtful is characterized by the fact that we do not know what to do when we are confronted by it. What shall we do, then, when what is happening to us is precisely that we do not know what to do, because the world—that is, a portion thereof—appears to us [riddled with] ambiguity? There is nothing for us to do about it. But it is in a situation like that that a human being engages in an odd form of doing that seems to be almost no doing at all: he or she sets out to think. To think of something is the least thing we can do about it. We do not even have to touch it. We do not even have to move. When everything around us is failing, the possibility of meditating on what is failing us remains, however, available to us. Of the devices a human being counts on, the intellect is the closest. He or she always has it at hand. As long as a human being engages in believing, he or she does not put it to use, because that would be an arduous effort. But when a human being falls in doubt, he or she holds on to it as if it were a lifesaver.

The gaps in our beliefs thus constitute the living locus wherein the intervention of the ideas finds its point of insertion. In the matter of ideas, it is always a question of substituting a world from which ambiguity vanishes for the unstable, ambiguous world of the doubt. How is that achieved? By fantasying or inventing worlds. An idea is an imagination. No world already predetermined is given to human beings. Only the sorrows and joys of life are given to them. Under their guidance, they have to invent the world. They have inherited a major portion of it from their elders, the portion in question being operative in their lives as a system of firm beliefs. But each and every one [of us] has to have it out, on his or her own, with everything that is doubtful, with everything that has been called into question. To this end, he or she would test [various] imaginary shapes of worlds and of his or her possible behavior therein. One among them would seem to him or her to be *ideally* firmer, and he or she would call that the truth. Let it be clearly noted, however, that that which is true, even that which is *scientifically* true, is nothing but a particular case of the fantastic. There are exact fantasies. And what is more: only the fantastic can be exact. There is no way of understanding human beings adequately, unless one takes notice of the fact that mathematics and poetry spring up from the same root, namely, our imaginative gift.

# Chapter Two

# Inner Worlds

∽

## I

*The Philosopher's Ridiculousness. A Car's Breakdown and the Breakdown of History. "Ideas and Beliefs," All Over Again.*

The matter in question is this: the preparation of today's minds, so that clarity may prevail about what is perhaps the ultimate root of all present forms of distress and wretchedness, namely, that, after several centuries marked by continual and abundant intellectual creation, human beings, who had expected everything to flow from it, are beginning to be at a loss as to what to do with ideas. They do not dare, without further ado, radically to have nothing to do with them, because they still believe, deep down, that the intellective function is something marvelous. But, at the same time, they are under the impression that the role and place belonging in human life to everything intellectual are not those attributed to it in the last three centuries. Which ones should they be? This is what is unknown.

When one is suffering, with inexorable immediacy, from the forms of distress and wretchedness of the times in which we live, it seems ridiculous at first to say that they derive from, or have as their root, as it were, something so abstract and thoroughly spiritual as that which I have indicated. When one places it face to face with the terrible aspects of what we are suffering from (e.g., an economic crisis, war and murders, anxiety, hopelessness), one discovers no resemblance at all. In rebuttal, I would only advance two observations:

(1.) I have never found the root of a plant to resemble its flower or its fruit at all. It is probable, then, that the nature of a cause is such that it does not resemble its effect in the least. To entertain the opposite belief was the error committed by [those who lived according to] the magical interpretation of the world: *similia similibus* [similar to similar]. The work [to be done] is this: there are certain ridiculous things that have to be said, and philosophers exist for that purpose. At least, Plato literally stated—in the most formal of ways and in the most solemn of occasions—that the philosopher's mission is to be ridiculous.[12] Don't you think that it is a task easy to discharge. It demands a courage of a sort that great warriors and the cruelest of revolutionaries have usually lacked. Both [groups] have usually [consisted of] rather vain people who got cold feet when, simply, it was a question of becoming ridiculous. Hence, it would be advisable for humanity to take advantage of the philosopher's special brand of heroism.

[(2.)] We cannot live without a last recourse, the full validity of which we would feel to be upon us. We would refer to it every single doubt and argument of ours, as if it were a court of last resort. During the last few centuries, the ideas, i.e., what used to be called "reason," constituted that sublime recourse. Presently, our faith in reason is [becoming] hesitant, clouded. Since it serves as the support of the rest of our lives, we cannot, consequently, live or live together, since, as it turns out, there is no other faith on the horizon that would be capable of replacing it. Hence, we would have that appearance of uprootedness that has been acquired by our existence and the impression we are under that we are falling, that we are falling into a bottomless void, so that, no matter how much we flap our arms, we do not find anything to hold on to. Now then, it is not possible for a faith to die, unless another has been born, just as it is impossible to come to the realization that we are in error, unless we find ourselves, by that very fact, standing on the ground of a new truth. In our case, then, it would be a question of an ailment our faith in reason is suffering from, not of its death. Let us make ready its convalescence.

Let me remind the readers of the minor drama set off in their minds when, during a trip, their car broke down, and they were ignorant of its mechanical aspects. *First act:* to the effects of the trip, this event exhibits an absolute character, because the car has stopped, not just a little or halfway, but completely. Since they are not familiar with the parts making it up, the car, so far as they are concerned, is an undivided whole. If the car breaks down, that means that it has done so altogether. Hence, the uninitiated mind would go in search of a cause for the absolute fact that the car has stopped, a cause that would be absolute too; and, further, every breakdown would seem to it, at first, to be definitive and hopeless. Grief, pathetic gestures. [We would be saying to ourselves:] "We'll have to spend the night here!" *Second act:* the mechanic approaches the motor with astonishing presence of mind. He or she handles this or that bolt. [He or she] takes hold of the steering wheel again. The car starts triumphantly, as if reborn from itself. Rejoicing. The feeling of being saved. *Third act:* under the torrent of joy flooding us, a small measure of the opposite feeling trickles in, to wit: an aftertaste of shame, as it were. It seems to us that our first and fatalistic reaction was absurd, rash, childish. How was it that it did not occur to us that a machine is an assemblage of many parts, so that the slightest maladjustment affecting one of them could bring about the ceasing of its functioning? We [then] realize that the "absolute" fact of the stoppage is not necessarily produced by a cause that would be absolute too, but that a slight change would perhaps suffice to bring the mechanism up to par. In short, we feel ashamed that we did not possess the [requisite] presence of mind, and full of respect for the mechanic, for the human being who is familiar with the matter.

We are just living through the first act of the formidable breakdown endured by historical life today. The case in question is all the more serious because, in a matter involving collective affairs and concerning the public machine, it is not easy for the mechanic to handle the bolts with presence of mind and efficiently, unless he or she [can] count, before the fact, on the trust in and respect for him or her on the part of the travelers, unless they believe there is someone who is "well up in the matter." In other words, the third act would have to precede the second, which is no easy thing to do. Besides, the number of bolts requiring adjustment would be large, and the bolts would be located in various places. Well, let each person take care of his or her job without conceit, without histrionics. This is the reason why I am engaged, while lying under the belly of the motor, in repairing one of its most recondite roller bearings.

Let us return to the distinction I introduced between beliefs and ideas or occurrences. Beliefs are all those things we absolutely count on, even though we do not think of them. On the grounds of the sheer fact of being certain that they exist, and that they are as we believe [them to be], we do not call them into question; rather, we behave automatically while taking them into account. When we walk along a street, we do not attempt to go through buildings: we automatically avoid colliding with them, without the express idea, "walls are impenetrable," having to arise in our minds. Our lives are riding every moment upon a huge stock of analogous beliefs. But there are things and situations before which we find ourselves bereft of any firm belief: we find ourselves doubting whether or not they exist and whether or not they are one way or another. Then we have no choice but to *fashion* for our use an idea, an opinion about them. Thus, ideas are "things" we consciously construct or elaborate, precisely because *we do not believe in them*. I think this is the best, the most pointed formulation, the one leaving the least room for avoidance [, on our part,] of the major question as to which is the odd and most subtle role that ideas play in our lives. Please note that under that name all of them are included, whether they are commonplace or scientific, be they religious ideas or of any other sort, because nothing is a complete and genuine reality for us, except one in which we believe. But ideas are born of the doubt, that is to say, of a void or gap in our beliefs. Therefore, what we ideate is not a complete and genuine reality for us. What is such a thing for us, then? One [may] certainly take note of the orthopedic character exhibited by ideas: they function wherever a belief has broken down or become weak.

Now it would not be advisable to inquire into the specific origin of our beliefs, or into that from which they derive, because the answer, as we will have an occasion to see,[13] would require that we first adequately understand what ideas are. It is better to proceed by making our departure on the basis of the present situation, of the unquestionable fact that we consist, on the one hand, of beliefs—whatever their origin may be—and, [on the other,] of ideas; and [further] that the former constitute our real world, while the latter are something we do not adequately know.

## II

### *The Ingratitude of Human Beings and Naked Reality.*

A human being's most serious [d]efect is his or her ingratitude. I base this extreme assessment on the fact that, since a human being's substance amounts to his or her history,[14] every anti-historical behavior acquires a suicidal character in him or her. An ingrate is oblivious of the fact that most of what is his or hers is not of his or her own making, but that it is a gift bestowed on him or her by others who strived to obtain it. Now then, in being oblivious of that, a human being radically fails to be aware of the true condition of what he or she has got. A human being believes that it is a gift spontaneously bestowed [on him or her] by Nature, and that, like Nature, it is indestructible. This makes a human being err thoroughly in managing the advantages he or she finds and gradually lose them to a greater or lesser degree. Today we are witnessing [the occurrence of] this phenomenon on a large scale. Contemporary human beings do not effectively realize that almost everything we nowadays possess in order to measure up to our existence with some ease is owed by us to the past; that, therefore, we have to move with great attentiveness, tact, and insight in our dealings with it; and, above all, that we must take it very much into account because, strictly speaking, it is present in its legacy to us. To be oblivious of the past, to turn our backs on it, has the effect we are witnessing today, namely, that human beings are becoming barbarians again.

But now I am not concerned with such extreme and transitory forms of ingratitude. I am more interested in the normal measure thereof that is permanently attendant on human beings and prevents them from realizing their true condition. But, since philosophy consists in perceiving ourselves and becoming aware of what we are and what the genuine and primordial reality of everything surrounding us is, it would mean that ingratitude breeds philosophical blindness in us.

If someone asked us what the real nature is of that which our feet are treading upon, we would at once reply that it is the Earth. By means of this locution we mean a heavenly body of given makeup and size, that is to say, a mass of cosmic matter that turns around the sun with regularity and certainty sufficient for us to be able to trust in it. Such is the firm belief in which we find ourselves placed, and that is why it is reality *itself* for us; and because it is reality itself to us we count on it without further ado: we do not call the topic into question in our everyday lives. But it so happens that, had the same question been posed to human beings living in the sixth century B.C., their answer would have been very different. For them, the Earth was a goddess, the mother goddess, Demeter.[15] It was no heap of matter, but a divine power endowed with its own will and fancies. This is enough for us to come to the realization that the genuine and primordial reality of the Earth is neither what one [interpretation] or the other says, i.e., that the Earth as a heavenly body and the Earth as a goddess are not reality pure and simple. Rather, they are two ideas. If you will, one is a true idea and the other an erroneous one *about* that reality, [two different interpretations] that were invented by particular human beings one good day at the expense of great efforts. Accordingly, the reality the Earth is for us does not proceed from it without further ado. We *owe* it, instead, to a human being, to many human beings who were our predecessors; furthermore, its truth depends on many difficult considerations; in brief, it *is* a problematic reality that is not unquestionable.

We could make the same observation about everything, and this would lead us to discover that the reality in which we believe we are living, the one we count on and to which we ultimately refer all our hopes and fears, is the work and achievement of other human beings, not the genuine and primordial reality. To come across it as it is in its actual nakedness, it would be necessary to remove from it all present and past beliefs, which are nothing but interpretations ideated by human beings about what they encounter in living, [both] in themselves and in their surroundings. Prior to any interpretation, the Earth is not even a "thing," because a "thing" is already a shape of being, a way of behaving belonging to something (as opposed, say, to a "phantom"), which has been constructed by our minds in order to explain that primordial reality to ourselves.

What the Earth qua reality signifies for us does allow us—to no inconsiderable degree—to know what to abide by in respect of it, to be reassured, and not lo live [feeling] constricted by unending terror. If we were grateful, we would certainly have realized that we owe all of that to the effort and inventiveness of other human beings. Had they not intervened, we would [still] be related to the Earth (and, likewise, to everything else found in our surroundings) as the first human beings were; that is to say, we would be terrified. We have inherited all those efforts by way of our beliefs, which constitute the capital on which we live. The great and, at the same time, the most elementary discovery that the West is going to arrive at in the next few years—when its period of intoxication with foolishness, with which it was overcome in the eighteenth century, is finally over—is that human beings are heirs, above all. And this and nothing else is what makes them radically different from animals. But to be aware that one is an heir is to possess historical consciousness.

The genuine reality of the Earth is shapeless; it is not endowed with a modality of being; it is a sheer enigma. Taken according to its primordial and naked "substance," it is the ground that serves to support us at the moment, without providing us with the slightest assurance that it is not going to fail us the next; it is that which has facilitated our flight from danger, but it is also that which, in the form of "distance," separates us from the woman we love or from our children; it is that which, at times, presents [us] with the annoying character of going uphill and, at times, with the delightful condition of going downhill. The Earth, taken by itself and stripped of the ideas human beings have been fashioning about it for themselves, is not, then, any "thing" at all, but [just] an uncertain stock of facilities and difficulties for our lives.

It is in this sense that I assert that the genuine and primordial reality is shapeless, when taken by itself. That is why it is not possible to call it a "world."[16] It is an enigma proposed to our existence. To encounter ourselves living is to encounter ourselves irrevocably immersed in an enigmatic medium. A human being reacts to this primordial and pre-intellectual enigma by setting his or her intellectual apparatus to work, an apparatus that is, above all, imagination. He or she creates the world of mathematics, the world of physics, the worlds of religion, morality, politics, and poetry. These are actually "worlds," because they have a shape and [each of them] is an order, a chartered whole. Those imaginary worlds would [then] be compared with the enigma genuine reality is, and they would become accepted when they seem to be consistent with it to the greatest possible degree.[17] But, of course, they are never identical with reality itself. At this or that point, the correspondence would be so close that they would be partly identified [with reality]. (Later we shall have an occasion to see the consequences of this.[18]) But, since the points where they would dovetail perfectly are inseparable from the rest, where no satisfactory dovetailing takes place, such worlds, when each is taken as a whole, would remain being what they are, namely, imaginary worlds, worlds existing only thanks to us; in brief, they would remain being "inner" worlds. That is why we may call them "ours." Now, every one of us has his or her world, as evinced, [for example, by the fact] that the mathematician qua mathematician and the physicist qua physicist have *their own*.

If what I am saying is true, isn't it clear how astonishing it is? Genuine reality is enigmatic and thus terrible. A problem that is a problem only for the intellect, and therefore a problem that is irreal, is never something terrible, while a reality that consists in being an enigma, when taken precisely as such and by itself, is the terrible itself. Now, it so happens that human beings, when confronted by genuine reality, react by secreting an imaginary world within their own selves. In other words, to begin with, they withdraw from reality—imaginarily, of course—and retire into their own inner world to lead their lives. This is what an animal cannot do. An animal always has to heed reality as it presents itself; an animal always has to be "beside itself." In his *Man's Place in Nature*,[19] [Max] Scheler catches a glimpse of this difference between the animal and the human condition, but he does not adequately understand it; he is not acquainted with the reason for it and its possibility. An animal has to be beside itself for the simple reason that it is not endowed with a "realm within itself," a *chez soi* [a place called home], an interiority where to repair when it endeavors to withdraw from reality.[20] And it is bereft of an interiority, that is, of an inner world, because it is devoid of imagination. What we call our inner realm is nothing but our imaginary world, the world comprised of ideas. The move by virtue of which we momentarily are oblivious to reality in order to heed our ideas is the specifically human [act] which is referred to [by the phrase,] "entering into and abiding in oneself" *[ensimismarse]*. Human beings would later leave [the state consisting in] "having entered into and abided in themselves" in order to return to reality, but, at that point, they would be regarding the latter—as if through some optical device—from [the standpoint of] their inner world, of their ideas, some of which would have become consolidated as beliefs. And this is the astonishing thing I announced earlier:[21] that human beings find themselves existing in two dimensions, being situated at once in the enigmatic reality and in the luminous world consisting of the ideas that have occurred to them. This other manner of existence is, for that very reason, an "imaginary" one. Please note, however, that to have an imaginary manner of existence pertains as such to the absolute reality of human beings.[22]

## III

*Science as Poetry. A Triangle and Hamlet. The Treasury of Errors.*

Let it be clearly understood, then, that what we usually call the real or "external" world is not the naked, genuine, and primordial reality that human beings encounter; rather, it already is an interpretation which they have given of that reality. It is, therefore, an idea, [but] an idea consolidated as a belief. To believe in an idea means to believe that it is reality and no longer, therefore, to see it as a mere idea.

But the fact is, of course, that those beliefs began by "being just" occurrences or ideas properly so called. They arose one good day as the work of the imagination of a human being who, in them, entered into and abided in him- or herself, and [thus] for a moment became oblivious of the real world. The science of physics, for example, is one of those ideal architectures that human beings construct for themselves. Some of the ideas belonging to that science are today operative in us as beliefs, but the majority of them constitute, for us, [the content of a] science—nothing more, nothing less. When the "physical world" is spoken of, then, please note that we do not take it to be, for the most part, as the real world; it is, rather, an imaginary or "inner" world.

Now, the question I am proposing to the reader is one that consists in determining, [for example,] the attitude according to which the physicists live when they are thinking the truths of their science, and in doing so in all strictness, without allowing [the use of] vague or indistinct expressions. Or to put it otherwise: [it is the question,] what is the world of the physicists, the world of the science of physics, to them? Is it reality to them? Obviously not. Their ideas seem true to them, but such an assessment serves to underscore the character of mere thoughts that those ideas exhibit to them. It is no longer possible—as it was in happier times—elegantly to define truth by saying that it is the adequacy of thought to reality.[23] "Adequacy" is an equivocal term. If one takes it to mean "equality," [the contention] turns out to be false. An idea is never equal to the thing it refers to. But if one takes it in the sense of "correspondence," which is vaguer, one would already be acknowledging that ideas *are not* reality, but something opposite [to that] altogether, namely, ideas and just ideas. The physicists know very well that *what* their theories convey *does not exist* in reality.

Besides, [to see that], it would be enough to note that the world of physics is incomplete, [that it is] crowded with unsolved problems obliging [the physicists] not to confuse it with reality itself, which is precisely what is posing those problems to them. [The science of] physics, therefore, is not reality for them, but an imaginary realm in which they imaginarily live while, at the same time, they continue to live the genuine and primordial reality of their lives.

Now then, this point is [admittedly] somewhat difficult to understand when we speak of physics and, in general, of science, but is it not obvious and clear when we observe what happens to us when we read a novel or attend a play? The one reading a novel is living, of course, the reality of his or her life, but this reality of his or her life at that moment consists in having escaped it through the virtual dimension of fantasy and in quasi-living in the imaginary world described for him or her by the novelist.

Here is the reason why the doctrine I began [to develop] in the first chapter of this essay is, in my opinion, so fruitful, to wit: that we only adequately understand what something is to us when it is not a reality for us but an idea, if we think of what poetry represents to human beings, and courageously succeed in regarding science *sub specie poieseos* [in the guise of poetry].

The "world of poetry" is, in effect, the most transparent instance of what I have called "inner worlds." The characteristics proper to them appear in it with a carefree cynicism and, so to speak, in the open. We are aware that it is a sheer invention of ours, a child of our fantasy. We do not regard it as reality, and yet we occupy ourselves with its objects just as we do with the things of the external world; that is to say, since to live is to be occupied with [something], we live—for many stretches [of our lives]—lodged in the world of poetry and absent from the real one. In passing, it would be advisable to acknowledge that, up to the present, no one has been able to provide a fair answer to the question of why human beings make poetry; of why, investing no minor effort, they create a realm of poetry for their own benefit. But the truth of the matter is that it could not be stranger. As if human beings did not have plenty to do with their real world for an explanation not to be required for the fact that they amuse themselves in deliberately imagining irrealities!

But we have become used to speaking of poetry without great pathos. When someone says that poetry is no *serious* matter, only the poets become irritated, for, as is well known, they are of the *genus irrita-bile* [irritable race].[24] It does not take a lot, then, for us to acknowledge that something so much lacking in seriousness may be pure fantasy. Fantasy is famous for being the madwoman about the house.[25] But what are science and philosophy but fantasy? The mathematical point, the geometrical triangle, and the physical atom, [for example,] would not possess the precise qualities constituting them, if they were not mere mental constructions. When we want to find them in reality (that is, in the sense-perceptible, not in the imaginary, domain), we have to resort to measurement, but, by that very fact, their precise character is degraded, and they are inevitably [affected by the qualification,] "a little more or less." What a coincidence! The same thing happens to characters in poetry. It is beyond doubt: a triangle and Hamlet have the same pedigree.[26] They are the offspring of the madwoman about the house; they are phantasmagories.

The fact that [the proponents of] scientific ideas are, with regard to reality, subject to obligations different from the ones to which those who accept poetical ideas are subject, and that the former's relationship with things is closer and more *serious* [than the latter's], should not hinder us from acknowledging that ideas are just fantasies and that we should only live them as such, despite their serious character. If we do the opposite, we distort the correct attitude [to be adopted] toward them: we would take them as if they were reality. Or what amounts to the same thing: we would confuse the internal with the external world. [But] this is, on a somewhat larger scale, what the lunatic usually does.

Let the reader revive, in his or her mind, the originary situation of human beings. In order to live, they would have to do something; they would have to have it out with what is in their surroundings. But in order to decide what they are going to do with all that, they would have to know what to abide by about it; that is to say, they would have to know *what it is*. Since that primordial reality does not amicably disclose its secret to them, they would have no choice but to set in motion their intellectual apparatus, the main organ of which—I contend—is the imagination. Human beings would imagine a certain shape or manner of being reality. They would entertain the supposition that it is thus or otherwise; they would invent the world or a portion thereof, just as novelists do in respect of the imaginary characters they create. The difference lies in the purpose for the sake of which they create. A topographical map is just as fantastic as a painter's landscape. However, a painter would not have painted his or her landscape in order to use it as a guide in a trip he or she would take through some region, while the map has been made for that purpose. The "inner world" of science is a huge map we have been engaged in developing in the last three-and-a-half centuries in order to travel among things. It is as if each one of us had said the following to him- or herself: "*Supposing* reality is just the way I imagine it, then the best way of behaving in and with it would have to be such and such. Let us put it to the test in order to see whether the outcome is good." [To perform] that test is a risky business; it is no game. To do well in our lives is at stake. Wouldn't it be foolish to have our lives hang on the unlikely coincidence of reality and one of our fantasies? It would be foolish, to be sure. But it is not a matter of choice, because we can choose—we will see to what extent [we can]—between one fantasy and another in order to direct our behavior and to carry out our test, but we cannot choose between exercising and not exercising our fantasy. Human beings are condemned to be novelists. The possible correctness of their phantasmagories may be as impossible as you wish; yet, even so, it is the only probability human beings count on in order to survive. The test in question is so risky that human beings have not yet managed to solve their problem with a degree of sufficiency ample enough to *be right,* or to be right on target. And the small measure of success they have achieved in this order [of things] has required several millenia, a measure of success they have won by dint of errors, that is to say, by setting sail on absurd fantasies, which were, so to speak, blind alleys from which they had to back up in a sorry state. But such errors, [when] experienced as such, are the only *points de repère* [reference points] that they possess, the only things they have truly obtained and consolidated. They know today, at least, that the shapes of the world imagined by them in the past *are not* reality. By dint of errors, the area of possible success is in the process of being delimited. *Hence the importance of the preservation of errors,*[27] history being such a preservation. At the level of individual existence, we call it "life experience,"[28] something that is of little profit, for the same subjects have to err first in order to be right later, but later is, sometimes, too late. However, at the level of history, it is the earlier time which was in error, while ours is the one that may profit by the experience.

## IV

### *The Articulation of the Inner Worlds.*

My greatest concern is that the readers, even the least cultivated ones, should not get lost in the rugged paths I have gotten them into. This obliges me to repeat the [same] things several times and to emphasize the stations [passed] along our way.

What we usually call reality or the "external world" is [for us] no longer the primordial reality stripped of every human interpretation;

rather, it *is that which we believe,* with a firm and consolidated belief, to be reality. Everything we find to be doubtful or insufficient in the real world obliges us to form ideas about it. Those ideas constitute the "inner worlds" in which we live knowing full well that we have invented them, in the same way we live the map of a region while we travel through it. But one should not think that the real world forces us to react only by means of scientific and philosophical ideas. The world of knowledge is just one of the many inner worlds. Next to it are the world of religion and the world of poetry and the world of *sagesse* ["wisdom"] or "life experience."

The question at hand is precisely this: to make somewhat clear why and to what extent human beings are in possession of that plurality of inner worlds. Or what amounts to the same thing: [to make somewhat clear] why and to what extent a human being is religious, a scientist, a philosopher, a poet, a bearer of "wisdom," and "a person of the world" (i.e., what our Gracián used to call "discreet"[29]). To this end, I invited the reader, above all, to become well aware of the fact that all those worlds, even the world of science, have a dimension in common with poetry, to wit: that they are the products of our fantasy. What one calls scientific thought is nothing but an exact fantasy. Moreover, if one reflects at all, one would [readily] observe that reality is never exact, that only the fantastic (e.g., a mathematical point, an atom, a concept in general, or a character in poetry) may be exact. Now then, there is nothing more opposed to the real than the fantastic; in effect, every world created on the basis of our ideas is placed in us in opposition to what we sense to be reality itself, to the "external world."

The world of poetry represents the maximal degree of the fantastic; in comparison with it, the world of science seems to us to be closer to the real one. Agreed, but let us not be oblivious of the [twofold] fact that: [(1)] even if the world of science seems almost real to us *compared* with the world of poetry, let us not forget that it is of a fantastic character too; and [(2)] *compared with reality,* it is nothing but a phantasmagory. This two-part observation permits me to point out that those various "inner worlds" are fitted by us in the real or external world, thus forming an articulated conjunction of major proportions. I mean that one of them—for example, the religious or the scientific world—seems to us the closest to reality; that the world of *sagesse* or spontaneous life-experience rides upon it, and that the world of poetry is [set] about the latter. The fact of the matter is that we live each one of those worlds according to a different measure of "seriousness" or, vice versa, according to various degrees of irony.

As soon as this is noted, an obvious recollection wells up in us to the effect that such an order of articulation between our inner worlds has not always been the same. There have been periods in which religion, not science, was, for human beings, the [world] closest to reality. There was a period of Greek history in which the "truth" was, for the Hellenes (and, therefore, for Homer), what is usually called poetry.

This leads us to the great question. I contend that European consciousness drags along the sin of speaking lightly of that plurality of worlds, [for] it has never truly endeavored to clarify the relations obtaining between them and the ultimate nature thereof. The sciences, [in terms of] their own contents, are marvelous, but when anyone asks point-blank what science is—as an occupation engaged in by human beings, and by contrast with philosophy, religion, experiential wisdom, etc.—only replies [containing] the vaguest of notions are forthcoming.

It is evident that all of them—science, philosophy, poetry, religion—are things human beings do,[30] but everything done is done because of something and for the sake of something.[31] Well, but why is it that they do such diverse things?

If human beings occupy themselves with knowing, if they do science or philosophy, it is, to be sure, because one good day they find themselves *placed in the doubt* concerning affairs that matter to them and aspire to find themselves *placed right in the truth*. But one must come to an adequate realization of what such a situation would imply. To begin with, we may note that that cannot be an originary situation; in other words, to *find oneself placed* in the doubt presupposes that one has *fallen* therein one good day. Human beings cannot begin by doubting. The doubt happens suddenly to people who previously had a given faith or belief, in which they had always found themselves placed without further ado. To be occupied with knowing is not, then, something that is not dependent on an antecedent situation. Someone who believes—i.e., someone who does not doubt—does not set in motion his or her distressful cognitive activity. Knowledge is born of the doubt and always keeps alive the force that begot it. A scientist must constantly attempt to cast doubt on his or her own truths. These are only cognitive truths to the extent that they are resistant to any possible doubt; they live, then, on the basis of our permanent struggle with skepticism.[32] And "proof" is the name for this struggle.

On the other hand, this serves to uncover the fact that the knower—whether scientist or philosopher—is not seeking after [just] any form of certainty. Believers possess certainty precisely because they have not fashioned it. A belief is a certainty in which we find ourselves placed without our knowing how or where we have come into it. Every faith has been received. That is why its prototype is "the faith of our fathers." However, when we occupy ourselves with knowing, we have lost precisely that certainty we had received as a gift, and in which we had found ourselves placed, and we find ourselves having to invent [a new] one exclusively on our own strength. Yet this is impossible, unless human beings *believe* that they have the strength to do it.

Having exerted just minimal pressure on the most obvious notion of knowledge has proven sufficient for this peculiar form of human doing to appear limited by an entire set of conditions; that is to say, for the discovery that human beings do not engage in knowing without further ado and under any set of circumstances. Wouldn't this also be true of all those other great occupations of the mind, namely, religion, poetry, etc.?

However, thinkers have not yet made an effort, strange as this may seem, to specify the conditions of such occupations. Strictly speaking, they have not even brought them to a closer confrontation with one another. To my knowledge, only [Wilhelm] Dilthey has dealt with the question to some extent and has thought himself obliged, in order to tell us what philosophy is, to tell us, as well, what science is, what religion is, and what literature is.[33] For it is quite clear that all of them have something in common. Cervantes or Shakespeare provided us with an idea of the world, just as Aristotle or Newton did. And religion [too] is not something that would have nothing to do with the universe.

As it turns out, when philosophers have described the multiplicity of directionalities [followed], say, by the intellectual activity[34] of human beings, they rest their case and believe they have done all they had to do with the topic. It is beside the point to add myth, as some of them have done, to [the list of] such directionalities, while distinguishing it from religion in some obscure way.[35] What is certainly to the point is the realization that for all of them, even for Dilthey, those directionalities are permanent and constitutive modalities of [being] human, of human life.[36]

[Accordingly,] a human being would be an entity essentially endowed with those dispositions to activity, just as he or she has legs, an apparatus to emit articulate sounds, and a system of physiological reflexes. [We would have,] therefore, that a human being is religious as a matter of course, that he or she engages in knowing in [the area of] philosophy or mathematics as a matter of course, and that he or she does poetry as a matter of course. By using the phrase, "as a matter of course," I mean to signify that a human being would be endowed with religion, knowledge, and poetry as his or her "faculties" or permanent resources. At every moment, a human being would be all those things (i.e., a religious person, a philosopher, a scientist, [and] a poet), albeit according to one or another measure and proportion.

When [the philosophers in question] entertained such a thought, they acknlowledged, of course, that the concept of religion, philosophy, science, [or] poetry can only be formed in view of certain human tasks, manners of behavior, [and] very specific endeavors, [all of] which arise at certain times and places in history. Just to linger about the clearest of cases, [let me point to] the examples [of] philosophy, which only took a definite form in the fifth century [B.C.] in Greece, and [of] science, which has only acquired a special and unequivocal aspect since the seventeenth century [of our era] in Europe. But, once one has fashioned a clear idea about a chronologically specific human doing, one would go in search of something similar to it in every historical period, even if the similarity is scant. In view of that, one would come to the conclusion that human beings, in the given historical period, also were religious persons, scientists, [or] poets. In other words, forming a clear idea of each of those things would have proven useless; instead, it is later transformed into something vague and ethereal, in order to be able to apply it to phenomena very different from one another.

Such a transformation would amount to this: that we would drain every concrete content from all those forms of human occupation, that we would regard them as being clear of every specific content. For example, we would consider religion not only every belief in a god, no matter which, but we would also call Buddhism a religion, despite the fact that Buddhism contains no belief in any god. Likewise, we would say that every opinion about what exists is to be called knowledge, no matter what the opinions entertained by human beings about what exists, or the modality of their opining itself, may be. Furthermore, we would call poetry any human work in words which pleases [us], whatever the appearance of that verbal product we take pleasure in may be. Moreover, with exemplary magnanimity, we would ascribe the untamable and contradictory variety of poetical contents to a boundless variation in styles, pure and simple.

In my judgment, accordingly, this so firm a practice is to be subjected at least to some revision, and probably to a profound reform. This is what I am attempting to do elsewhere.[37]

December, 1934

# Notes

## Translator's Introduction

1. For its preparation on the basis of Ortega's posthumous writings, see "Spanish Editor's Note," infra, p. 30.

2. Ibid.

3. Ibid.

4. Ibid., p. 29.

5. For the term *Erkenntnistheorie* or theory of knowledge, see Karl L. Reinhold, *Versuch einer neuen Theorie des menschlischen Vorstellungsmögen* (Prague and Jena: Mauke, 1789) and Nicola Abbagnano, *Dizionario di filosofia* (Turin: Unione Tipografica Editrice Torinese, 1961), "Conoscenza." (Translation: *Diccionario de filosofía*, 2nd ed., trans. A. N. Galletti [Mexico City: Fondo de Cultura Económica, 1991], p. 227. All references are given according to the Spanish edition.)

6. D. M. Hamlyn, "Epistemology, History of" in *The Encyclopedia of Philosophy*, ed. P. Edwards (New York: Macmillan and The Free Press, 1967), III, pp. 8–9.

7. Ibid., pp. 9ff.

8. Cf. infra, pp. 55ff.

9. Cf. infra, p. 7 and Aloys Müller, *Einleitung in die Philosophie* (1925), chapter 2, §1. (Translation: *Introducción a la filosofía*, trans. J. Gaos [Madrid: Revista de Occidente, 1934], p. 80. All references are given according to the Spanish edition.)

10. Cf. D. M. Hamlyn, loc. cit., p. 9.

11. A. Müller, op. cit., p. 80.

12. Ibid. Cf. M. Blondel, Note to "Connaissance" in *Vocabulaire technique et critique de la philosophie*, by André Lalande, 8th ed. rev. and enl., ed. Société Française de Philosophie (Paris: Presses Universitaires de France, 1960), p. 171, and N. Abbagnano, op. cit., p. 237.

13. N. Abbagnano, op. cit., p. 217.

14. Cf. infra, n. 104.

15. Cf. infra, Part IV, pp. 155, 158, and 159ff. *Vide* N. Abbagnano, op. cit., pp. 224–225: "The [romantic] historical perspective . . . [takes as opposite] the 'classical' (or ancient and medieval) conception, according to which the operation of knowing would be ruled by the object, and the modern or romantic understanding, according to which knowledge would be the activity of the subject and a manifestation of its creative power. . . ." See José Ferrater Mora, "Conocimiento" in *Diccionario de filosofía*, 5th ed. (Buenos Aires: Editorial Sudamericana, 1965), I, p. 341, right-hand column.

16. Cf. N. Abbagnano, op. cit., p. 218, and St. Thomas Aquinas, *Summa contra gentiles,* II, 77 (Rome: Forzani, 1894), p. 235.

17. St. Thomas Aquinas, *Summa theologiae,* Latin/English ed., Blackfriars (New York: McGraw-Hill), III (1964), i, q. 2, a. 4, "Responsio," p. 14. Cf. infra, Part IV, p. 162.

18. Cf. N. Abbagnano, op. cit., p. 218.

19. Ibid. Cf. Aristotle, *On the Soul,* trans. J. A. Smith, II.5, 417 a 19–20, in *The Complete Works of Aristotle,* ed. J. Barnes, rev. Oxford ed. (Princeton: Princeton University Press/Bollingen Series LXXI-2, 1984), I, p. 664.

20. Cf. N. Abbagnano, op. cit., p. 221.

21. Ibid. Cf. René Descartes, *Rules for the Direction of the Mind,* v, in *The Philosophical Works of Descartes,* trans. E. S. Haldane and G. R. T. Ross (New York: Dover, 1955), I, p. 14.

22. N. Abbagnano, op. cit., p. 222. Cf. Immanuel Kant, *Kritik der reinen Vernunft* (Hamburg: Felix Meiner, 1956), B 263.

23. Cf. N. Abbagnano, op. cit.

24. This does not mean, of course, that one would initiate cognitive activity indifferently or at pleasure. After all, thinking is a reactive effort into which we are obliged by our pre-intellectual existence (see infra, Part III, p. 108), but it is nonetheless an effort we freely decide to make, even if it is for the purpose of meeting a survival need of ours and of resolving a conjoint worldly difficulty.

25. N. Abbagnano, op. cit., p. 225. Concerning Husserl in this respect, cf. ibid., p. 224, and Edmund Husserl, *Ideas Pertaining to a Pure Phenomenology and to a Phenomenological Philosophy,* I, trans. F. Kersten (The Hague: Martinus Nijhoff, 1982), §79, p. 187 [157]. Henceforth, I shall refer to this work as *Ideas,* I.

26. Johannes Hessen, *Lehrbuch der Philosophie, I. Wissenschaftslehre* (Munich: Ernst Reinhardt Verlag, 1950), Book II, Introduction, §1, p. 175.

27. Cf. supra, p. 2 and n. 11. Abbagnano essentially agrees with this interpretive point, although he adds the important specification that transcendence aims at, or finds its terminus in, being-in-itself. (Cf. op. cit., p. 224.)

28. Nicolai Hartmann, *Grundzüge einer Metaphysik der Erkenntnis,* 2nd ed. enl. (Berlin and Leipzig: Walter de Gruyter & Co., 1925), Part I, ii, chap. 5, pp. 43 ff. For an apt summary of Hartmann's analysis, cf. J. Hessen, *Erkenntnistheorie* (1926), Part I, "Preliminary Phenomenological Investigation." (Translation: *Teoría del conocimiento,* trans. J. Gaos [Madrid: Revista de Occidente, 1932], pp. 30 ff. All references are given from the Spanish edition.)

29. N. Hartmann, op. cit., No. 1, p. 43. Emphasis added.

30. Cf. ibid., No. 2.

31. Cf. ibid., No. 3.

32. Ibid., No. 4.

33. Cf. ibid., No. 5.

34. Cf. ibid., No. 6.

35. Ibid., p. 44.

36. Cf. ibid., No. 7.

37. Ibid.

38. J. Hessen, *Erkenntnistheorie,* p. 31.

39. Cf. infra, Part IV, pp. 170–171.

40. Cf. N. Hartmann, op. cit., No. 7, p. 44. Cf. Blondel's conception of the third factor at play in cognition, namely, "le résultat détaché par abstraction (l'objet connu)." See supra, n. 12.

41. Cf. ibid., No. 6, p. 43.

42. Cf. J. Hessen, *Erkenntnistheorie,* p. 33. This has to do with what Ortega called the "paradox of knowledge," which he illustrated by means of this example: ". . . [the] chair's 'being independent of me' is just a way of dependence [on me], on my [theoretical] action on it. . . ." (See infra, Part III, p. 126; cf. Part IV, p. 158). *Vide* J. Ferrater Mora, op. cit., I, p. 341: ". . . if this were not so, there would be [in cognition] no 'apprehension' of something external: the subject would somehow be 'apprehending' itself. . . . [The object] is not in . . . [the subject] either physically or metaphysically: it is therein only 'representationally.'"

43. See infra, Part III, p. 139.

44. Ibid. This allowed Hartmann to employ the unexamined notion of "apprehension" to deal with the subjective side of the cognitive relationship of transcendence, but that concept is, according to Ortega, both impossible and superfluous, because, respectively, "things out there" are extended, while the mind is not, and I already have, or encounter, the "things out there." (Cf. infra, Part III, p. 140). What is "apprehended" in cognition is not a thing but its essence, and "apprehension" begins as an act of hypothetical thinking, that is, as an act of postulation and invention. (Ibid.) Hence, the cognitive act does not resemble at all an "apprehending."

45. Ibid., p. 44.

46. Ibid.

47. I will not dwell any further on the third question, since, for our purposes, it is my opinion that it has been sufficiently taken into consideration.

48. J. Ortega y Gasset, "Apuntes sobre el pensamiento: su teurgia y su demiurgia," *Obras Completas,* V, p. 529. Henceforth I will be referring to this collection as *OC* and to this particular essay as "Apuntes sobre el pensamiento." (Translation: "Notes on Thinking—Its Creation of the World and Its Creation of God," in *Concord and Liberty,* trans. H. Weyl [New York: W. W. Norton & Co., 1946], p. 63.)

49. Cf. Martin Heidegger, *Sein und Zeit,* in GESAMTAUSGABE, I.2 (Frankfurt am Main: V. Klostermann, 1977), §13, pp. 81 (60) and 82 (61). (Translation: *Being and Time,* trans. J. Macquarrie et al. [New York: Harper & Row, 1962], pp. 87 and 88.) As Abbagnano points out, ". . . [t]he 'problem of knowledge' and the 'problem of reality', . . . [as] formulated in nineteenth-century philosophy, are, therefore, eliminated by Heidegger" (op. cit., p. 225). The same can be said in Ortega's case.

50. J. Ortega y Gasset, "Apuntes sobre el pensamiento," p. 523 (trans., p. 57).

51. Cf. infra, "Appendix," pp. 187–188, 191–192, and 201.

52. J. Ortega y Gasset, "Apuntes sobre el pensamiento," p. 525 (trans., p. 59).

53. Ibid.

54. Ibid. (trans., p. 60).

55. Ibid.

56. Cf. ibid., p. 529 (trans., p. 64). It is also certain that human beings actually engage in knowing and that they need to do so. (Cf. infra, Part II, p. 86.)

57. J. Ortega y Gasset, "Apuntes sobre el pensamiento," p. 526 (trans., p. 60). "Not only modern . . . [psychologism] but even Aristotle . . . identifies thinking with the simple execution of intellectual activities." (Ibid.) Cf. E. Husserl, "Prolegomena to Pure Logic," chaps. 3–5 and 7–8, in *Logical Investigations,* trans. J. N. Findlay (New York: Humanities Press, 1970), I, pp. 90–128 and 135–196, and infra, Part II, p. 85.

58. Aristotle, *Metaphysics,* I.1, 980 a 22–23, in *The Complete Works of Aristotle,* rev. Oxford ed., II, p. 1552.

59. See infra, Part II, p. 85. As Aristotle immediately added, the grounds for this interpretation lie in the delight we take in our senses (cf. op. cit.). Moreover, his implicit appeal to curiosity as a motive will not do to justify his view of knowledge. Cf. infra, Part II, pp. 78 and 86).

60. See infra, Part II, p. 85.

61. See ibid., p. 86. Cf. Part III, p. 140.

62. Cf. infra, Part II, p. 86. In fact, such a view would amount to an unwarranted assumption of success. *Vide* J. Ortega y Gasset, "Apuntes sobre el pensamiento," p. 532 (trans., p. 67) and infra, Part III, p. 150: ". . . the intellect sets itself to work . . . not because one is in possession of it . . . [but] to be saved from being at a loss in chaos."

63. Cf. E. Husserl, "Prolegomena to Pure Logic," chap. 12 in op. cit., I, pp. 74ff.

64. J. Ortega y Gasset, "Apuntes sobre el pensamiento," p. 527 (trans., pp. 61–62).

65. Ibid. (trans., p. 60).

66. Cf. infra, "Appendix," chap. 2, iii and iv, pp. 196ff.

67. J. Ortega y Gasset, "Apuntes sobre el pensamiento," p. 528 (trans., p. 63).

68. Ibid.

69. Cf. ibid. (trans., p. 62): "When a serious attempt was made to construe logic logically—in logistics, symbolic logic, mathematical logic—it appeared that this was impossible . . . ," every single requirement stipulated for it having been shown to be eventually but necessarily violated by it. "[I]n consequence, . . . there are illogical truths. . . . Logic that reveals itself to be pervaded by illogical elements loses its *emphatic aloofness from other forms of thinking* . . ." (ibid.) and therefore its privileged status as legitimate claimant to the title of royal road to the truth. Cf. J. Ortega y Gasset, *La idea de principio en Leibniz y la evolución de la teoría deductiva,* in OC VIII, p. 335. (Translation: *The Idea of Principle in*

*Leibnitz and the Evolution of Deductive Theory,* translated by M. Adams [New York: W. W. Norton & Co., 1971], p. 355.) Henceforth I shall refer to this work as *La idea de principio.*

70. J. Ortega y Gasset, "Apuntes sobre el pensamiento," p. 529 (trans., p. 64).

71. Ibid.

72. Ibid., pp. 530–531 (trans., p. 65).

73. Ibid., p. 532 (trans., p. 67). For the notion of belief as the functional counterpart of idea (and the notions of reality and ideality, respectively, cf. infra, "Appendix," pp. 179 and 181–182 and Part III, p. 150: ". . . [the] outline of the universe [resulting from the *consolidation* of the ideas we form in our effort to know] is the system of our convictions in force, . . . of *beliefs* concerning what things are" (emphasis added). In their "objective" sense, ideas and beliefs are constituents of the *world,* i.e., of the interpreted part of the circumstance Ortega called "theoretical culture" (see infra, Part I, "The 1929–1930 Course," p. 64).

74. Cf. J. Ortega y Gasset, "Apuntes sobre el pensamiento," p. 526 (trans., p. 60).

75. Ibid.

76. Cf. ibid., n. 2 (trans., p. 61, n. 8): "[Perceiving, imagining, comparing] . . . , even reasoning are constantly and *automatically* at work in our mind. They are therefore not our doing, not *action.* The difference between an *action* and a mechanism lies in the intervention of the will and therewith of an intention, [purpose, or] . . . end in view."

77. Ibid., n. 1 (trans., p. 60, n. 7). In this formula, I have substituted "*because of* " for "*by* something," which also appears in the body of the translated text, in light of Ortega's earlier and more fully worked out version of this factor. (Cf. infra, Part I, "The 1929–1930 Course," pp. 60 and 227 [n. 40] and Part III [1930], pp. 124–125 and 235 [n. 39].) A significant thing is to be noted in passing, to wit: that, in distinguishing between the motives of *para algo* or *en vista de que* ("for the sake of something") and *por algo* or *porque* ("because of") within the structure of action, he was anticipating (in 1930) Alfred Schutz's similar distinction (1932) between the *Um-zu-Motiv* (in-order-to motive) and the *Weil-Motiv* (because motive) in his *Der sinnhafte Aufbau der sozialen Welt,* 2nd ed. (Vienna: Springer Verlag, 1960; 1st ed., 1932). (Translation: *The Phenomenology of the Social World,* trans. G. Walsh et al. [Evanston: Northwestern University Press, 1967].) For the similarity between Ortega's notion of action and Schutz's, cf. ibid., §9, p. 59 (trans., p. 61) and "On Multiple Realities," in *Collected Papers,* vol. 1, ed. M. Natanson (The Hague: Martinus Nijhoff, 1962), pp. 214–215.

78. J. Ortega y Gasset, "Anejo [a] Apuntes sobre el pensamiento," p. 541 (trans., "Appendix," p. 76). Emphasis added.

79. Ibid.

80. J. Ortega y Gasset, "Apuntes sobre el pensamiento," p. 530 (trans., p. 64).

81. For the notion of belief and its implications, cf. supra, n. 73.

82. Cf. J. Ortega y Gasset, *¿Qué es filosofía?* in OC VII, chaps. 7–8, pp. 360ff., and Antonio Rodríguez Huéscar, *José Ortega y Gasset's Metaphysical Innovation. A*

*Critique and Overcoming of Idealism,* trans. J. García-Gómez (Albany, NY: State University of New York Press, 1995), Part I, chap. 2.

83. E. Husserl, *Ideas Ideas,* I, §§30–31, and A. Rodríguez Huéscar, op. cit., Part I, chap. 3.

84. Cf. supra, n. 51 and infra, Part IV, p. 201.

85. J. Ortega y Gasset, "Apuntes sobre el pensamiento," p. 530 (trans., p. 64).

86. Cf. ibid., pp. 536–537 (trans., pp. 71–72).

87. Cf. supra, n. 66.

88. J. Ortega y Gasset, "Apuntes sobre el pensamiento," p. 530 (trans., p. 65).

89. Ibid. Emphasis added.

90. Ibid., p. 532 (trans., p. 67). For a brief because-motivational account of theoretical thinking, as a special case of cognition, cf. infra, Part I, "The 1929–1930 Course," p. 60; *vide* pp. 63–64.

91. Cf. supra, pp. 6–7.

92. Cf. infra, "Appendix," p. 202.

93. J. Ortega y Gasset, "Apuntes sobre el pensamiento,," p. 533 (trans., p. 68).

94. Ibid. (Emphasis added). Another way of conveying Ortega's thesis is to say, with him, that cognition is not a natural activity performed by human beings, as intellection or sensation for example are, but a "life form" historically constituted, i.e., "invented and developed in the course of history by way of an answer to certain experiences and liable to be dropped in view of others. . . " (ibid., p. 537; trans., p. 72). Cf. ibid., p. 538 (trans., p. 74), and infra, "Appendix," pp. 202f.

95. J. Ortega y Gasset, "Apuntes sobre el pensamiento," p. 539 (trans., p. 74).

96. Ibid., p. 538 (trans., p.74).

97. Ibid., p. 539 (trans., p. 75).

98. Cf. E. Husserl, *Logical Investigations,* i, chap. 3, §26, I, pp. 313ff.

99. J. Ortega y Gasset, "Apuntes sobre el pensamiento," p. 539 (trans., p. 74). Not only are the abstract notions of human being, environment or circumstance, and adjustment to the circumstance to be taken, at every juncture, according to their prevailing concrete historical value, if we are, at every turn, to understand an individual or collective life adequately for what it actually is, but so must the intellect be, which is "no fixed entity . . . [for] it varies incessantly in the course of history with the varying use it is put to and the varying education . . . it is subjected to" (ibid.) The actual values assigned to each abstract term are to be "determined . . . *[chronologically]*" (ibid.). Living, historical reason amounts, in principle, to such an exercise when it is conducted systematically.

100. Cf. supra, pp. 5 and 207, n. 48.

101. Cf. supra, pp. 9ff.

102. J. Ortega y Gasset, "Apuntes sobre el pensamiento," p. 531 (trans., p. 65).

103. Ibid. Emphasis added.

104. Ibid. Emphasis added.

105. Ibid.

106. Consequently, being is *not* given, but *latent* (ibid.; trans., p. 66), albeit in the sense of a conceptual, not a perceptual, task, as can be gathered from the following: if being exhibits the character of fixity and stability, then it would also present itself as self-identical (ibid., p. 531; trans., p. 66); accordingly, for Ortega the notion of being and the traditional concept of *essence* are synonymous (cf. ibid., p. 525; trans., p. 59). It is then not surprising to hear that ". . . [a]s . . . [the] . . . character [of identity] is proper to concepts also, *being* and thinking [qua cognition] turn out to . . . [be comprised of the same attributes], and the laws that hold for concepts hold for being" (ibid., p. 532; trans., p. 66; cf. "Ni vitalismo ni racionalismo," in *OC* III, p. 279). Only in the times of classical Greece, however, was there unqualified human trust in *being* and, therefore, an "unshaken belief that reality consists in being, wholly and exclusively . . . ," and only then did human beings pursue it, in cognition, "without reserve" ("Apuntes sobre el pensamiento," p. 533; trans., p. 68). By contrast, ". . . [w]e have been left with . . . [such a] conviction minus the faith on which it is based" (ibid., p. 535; trans., p. 70); that is to say, we have been left with the idea of being, not with a belief therein.

107. Ibid., p. 531 (trans., pp. 65–66). The emphasis on "natural" is my responsibility.

108. Ibid. (trans., p. 66). Ortega illustrated his meaning by means of the example of light, which, as long as it works well, is *indubitably* what it immediately shows itself to be, i.e., the living function of illuminating me. This he opposed to the being of light, which is not part and parcel of its function, but rather the nonevident (or conceptual) ground thereof (ibid., pp. 531–532; trans., p.66).

109. Cf. J. Ortega y Gasset, *¿Qué es filosofía?*, chap. 5, and infra, Part I, "The 1929–1930 Course," p. 45.

110. J. Ortega y Gasset, "Apuntes sobre el pensamiento," p. 536 (trans., p. 71). Cf. infra, Part II, pp. 79–80. Ortega availed himself of this classical characterization of philosophy to contrast it with prayer, as the form of thinking or conduct of the believer in God ("Apuntes sobre el pensamiento," pp. 535–537; trans., pp. 70–72), and to oppose *alétheia* to "the *amen* of faith . . ." (ibid., p. 536; trans., p. 71). This allowed him to establish a *gamut* of forms of thinking (and another consisting of the products thereof), to wit: mythology, magic, wisdom or life experience, religion, science, and philosophy, all of which, despite their differences as ways of thinking and in terms of the results obtainable thereby, have nonetheless something in common, namely, being inventions originally proposed by human beings—at various historical junctures—so as to meet the radical doubt or perplexity affecting them at that point, and thus to secure for themselves a new life settlement in the wake of the loss of their former grounds of credibility (cf. ibid., p. 537; trans., p. 72). The word "gamut," however, may lend itself mistakenly to the suggestion that there is a continuity of life forms, but that is what is negated precisely by Ortega's use of the term "invention" and his connecting it with the settings of various historical crises. Accordingly, every such form of thinking is distinctive and discrete, and it enjoys its "lifespan" between its points of insertion (invention) and disappearance (dissolution). This is even true of philosophy, although philosophy, given its radicalism, may eventually come to the full awareness of its finiteness and contingency. This "privilege"

Ortega claims for his own philosophy, inasmuch as it ". . . [pre-forms] further forms of human reaction destined to supersede it" (ibid., pp. 537–538; trans., p. 73). Cf. J. Ortega y Gasset, *Origen y epílogo de la filosofía*, in OC IX, pp. 347ff. (Translation: *The Origin of Philosophy*, trans. T. Talbot [New York: W. W. Norton & Co., 1967].)

111. Cf. J. Ortega y Gasset, "[Prólogo] A 'Historia de la Filosofía' de Émile Bréhier" in OC VI, pp. 377ff. (Translation: "Prologue to a History of Philosophy" in *Concord and Liberty*, pp. 83ff.).

112. J. Ortega y Gasset, "Apuntes sobre el pensamiento," p. 540 (trans., p. 76). Emphasis added. Even the sciences are naïve in this sense, but not because of choice or as a failure to be themselves; rather, it is so by virtue of a constitutive necessity. (ibid., p. 541; trans., p. 76).

113. Cf. supra, p. 8.

114. "Apuntes sobre el pensamiento," p. 542 (trans., p. 78).

115. For an application of this principle to the interpretation of Locke's and Husserl's philosophies, see the following: for Locke, "Anejo [a] 'Apuntes sobre el pensamiento,'" pp. 542–544 (trans., "Appendix" to "Notes on Thinking," pp. 78–80); for Husserl, "Apuntes sobre el pensamiento," p. 521 (trans., p. 55), and "Anejo . . . ," pp. 544–546 (trans., pp. 80–82) and p. 547, n. 1 (trans., p. 82, n. 19); John Locke, *An Essay Concerning Human Understanding*, ed. J. W. Yolton (London: Dent/Everyman's Library, 1964), Book I, chap. 1, §6 (Vol. I, p. 8); Edmund Husserl, *Ideas* I, Part IV, chap. 2; E. Husserl, *Formal and Transcendental Logic*, trans. D. Cairns (The Hague: Martinus Nijhoff, 1969), p. 5; and Husserl, *The Crisis of the European Sciences and Transcendental Phenomenology*, trans. D. Carr (Evanston: Northwestern University Press, 1970), Part I, pp. 3ff. and Appendix VI, pp. 353ff. *Vide* Antonio Rodríguez Huéscar, *José Ortega y Gasset's Metaphysical Innovation*, Part I, chap. 3.

116. Cf. supra, pp. 5ff.

117. Cf. J. Ortega y Gasset, *Investigaciones psicológicas* in OC XII, chaps. 10–14. (Translation: *Psychological Investigations*, trans. J. García-Gómez [New York: W. W. Norton & Co., 1987].)

118. Cf. J. Ortega y Gasset, *El tema de nuestro tiempo* in OC III, chaps. 3–6 (translation: *The Modern Theme*, trans. J. Cleugh [New York: Harper & Row, 1961]); "Historia como sistema" in OC VI, pp. 11ff. (translation: "History as a System" in *History as a System*, trans. H. Weyl [New York: W. W. Norton & Co., 1941], pp. 163–233); "Ideas y creencias" in OC V, pp. 377ff. (translation: "Ideas and Beliefs," see infra, pp. 175ff.); and *Sobre la razón histórica* in OC XII, pp. 143ff. (translation: *Historical Reason*, trans. Ph. W. Silver [New York: W. W. Norton & Co., 1984]).

119. For a critique of Descartes's search for indubitable knowledge and Ortega's own conception of such a pursuit, cf. J. Ortega y Gasset, *¿Qué es filosofía?*, chaps. 7–8, and A. Rodríguez Huéscar, *José Ortega y Gasset's Metaphysical Innovation*, Part I, chap. 2.

120. See infra, Part I, "The 1929–1930 Course," p. 42.

121. As opposed to scientific truths, cf. ibid., pp. 44f.

122. Cf. ibid., p. 65 and supra, p. 11.

123. Cf. infra, Part I, "The 1929–1930 Course," p. 65.

124. Ibid.

125. Cf. J. Ortega y Gasset, *Meditaciones del Quijote* in OC I, p. 322. (Translation: *Meditations on Quixote,* trans. E. Rugg et al. [New York: W. W. Norton & Co., 1961], p. 45: "I am myself . . . [and] my circumstance, and if I do not save it, I cannot save myself.") See infra, III, pp. 116, 126, and 127–128; also p. 118: "Life consists . . . of three things: myself, my being at, and the [living] universe." (Cf. Martin Heidegger, *Sein und Zeit,* §§9 and 12.) Moreover, life is never identifiable with its instruments (be they bodily, mental, or part of the circumstance) or with the activities thereof. (Cf. infra, Part II, pp. 97f. and 99.)

126. Cf. infra, Part I, "The 1929–1930 Course," p. 68.

127. Cf. infra, Part III, p. 106.

128. Cf. supra, n. 125.

129. See infra, Part III, p. 118.

130. In Ortega's early formula for life, "I am myself and my circumstance" (cf. supra, n. 125), the first "I" is tantamount to life's non-objectivating, continuous awareness of itself taken as a totality. In this sense, life is always open, at particular points or nodes in which the need arises, to self-objectivation, which is the activity of the second "I" (myself) of the said formula. The need in question amounts to one's encounter with the problematic, in the sense of that which exceeds the body of beliefs in force, either as a whole or in part, that life, at its core, consists of. (Cf. infra, Part IV, pp. 175ff.)

131. See infra, Part III, p. 119. Emphasis added.

132. Ibid., p. 123. Cf. pp. 125–126.

133. Cf. supra, p. 12.

134. See infra, Part IV, p. 166.

135. Cf. ibid. Moreover, according to Ortega, the fundamental misunderstandings found in the history of philosophy, in this connection, are of two sorts, namely, that the question about the being of things has been taken to mean a concern with an abstract, indeterminate entity (cf. ibid.) or with things taken as a whole (ibid.).

136. Cf. infra, Part I, "The 1929–1930 Course," p. 65 and passim.

137. See infra, Part I, p. 65.

138. Cf. ibid., pp. 64ff. The possibility of philosophy rests with the possibility of gaining access to what things are non-mediately. This is assured, on the one hand, if philosophy itself is a modality of life as self-positing (cf. ibid., pp. 65f.) and, if on the other hand, things are spontaneously available to me as "what refers to and exists for me" at every turn. This normal condition does not require objectivation (although it is in principle open to it), and therefore its being propounded as a first metaphysical thesis has nothing to do with idealism, but implicates that the metaphysical theses of the latter have been overcome, for, as Ortega put it, "I have specified that . . .

[the] way of referring to and existing for me [which is proper to things at the level of immediacy] is tantamount to their *acting* on me . . ." (cf. infra, Part III, p. 124; cf. p. 126), just as I spontaneously consist in my acting on them on the basis of my past decisions and the needs they imply (i.e., my because-motivational grounds) and in view of my vocation qua project or program (i.e., my ultimate or global for-the-sake-of motivational grounds). Cf. A. Rodríguez Huéscar, *José Ortega y Gasset's Metaphysical Innovation,* Part I, chaps. 2–3.

139. Its truths would have to be characterized as autonomous (i.e., as completely presuppositionless) and pantonomous (i.e., as altogether encompassing and universal). Cf. supra, n. 109.

140. Cf. supra, pp. 2 and 205, n. 11.

141. For a more complete account of the life categories, *vide* A. Rodríguez Huéscar, *José Ortega y Gasset's Metaphysical Innovation,* Part II, and my paper, "José Ortega y Gasset's Categorial Analysis of Life," *Analecta Husserliana* LVII (1998), pp. 135 ff.

142. Ortega, simplifying matters, contended that life is absolute in two senses of the term, to wit: as the all-encompassing reality and as the reality that is independent of everything else (cf. infra, Part I, "Problems," §7, pp. 36f. and Part III, pp. 112f [cf. pp. 117–118]). And this of course applies to every ingredient and activity therein, when it is taken performatively. Hence, as to universality, ". . . [w]hat is lived by us serves to delimit the sphere containing every reality." (See ibid., p. 112).

143. Cf. infra, Part I, "Problems," §§4–6, pp. 33–34.

144. See ibid., "The 1929–1930 Course," p. 73. Cf. A. Rodríguez Huéscar, *José Ortega y Gasset's Metaphysical Innovation,* Part I, p. 83.

145. Cf. infra, Part I, "Problems," §9, p. 38.

146. Cf. infra, Part I, "Problems," pp. 36–37 and "The 1929–1930 Course," p. 66. Or expressed even more bluntly: life's being is performative; it is doing, action. (Ibid., "Problems," §7, p. 34).

147. Ibid., "The 1929–1930 Course," p. 68.

148. Cf. ibid.

149. Cf. ibid., p. 59. Cf. supra, n. 130, and infra, Part III, p. 111: "I am inexorably confined within my life. . . ." In other words, my life includes myself and the "universe" in actional reciprocity. The circumstance, however, does not amount to a stock of actual or present things favoring or opposing my life designs. I "sense" that it encompasses "also . . . [the stock of] things past, as well as . . . [that] of things future." (Ibid.). Cf. ibid., pp. 129, 147, and also p. 131, and A. Rodríguez Huéscar, *José Ortega y Gasset's Metaphysical Innovation,* Part II, chap. 4, §8, pp. 132 ff. and §9, for the notion of vocation (i.e., one's life global project or program) which exerts its pressure on me to be myself and therefore on the circumstance, as the stock of "things" that would assist or hinder me in carrying out my vocation.

150. See infra, Part I, "The 1929–1930 Course," p. 61.

151. Cf. ibid., p. 70, and cf. supra, n. 125. The subject or "I" that explicitly confronts

the circum-stance (i.e., the second "I" of Ortega's formula for life's actional structure of reciprocity) is my objective presence to myself, which, as opposed to the global subject of life, or first "I" of the said formula, is not global but partitive. (Cf. infra, Part I, "The 1929–1930 Course," p. 71–72.)

152. See ibid., p. 68. "Counting on" is a manner of acting, of doing (ibid.); indeed, it is the basic style or form thereof.

153. Cf. ibid. and A. Rodríguez Huéscar, *José Ortega y Gasset's Metaphysical Innovation,* pp. 87–119.

154. See infra, Part III, p. 114. The failure to reject the pair "substance/accident" as inapplicable to life would lead to the absurd proposition that life and "things" are both substances and accidents. (Cf. ibid.)

155. Cf. ibid., p. 124.

156. See ibid., p. 111.

157. Cf. ibid.: ". . . any reality or thing that is not my life is either a part or (ingredient of it [a 'thing' or a 'subjective modality']) or something which would have to be made known to me in some modality of life [e.g., God]."

158. Ibid., p. 132. Even though I cannot go into the matter here, at least I must say— if I want to do it minimal justice—that life's essential future-tending character (and its ongoing retroactive effect on my sense of the present and of the past, including its selection and re-interpretation; cf. supra, n. 149) is the ground for the dimension of self-realization. Self-realization is not simply the carrying into effect of directionalities pre-inscribed in my life, as if life were conceivable according to the Aristotelian idea of substance as *tò tí en einai.* (Cf. e.g., Aristotle, *Metaphysics* I, 983 a27, in *The Metaphysics,* trans. H. Tredennick, Greek/English ed. [Cambridge, Mass.: Harvard University Press/The Loeb Classical Library, 1961], I, pp. 16 [Greek] and 17 [English]: "the essential nature of the thing. . . .") Rather, it is an evergoing determination of my present resulting from the pressure exerted on it by my future, i.e., by my vocation or what I *have* to be, whether I succeed in carrying it out or not (even in part). Cf. infra, Part III, p. 136.

159. Cf. ibid., pp. 146f.

160. Cf. ibid.

161. Cf. infra, pp. 17–18.

162. See infra, Part III, p. 150.

163. See ibid.

164. See ibid., p. 147.

165. See ibid.

166. See ibid., p. 151.

167. See ibid.

168. See ibid. Or perhaps even more pointedly: "the problem of knowledge does not originally arise with the relationship between its two termini, namely, the act of 'apprehending' and 'being,' but already with each of them" (ibid., p. 139).

169. Cf. supra, p. 14.

170. Primarily to oneself, secondarily or derivatively to another. The former is thinking proper, the latter is conversing. Cf. infra, Part II, p. 92.

171. Cf. ibid., p. 87–88.

172. Cf. ibid.

173. See ibid., p. 88. Emphasis added.

174. See ibid. Cf. infra, Part III, p. 142.

175. See infra, Part II, p. 89.

176. Cf. ibid., Part III, pp. 107 and 139.

177. J. Ortega y Gasset, "Comentario al 'Banquete' de Platón," i, in OC IX, p. 764.

178. *Apud* J. Ortega y Gasset, ibid., p. 756.

179. Cf. ibid., p. 764.

180. Cf. Karl Bühler, *Sprachtheorie* (Jena: Gustav Fisher, 1934), i, §4.1 and ii, §10, and Eugenio Coseriu, "Determinación y entorno. Dos problemas de una lingüística del hablar" in *Teoría del lenguaje y lingüística general* (Madrid: Gredos, 1967), pp. 282ff.

181. Cf. infra, pp. 20ff.

182. Anything that would exert such pressure on me, as part and parcel of my given living situation, belongs, paradoxically, to the order of external ends, inasmuch as what would play such a role is that which Ortega called *being,* of which we know nothing to begin with, except, "subjectively," that we are in need of it as a possible measure to overcome the chaotic nature of the situation in which we may find ourselves, and, "objectively," that it is what is being *sought after* by us in what Ortega called the "world beyond."

183. See infra, Part III, p. 106. Ortega said "begin . . . to pose" because, I think, he was keeping in mind the distinction between this kind of question (i.e., the scientific question) and the sort of question one would end up with (i.e., the metaphysical question proper, namely, "what is the being of things in general?"), if one pursues cognitive action relentlessly to its ultimate consequences.

184. For Ortega's examination of curiosity, cf. infra, Part II, pp. 78ff. and 86–87.

185. Cf. Plato, *Symposium,* 200.

186. See infra, Part III, p. 107.

187. Cf. ibid., p. 142.

188. Cf. infra, Part II, p. 94. *Vide* p. 96 for Ortega's employment of the case of light to illustrate this thesis. He often availed himself of this example to make this and related points.

189. See infra, Part III, p. 143.

190. "Formal" is used here in the sense of "formally categorial" or "materially empty and functionally historical." Cf. supra, p. 10.

191. See infra, Part III, p. 143. (Cf. p. 144.) Ortega obviated a possible, indeed a disastrous, misunderstanding of this thesis when he argued that life's neediness can-

not be understood in terms of a notion of the self as a bundle of needs and reactions, merely existing in reciprocity with the various pressures exerted on it by the circumstance. And it cannot be so understood because, at every turn, we are not pure passivity and receptivity, since we "come" to our present by virtue of a prior decision to do something, a decision that is not usually the result of reflection and deliberation. Such decisions—intelligent or not, beneficial or not—are the spontaneous "means" by which we ongoingly *unify* our lives. Those decisions include not only those pertaining to what we are going to do next (that is to say, what we are going to be next), but the decision to continue to live as well. Cf. ibid., p. 124.

192. See infra, Part II, p. 84.

193. Ibid., p. 82.

194. Cf. ibid.

195. Cf. infra, Part III, p. 111.

196. Cf. infra, Part IV, p. 168.

197. Ibid., pp. 162–163.

198. Ibid., p. 163. (Emphasis added.) For Ortega's critique of Plato's Theory of Ideas or Forms as a solution to this problem, cf. ibid., pp. 168 ff.

199. Ibid., p. 170.

200. See ibid., p. 168.

201. Cf. J. Ortega y Gasset, *El hombre y la gente* in OC VII, pp. 128–129. (Translation: *Man and People,* trans. W. R. Trask [New York: W. W. Norton & Co., 1957], pp. 77–79).

202. See infra, "Appendix," p. 188.

203. Ibid. Accordingly, the "world" and "things" (as the components thereof) are not originarily encountered by us. A world is an order we construct, however well or poorly, in order to live in the actual circumstance; it is the fruit of our imaginative or interpretive work, while the circumstance is not, comprised as it is of *prágmata* or *importances* exclusively. It is not out of curiosity, not even out of a contemplative disinterest, but for the purposes of survival *(pervivencia)* and meaningfulness that our lives consist in transforming the circumstance into a world. Cf. infra, "Appendix," passim.

204. Cf. ibid., pp. 194–195: "A human being reacts to the primordial and preintellectual enigma [which genuine or naked reality is] by setting his or her intellectual apparatus to work, an apparatus that is, above all, imagination."

205. See ibid., p. 194. Take Ortega's own example: the "Earth, taken by itself . . . is not any 'thing' at all, but [just] an uncertain stock of facilities and difficulties in our lives" (ibid.). At that level, it is, for instance, the support offered to our feet (its "subjective" counterpart being the certainty and the ease of motion it provides for us); it is uphill or downhill (its "subjective" counterpart being, respectively, the vexation or the delight it produces in us); it is that which separates us from our loved ones or our enemies (its "subjective" counterpart being, respectively, the emotional upheaval and suffering or the relief it causes in us), etc.

Moreover, whatever it is, it is not even a "thing," which is "already a shape of being" (say, the bearer of qualities), "a way of behaving belonging . . . to [it], which has been constructed by our minds in order to explain the primordial reality to ourselves" (ibid.).

206. See infra, Part II, p. 78. (Cf. p. 87). In fact, originally, "'[k]nowledge' is [just] the name usually given to our effort to arrive at being, of which the . . . question ['what is the being of this or that?'] marks the beginning" (ibid., p. 85).

207. Cf. infra., Part III, p. 111.

208. Cf. ibid., p. 115.

209. Cf. infra, Part II, p. 84.

210. Cf. infra, Part III, p. 115.

211. Cf. ibid.

212. Cf. supra, n. 206.

213. See infra, Part III, p. 140.

214. Ibid., p. 141. Emphasis added.

215. This cannot be otherwise, for being, originarily or at the level of my proposing it as a hypothesis or postulate, is a *finite* foreshortening of the world, of the *infinity* of the world. In principle, being thus cannot be found therein. (Cf. ibid., p. 147.) Accordingly, being, as our formula, must be finite, for it is "something projected onto a mind which lasts only for a while." (See ibid.; cf. supra, n. 149.) As Ortega pointed out, "we are in need of complementing the *paucity* of our time, its dearth and inexorable determination, by *anticipating* the things themselves . . . by means of an image or schema. . . . We are in need of being certain . . . , of discovering the *essence* or being . . . [of things]" (ibid.; emphasis added). But this point serves only to underscore the paradoxical character of knowledge, for thereby we seek certainty in order to live and live well, and yet we do so, to begin with, on the basis of postulating something (i.e., being) that is not certain at all, but hypothetical and problematic. Moreover, assuming that we succeed in our cognitive effort, knowledge would further require the demonstration of what we had proposed.

216. Cf. infra, Part IV, pp. 165–166 and infra, pp. 24f.

217. Cf. infra, Part IV, p. 164–165.

218. See ibid., p. 157. (Emphasis added.) This is in keeping, contended Ortega, with the evolution of metaphysics which, having started with what he characterized as the error of identifying being, entity, and thing (cf. ibid., p. 166), proceeded as the "ongoing establishment of a distance between being and things, . . . [resulting in] being . . . progressively becom[ing] . . . less [like] things and contain[ing] less of them." (See ibid., p. 158; for an interesting discussion of this development in Plato, cf. ibid., p. 169.)

219. Cf. ibid., pp. 155 and 164–165.

220. See ibid., p. 169.

221. Cf. ibid., pp. 170–171. *Vide* p. 171 for the use Ortega makes of Plato's *Meno*.

222. See ibid.; "Ideas y creencias," p. 401 (and infra, "Appendix," p. 195), and *El hombre y la gente,* chap. 1.

223. See infra, Part IV, p. 171.

224. It goes without saying that the inquirer does not rest his or her case at the level of a proposal, hypothesis, or postulate. He or she is under the obligation of testing and proving the ontological interpretation he or she advances, and of doing so in connection with the actual behavior of things, whether past (as a suggestive indicator) or future (for the purposes of confirmation).

225. See ibid.

226. J. Ortega y Gasset, *La idea de principio,* p. 161 (trans., p. 136).

227. See infra, Part III, pp. 115–116.

228. Cf. J. Ortega y Gasset, *La idea de principio,* p. 161 (trans., p. 136).

229. See ibid. and supra, pp. 19–20.

230. See J. Ortega y Gasset, *La idea de principio,* p. 208 (trans., p. 195).

231. Ibid., p. 211 (trans., p. 198).

232. Cf. ibid., p. 208 (trans., p. 195) and pp. 201 and 205 (trans., pp. 185 and 190). *Vide* J. Ortega y Gasset, "Principios metafísicos de la razón vital," Curso de 1933–1934, Universidad de Madrid; unpublished typescript (Fundación José Ortega y Gasset, Madrid), viii, pp. 44–45, and infra, Part IV, pp. 161ff. and 167ff.

233. Cf. J. Ortega y Gasset, *El hombre y la gente,* p. 117 (trans., p. 62).

234. J. Ortega y Gasset, "Comentario al 'Banquete' de Platón," p. 773.

235. Cf. ibid. For the signification of the pair "question/need," cf. supra, pp. 17ff.

236. According to Ortega, Hartmann's failure to make these distinctions is his fundamental error. (Cf. infra, Part III, p. 139.) *Vide* J. Ortega y Gasset, *La idea de principio,* p. 232, n. 2 (trans., p. 226, n. 9); "[Prólogo] A un diccionario enciclopédico abreviado," in *OC* VI, p. 360; and "Comentario al 'Banquete' de Platón," p. 783, n. 4.

237. Cf. J. Ortega y Gasset, *La idea de principio,* p. 234 (trans., p. 228).

238. Cf. J. Ortega y Gasset, *El hombre y la gente,* p. 110 (trans., p. 54).

239. See ibid.

240. Cf. Wolfgang-Rainer Mann, *The Discovery of Things. Aristotle's Categories and Their Context* (Princeton: Princeton University Press, 2000). For the question as to why "discovery" rather than invention, cf. p. 22, n. 31.

241. Ibid., p. 12.

242. Ibid., p. 11.

243. Ibid., p. 10. He explains the sense of "particular object" by means of Aristotle's construal of two sub-theses, to wit: "(i) [the distinction] . . . between *objects* and the *properties* of objects" (ibid., p. 8) and "(ii) that between what is *particular* and what is general" (ibid., p. 9).

244. Ibid., pp. 10–11.

245. Ibid., p. 13.

246. Ibid.

247. Ibid., p. 14.

248. Ibid.

249. Ibid., p. 19. Cf. pp. 87, 107, 124, and 201 (n. 18), and infra, Part IV, pp. 163 ff. and 169 ff.

250. Cf. J. Ortega y Gasset, "Principios metafísicos de la razón vital," viii, p. 44, and supra, n. 103.

251. W.-R. Mann, op. cit., p. 30. Cf. p. 34:

> "From Aristotle's perspective, Plato's quasi-Anaxagoreanism leaves him vulnerable to . . . [the] criticism . . . [that] Plato has no good way of distinguishing between a participant [in the Forms] *changing* (while remaining the same participant) and a participant being *replaced* (by some new participant), because he ultimately has no clear way of regarding a participant as anything other than a 'mixture,' that is, as anything other than a heap, rather than a thing. Thus, as a first approximation, what is wrong with the Platonic view is that it treats all predication in the sensible world as, in effect, accidental predication."

252. Cf. J. Ortega y Gasset, "Principios metafísicos de la razón vital," vii, pp. 40 and 42 and viii, pp. 44–45; see infra, Part IV, pp. 163–164.

253. Cf. W.-R. Mann, op. cit., pp. 23–24.

254. Cf. supra, p. 22 ff.

255. Cf. Parmenides, Fragment 8 in *Ancilla to the Pre-Socratic Philosophers,* trans. K. Freeman (Cambridge, Mass.: Harvard University Press, 1962), pp. 43 f.; J. Ortega y Gasset, *La idea de principio,* p. 104 (trans., p. 63); and A. Rodríguez Huéscar, *José Ortega y Gasset's Metaphysical Innovation,* Part II, chap. 4, 5B, p. 110.

256. J. Ortega y Gasset, *La idea de principio,* p. 104 (trans., p. 63).

257. Cf. ibid., pp. 209 and 211 (trans., pp. 196–198).

258. Cf. J. Ortega y Gasset, "Principios metafísicos de la razón vital," vii, p. 41, and infra, Part IV, pp. 164–166.

259. In the threefold sense of necessities, facilities, and difficulties. Cf. J. Ortega y Gasset, *El hombre y la gente,* p. 111 (trans., p. 54).

260. Ibid., p. 166 (trans., p. 129).

261. Ibid. For the moral and political questions rooted in the equation "man = human being," cf. ibid., chap. 10, pp. 227–228 (trans., pp. 213 ff.).

## Spanish Editor's Note

1. *Editor's Note:* Revista de la Facultad de Filosofía y Letras, Universidad Nacional de Tucumán (Argentina), XII (1964), No. 17.

2. *¿Qué es conocimiento?,* ed. P. Garagorri (Madrid: Revista de Occidente en Alianza Editorial, 1984).

3. *Ed.'s N.:* This course has also been published as part of the above-mentioned collection. [Cf. *¿Qué es filosofía?* in *Obras Completas* (Madrid: Alianza Editorial/

Revista de Occidente, 1983), VII, pp. 273ff. (henceforth this set will be referred to as *OC*). Translation: *What Is Philosophy?*, trans. M. Adams (New York: W. W. Norton & Co., 1960).]

4. Ibid., p. 275; cf. "Translator's Preface," *What Is Philosophy?*, p. 10: "in the profane surroundings of a theatre."

5. The word "radical" is taken here etymologically, i.e., as deriving from *radix* ("root"). Hence, "radical reality" is understood to mean "fundamental reality." The special sense of this expression will become apparent as it is used throughout the book.

6. *Ed.'s N.:* This course has also been published as part of the above-mentioned collection. [Cf. *Unas lecciones de metafísica* in *OC*, XII, p. 13, and "Note by the Spanish Publishers" in *Some Lessons in Metaphysics*, trans. M. Adams (New York: W. W. Norton & Co., 1969), p. 7.]

# 1. Problems

1. "Absolute" is taken, here and elsewhere, in its etymological sense, that is to say, as the past participle of *absolvo*, which derives from *ab-* (away, off) and *solvo* (I loosen), and thus means "that which is loosened or freed from." In other words, anything is absolute which stands altogether on its own to be what it is. Cf. *The American Heritage Dictionary of the English Language,* 3rd ed. (Boston: Houghton Mifflin Co., 1992), p. 7, left column. Ortega himself defines "absolute" as that which is "self-relative." Cf. J. Ortega y Gasset, "Apuntes sobre el pensamiento: su teurgia y su demiurgia," *OC* V, p. 545. ("Notes on Thinking— Its Creation of the World and Its Creation of God" in *Concord and Liberty,* trans. H. Weyl [New York: W. W. Norton & Co., 1946], p. 81.)

2. Cf. J. Ortega y Gasset, *Meditaciones del Quijote,* i, §11, *OC* I, p. 283 (translation: *Meditations on Quixote,* trans. E. Rugg et al. [New York: W. W. Norton & Co., 1961], p. 138: "The Renaissance discovers the inner world in all its extension, the *me ipsum* [I myself], the consciousness, the subjective.")

3. For the notion of belief in Ortega's sense, cf. infra, "Appendix: Ideas and Beliefs," pp. 177ff.

4. Cf. supra, n. 5 on this page.

5. For Ortega, the *fundamental* sense of words like "living" or "vital" seems to be the same as that of the term "performative" *(ejecutivo)*, as will become apparent in due course. One should therefore avoid taking them at the primordial level as if they had biological significance.

6. "Fact" is usually taken by Ortega in an etymological sense, i.e., as deriving from the Latin *factum,* the neuter past participle of *facio* ("I do"), hence as meaning "deed" or "that which is done or made." Cf. Charlton T. Lewis et al., *A Latin Dictionary* (Oxford at the Clarendon Press, 1966), p. 716, left column.

7. This is the name that was given to Ortega's doctrine in the 1920s. Cf., e.g., J. Ortega y Gasset, *El tema de nuestro tiempo,* iii–vi, *OC* III, pp. 157ff. (*The Modern Theme,* trans. J. Cleugh [New York: Harper & Row, 1961], pp. 28ff.) and

"Guillermo Dilthey y la Idea de la Vida," iv, *OC* VI, pp. 195–196, n. 2 ("A Chapter from the History of Ideas" in *Concord and Liberty,* p. 164, n. 28).

8. *Positum* is the past participle of *pono,* meaning "I put," "place," or "set." The *positum* is, then, that which is set forth or forward. Cf., e.g., *positio* (2) in Roy J. Deferrari, *A Latin-English Dictionary of St. Thomas Aquinas* (Boston: St. Paul Editions, 1960), p. 803, col. 1: "*setting down, putting down, affirmation,* synonym of *affirmatio,* the opposite of *negatio* and *remotio.* . . ." As is thus evident, the traditional usage of *positio* (positing) and *positum* (the posited) has been developed at the propositional and related levels, while Ortega's employment thereof reaches much deeper, as will become apparent in the text.

9. Cf. J. Ortega y Gasset, *El hombre y la gente,* ii in *OC* VII, p. 107 (translation: *Man and People,* trans. W. R. Trask [New York: W. W. Norton & Co., 1957], p. 49:

   "The radical solitude of human life, the being of man, does not, then, consist in there really being nothing except himself. . . . There is . . . an infinity of things but—there it is!—amid them Man in his radical reality is alone—alone *with* them. And since among these things there are other human beings, he is *alone with* them too. If but one unique being existed, it could not properly be said to be alone. Uniqueness has nothing to do with solitude").

10. Cf. Antonio Rodríguez Huéscar, *José Ortega y Gasset's Metaphysical Innovation. A Critique and Overcoming of Idealism,* trans. and ed. J. García-Gómez (Albany, N.Y. : State University of New York Press, 1995), pp. xxxv–xxxvi: ". . . each and every concept referring to human life [is] . . . 'a function of the given occasion.'" *Vide* J. Ortega y Gasset, "Historia como sistema," *OC* VI, pp. 35–36 ("History as a System" in *History as a System and Other Essays Toward a Philosophy of History,* trans. H. Weyl [New York: W. W. Norton & Co., 1941], pp. 205–207), "Apuntes sobre el pensamiento: su teurgia y su demiurgia," pp. 538 ff. (trans., pp. 73 ff.), and *El hombre y la gente,* chaps. 1–4 (trans. pp. 11–93). For the notion of occasional expression, see Edmund Husserl, *Logical Investigations,* i, §§26–27, trans. J. N. Findlay [New York: Humanities Press, 1970], I, pp. 313–320.)

11. *Vide* G. W. Leibniz, "First Truths" ("Primae veritates"), *Opuscules et fragments inédits de Leibniz,* ed. L. Couturat (Hildesheim: Georg Olms Verlag, 1966; a reissue of the Paris, 1903 ed.), p. 519, in *Philosophical Papers and Letters,* ed. and trans. L. E. Loemker, 2nd ed. (Dordrecht: D. Reidel, 1969), p. 268: "*there cannot be two individual things in nature which differ only numerically.*" See also Leibniz, *Discours de métaphysique et correspondance avec Arnauld,* ed. and comm. G. le Roy (Paris: J. Vrin, 1957), §9, p. 44 and pp. 218–219 (Comm.); *The Monadology* in *Discourse on Metaphysics. Correspondence with Arnauld. Monadology,* trans. G. R. Montgomery (La Salle: Open Court, 1957), §9, p. 252; *Nouveaux essais sur l'entendement humain* (Paris: Garnier/Flammarion, 1966), ii, chap. 27, §3, p. 197; *Leibniz-Clarke Correspondence,* ed. H. G. Alexander (Manchester, 1956), No. 5, 21 (*Die philosophischen Schriften von G. W. Leibniz,* ed. C. I. Gerhardt [Hildesheim: Georg Olms Verlag, 1978; a re-issue of the 1875–1890 ed.], VII, pp. 393–394; henceforth this edition will be referred to as G); and "Fourth Letter to Clarke," *Philosophical Papers and Letters,* ed. and

trans. L.E. Loemker, vii, §9, p. 687 (*G* VII, p. 372). Cf. John Dewey, *Leibniz's "New Essays Concerning Human Understanding"* (New York: Hillary House Publishers, 1961; a re-issue of the 1888 ed.), chap. 9, p. 185, and Frederick Copleston, *A History of Philosophy* (London: Burns & Oates, 1965), IV, pp. 290ff.

12. *Vide* J. Ortega y Gasset, "Historia como sistema," p. 36, n. 1 (trans., p. 207). Cf. J. García-Gómez, "Interpretación mundanal e identidad propia. Crítica del experimento mental de Bergson y de Schütz en torno a la naturaleza y los límites de la conciencia," *Revista de Filosofía* 3, No. 4 (1990) (Universidad Complutense de Madrid), 3rd epoch, pp. 111ff. and especially pp. 117ff.

13. *Vide* René Descartes, *Discours de la méthode,* iii in *Oeuvres de Descartes,* ed. Ch. Adam and P. Tannery (Paris: J. Vrin; a re-issue of the Paris 1897–1913 ed.), VI (1965), pp. 32–33, and *Meditationes de prima philosophia* in ibid., VII (1964), pp. 25 and 27. Cf. J. Ortega y Gasset, *¿Qué es filosofía?,* pp. 394ff. (trans., pp. 186ff.).

14. The word "thought" was added by the Spanish editor.

15. Cf. Antonio Rodríguez Huéscar, op. cit., ii, chap. 4, §2, p. 87: "In effect, to live is to *encounter myself [encontrarse] living.*" (Cf. also p. 171, n. 6.) In Ortega's text, however, the verb is *hallarse* rather than *encontrarse,* yet the basic meaning is the same, namely, "to find, encounter, or come across something or someone in the world." As opposed to this sense of "encounter," to which Ortega objected in the text, Rodríguez Huéscar identifies here a more fundamental signification, one that is consistent with the notion of life as a non-mediately self-aware performance and self-fashioning, managing at the same time to keep in view the duality inscribed in life. (Cf. *Meditaciones del Quijote,* p. 322; trans., p. 45, slightly modified: "I ["my life"] am myself [the objectivating ego] and my circumstance." *Vide* Julián Marías, "Comentario," jointly published with *Meditaciones del Quijote* [Madrid: Revista de Occidente/Ediciones de la Universidad de Puerto Rico, 1957], pp. 266ff.). This more fundamental sense of the word allows for the radical, active, and concomitant self-awareness of my living (which Ortega has here in mind), even as I am *conscious* of something else, i.e., as I engage with and objectivate it.

16. Cf. supra, n. 6. The Spanish verb used here is *hacer,* which has a dual sense corresponding to two separate English verbs (viz., "to do" and "to make"). Such a contextual duality, which at first glance may give rise to mere ambiguity, is nonetheless fruitful in keeping the *ad intra* and *ad extra* dimensions of life not just together, but intimately linked. For the related distinctions between *poíesis* and *prâxis* and "action" and "working," cf., respectively, Aristotle, *Nicomachean Ethics,* vi, 4, 1140 a, trans. W. D. Ross, rev. J. O. Urmson (in *The Complete Works of Aristotle,* rev. Oxford ed., ed. J. Barnes [Princeton: Princeton University Press/Bollingen Series LXXI-2, 1984], II, pp. 1799–1800), and Alfred Schutz, "On Multiple Realities," i, 2 in *Collected Papers* (The Hague: Martinus Nijhoff, 1962), I (ed. M. Natanson), pp. 211–212. *Vide* Xavier Zubiri, *Cinco lecciones de filosofía* (Madrid: Sociedad de Estudios y Publicaciones, 1963), i.ii, pp. 36–37.

17. *Vide* Jean-Paul Sartre, *L'existentialisme est un humanisme* (Paris: Les Éditions Nagel, 1970), p. 22: "l'homme n'est rien d'autre que ce qu'il se fait...." (See also

p. 58 and *L'être et le néant* [Paris: Gallimard, 1943], pp. 61 and 513. Cf. J. Ortega y Gasset, *Una interpretación de la historia universal* in OC IX, p. 216 [*An Interpretation of Universal History,* trans. M. Adams {New York: W. W. Norton & Co., 1973}, p. 285] and *La idea de principio en Leibniz y la evolución de la teoría deductiva* in OC VIII, p. 315 [*The Idea of Principle in Leibnitz and the Evolution of Deductive Theory,* trans. M. Adams {New York: W. W. Norton & Co., 1971}, p. 332].) For the grounds of the contrast between Sartre and Ortega on this point, cf. the discussion between members of the audience (particularly Maurice Merleau-Ponty) and Ortega on the occasion of his lecture entitled "Pasado y porvenir del hombre actual," which was delivered by him as part of the "Rencontres internationales de Genève" (1951) and was published, with the other papers presented there, in *La connaissance de l'homme au XXe. siècle* (Neuchâtel: Éditions de la Baconnière, 1952). The original text seems to have appeared first in the Spanish translation of that volume, namely, *Hombre y cultura en el siglo XX,* trans. M. Riaza (Madrid: Ediciones Guadarrama, 1957), pp. 321–347; the discussion in question appears on pp. 349ff. (the relevant parts being found on pp. 354–362). The text of the lecture is currently available in OC IX, pp. 645ff.

18. Cf. J. Ortega y Gasset, "Ensayo de estética a manera de prólogo," §§2–3, OC VI, pp. 250ff. and particularly p. 252 ("An Essay in Esthetics by Way of a Preface" in *Phenomenology and Art,* trans. Ph. W. Silver [New York: W. W. Norton & Co., 1975], pp. 131ff. and especially pp. 133–134).

19. Cf. E. Husserl, *Logical Investigations,* i, chap. 1, §9 (I, pp. 280 f.) and v, chap. 2, §10 (II, pp. 555–556), and *Ideas Pertaining to a Pure Phenomenology and to a Phenomenological Philosophy,* I, trans. F. Kersten (The Hague: Martinus Nijhoff, 1982), §§34 (p. 67), 36 (pp. 73ff.), and 84 (pp. 199ff.). Henceforth I shall be referring to the latter as *Ideas,* I. *Vide* J. Ortega y Gasset, *Investigaciones psicológicas* in OC XII, pp. 377f. (*Psychological Investigations,* trans. J. García-Gómez [New York: W. W. Norton & Co., 1987], pp. 87ff.).

20. Cf. supra, §4. [This remark is by the author.]

21. *Vide* Immanuel Kant, *Critique of Pure Reason,* B 131, trans. N. K. Smith (New York: St. Martin's Press, 1961), p. 152: "It must be possible for the 'I think' to accompany all my representations...."

22. Cf. supra, §8. [This remark is by the author.]

## I. The 1929–1930 Course

1. The equivalent of "derives from" has been added by the Spanish editor.

2. Cf. R. Descartes, *Meditationes de prima philosophia,* ii and iii in *Oeuvres de Descartes,* VII, pp. 28 (vv. 20–22) and 34 (vv. 18–20).

3. The text reads *intuición,* and it has been translated accordingly, but, given its antecedent use and immediate re-employment, Ortega may have meant *intención.* If, however, the actual text is correct, then some kind of reason justifying the identification of intuition with intention would apparently have been needed.

4. [*Vide* Pierre M. M.] Duhem, [*SOZEIN TA PHAINOMENA: Essai sur la notion de théorie physique de Platon à Galilée* (Paris: A. Hermann, 1908). (Translation: *To Save the Phenomena,* trans. E. Dolan et al. [Chicago: University of Chicago Press, 1969)].

5. Cf. J. Ortega y Gasset, "Prólogo para alemanes," *OC* VIII, p. 37. ("Preface for Germans" in J. Ortega y Gasset, *Phenomenology and Art,* pp. 46–47).

6. Cf. supra, p. 41.

7. Cf. J. Ortega y Gasset, "Ideas y creencias," *OC* V, pp. 392 and 394. (For the translation, *vide* "Appendix," infra, pp. 185–186 and 188).

8. Cf. ibid., pp. 393 and 397 (trans., infra, pp. 186–187 and 191) and "Historia como sistema," *OC* VI, pp. 14, 18, and 46 (trans. pp. 167, 174, and 224–225).

9. For the notion of the ridiculousness of philosophy, cf. infra, "Appendix," chap. 2, I, pp. 190–191ff.; for the concept of *àlétheia,* see J. Ortega y Gasset, *Origen y epílogo de la filosofía* in *OC* IX, pp. 384ff. (*The Origin of Philosophy,* trans. T. Talbot [New York: W. W. Norton & Co., 1967], pp. 60ff.)

10. Cf. J. Ortega y Gasset, *¿Qué es filosofía?,* pp. 335ff. (trans., pp. 101ff.).

11. Cf. supra, p. 43.

12. Cf. A. Rodríguez Huéscar, op. cit., ii, chap. 4, §5A, pp. 95ff.

13. Cf. infra, p. 50. The word used is *complica,* which literally means "complicates," but it seems here to signify "co-implicates" or just simply "implicates."

14. "Thought" *(pensamiento)* seems to refer here to a judging or act of propositional thinking, as opposed to its propositional correlate (or the content of the judgment).

15. Cf. supra, n. 14. For what follows, cf. supra, "First Day," p. 42.

16. Cf. Heraclitus, Fragments 1 and 89 in *Ancilla to the Pre-Socratic Philosophers,* trans. K. Freeman (Cambridge, Mass.: Harvard University Press, 1962), pp. 24 and 30.

17. Here, as well as in what follows, Ortega is deliberately underscoring the twofold sense of the word *salvar* ("to save"), namely, to gain the state of freedom from danger (i.e., the *safety* one is after when in peril of drowning) and to attain salvation (i.e., the deliverance from evil and one's admission to bliss).

18. Cf. supra, p. 45.

19. Ibid.

20. Cf. E. Husserl, *Prolegomena to Pure Logic,* chaps. 3–5 and 7–8 in *Logical Investigations,* I, pp. 90–128 and 135–196.

21. Cf. supra, Figure 1, p. 46.

22. Cf. infra, Part III, pp. 140 and 229 (n. 69).

23. Ortega is availing himself of two forms of the same Spanish verb, one non-reflexive (namely, *parecer,* which means to seem or appear) and another reflexive (viz., *parecerse,* which signifies to look like or resemble). That is how I have translated the two mentions of the verb (and, following Ortega, in that order). As a result, something is unavoidably lost in the translation, for in English words of

the same origin cannot, so far as I know, be used to convey the two verbal functions of the Spanish verb. Though, generally speaking, this phenomenon is common enough in translation and therefore trivial, it is not so in this case, given the centrality of the opposition between appearing and seeming and that between thinking and the content of thought in Ortega's argument.

24. Cf. supra, p. 49.

25. In the original, the multiplication symbol is used instead, at this point, to relate the subject *thesis* and what is predicated of it, while the sign "=" is employed in connection with the subjects *hypothesis, antithesis,* and *synthesis,* which follow immediately. I have taken "=" to mean *is* and substituted "signifies" for the multiplication symbol (and, by implication, for any other nexus of attribution). I believe that this is consistent with my construing the whole as an articulated series of sentences.

26. Cf. supra, "Problems," pp. 221 (n. 6) and 223 (n. 16).

27. Cf. supra, pp. 45–46 and 49 ff.

28. The expression in parentheses has been added by the Spanish editor.

29. The expression in parentheses has been added by the Spanish editor.

30. *Ed.'s N.:* Cf. [J. Ortega y Gasset,] *¿Qué es filosofía?* [particularly chaps. 3–5, pp. 299–343; trans., pp. 47–113].

31. Cf. R. Descartes, *Meditationes de prima philosophia,* ii in *Oeuvres de Descartes,* A.-T., VII, pp. 25 (vv. 10–13) and 27 (vv. 8–12).

32. Cf. ibid., p. 28, vv. 20 ff.

33. As will become apparent at once, the formula "seeing this light" is *not* the equivalent of the expression "the seeing of this light," which refers to a mere psychological fact and is reducible, when carried to the limit, to the idealist thesis. Furthermore, let me call the reader's attention to the fact that Ortega employs the expression *extra ser* later in this paragraph. That locution has been translated here, given the context, as "external being," though it may also mean "additional or surplus being" by virtue of the prefix *extra.* Not only is there no incompatibility between the two senses of Ortega's phrase, but I believe he has both in mind, and, though the English version does not lend itself easily to conveying this other signification, the reader, nonetheless, would be well advised to bear it in mind as an essential determination to which one gains access by means of his analysis.

34. Cf. *¿Qué es filosofía?,* chap. 9, pp. 388 ff. (trans., pp. 177 ff.).

35. The opening phrase has been added by the Spanish editor.

36. Cf. supra, "Problems," p. 36.

37. Cf. supra, p. 57.

38. As will become apparent immediately, Ortega is speaking here not just of doubting this or that, but of the universal doubt. Cf. R. Descartes, *Meditationes de prima philosophia,* ii.

39. I have read the original text as if it said *mi* ("my"), rather than *ni* ("neither/nor"), which makes no sense in the present context.

40. In what follows, please compare Ortega's distinction between *para algo* ("being for," "for the sake of," or "in order to") and *por algo* ("because" or "because of") with the similar differentiation introduced later by Alfred Schutz between the *Um-zu-Motiv* ("in-order-to motive") and the *Weil-Motiv* ("because motive") in his *Der sinnhafte Aufbau der sozialen Welt*, 2nd ed. (Vienna: Springer Verlag, 1960; 1st ed., 1932), §17 (p. 95) and 18 (p. 100); (translation: *The Phenomenology of the Social World*, trans. G. Walsh et al. [Evanston: Northwestern University Press, 1967]: "the act ... projected in the future perfect tense and in terms of which the action receives its orientation is the 'in-order-to motive' ... for the actor" (p. 88); "the in-order-to motive explains the act in terms of the project, while the genuine because-motive explains the project in terms of the actor's past experiences ... " [p. 91].) Cf. A. Schutz, "Projects of Action," iii in *Collected Papers* (The Hague: Martinus Nijhoff), I (1962, ed. M. Natanson), pp. 69ff. and *Reflections on the Problem of Relevance*, ed. R. M. Zaner (New Haven: Yale University Press, 1970), chap. 2, §E, pp. 45ff.

41. Whenever possible, *existir* has been translated as "existing" or "to exist." Occasionally, when Ortega himself employs *existencia* or when translating *existir* in the usual way would have been awkward, I have used "existence." In any case, however, all such words are always intended by Ortega to refer to the *act* of existing or living, not to something merely abstract, inert, or derivative.

42. Cf. J. Ortega y Gasset, *El tema de nuestro tiempo*, chap. 6, pp. 174ff. (trans., pp. 52ff.) and "Sensación, construcción e intuición" in OC XII, pp. 487ff. (trans.: "Sensation, Construction, and Intuition" in *Phenomenology and Art*, pp. 79ff.).

43. Vide "Ideas y creencias," pp. 384–385 (trans., cf. infra, pp. 178–179).

44. Cf. supra, pp. 40–46.

45. Cf. J. Ortega y Gasset, *Meditaciones del Quijote*, OC I, p. 322 (trans., p. 45).

46. Cf. ibid., pp. 320ff. (trans., pp. 43ff.). The expressions "theoretical culture," "theory," and the like are meant here to cover the whole range of interpretations that human beings may propose to meet the difficulties of living. Accordingly, they are *not* intended to refer exclusively, or even primarily, to the plane of scientific or philosophical meanings, which are a specialized and radical sort of concepts, judgments, and inferences within the field of interpretations *lato sensu*. See "Ideas y creencias," pp. 406ff. and infra, pp. 200ff.

47. Cf. J. Ortega y Gasset, *Meditaciones del Quijote*, OC I, p. 322 (trans., p. 45): "In short, the re-absorption of circumstance is the concrete destiny of man." As Julián Marías says in n. 7 to p. 172 of the translation, the "... reabsorption of the circumstance consists in its humanization, in its incorporation into that project of man. Man makes himself *with the things which are offered to him,* makes life out of them, his own life, he assumes them by projecting on them that sense, that *logos* or significance" which in themselves, or apart from my life, they do not have, so as "to convert that which simply 'is there around me' (circumstance) into a real *world,* into *personal human life*." (Cf. J. Marías, "Comentario," p. 264.)

48. Cf. E. Husserl, *Ideas*, I, §§31 (pp. 57ff.), 32 (pp. 60ff.), 33 (pp. 65–66), 50 (pp. 112ff.), and 90 (p. 220), and A. Rodríguez Huéscar, *José Ortega y Gasset's Metaphysical Innovation*, Part I, chap. 3, pp. 51ff.

49. Cf. E. Husserl, *Ideas,* I, §§51 ("Note," p. 117) and 58 (pp. 133–134).

50. Cf. J. Ortega y Gasset, "Prólogo para alemanes," pp. 47 and 52 (trans., pp. 60 and 67–68); *¿Qué es filosofía?,* p. 414 (trans., p. 216); and *Meditación de nuestro tiempo (Conferencias en Buenos Aires: 1928),* in *Meditación de nuestro tiempo. Las Conferencias en Buenos Aires: 1916 y 1928,* ed. J. L. Molinuevo (Mexico: Fondo de Cultura Económica, 1996), pp. 185, 186, and 188.

51. Cf. J. Ortega y Gasset, *¿Qué es filosofía?,* p. 404 (trans., p. 201).

52. Added by the Spanish editor.

53. Cf. Martin Heidegger, *Sein und Zeit* in *GESAMTAUSGABE* I.2 (Frankfurt: V. Klostermann, 1977), §§9 (pp. 56ff.) and 25 (pp. 153ff.). (*Being and Time,* trans. J. Macquarrie et al. [New York: Harper & Row, 1962], pp. 67ff. and 150ff.).

54. Cf. supra, "Problems," p. 38.

55. The expressions "extra-" and "pre-intellectual" are the English translations for the Spanish words *extra-noético* and *pre-noético,* respectively. The translations adopted here are consistent with the sense of *noético* as a derivative of the Greek words *noûs* ("intellect") and *noeîn* ("to intuit intellectually").

56. Cf. Henri Bergson, "Introduction à la métaphysique," *La pensée et le mouvant* in *Oeuvres* (Paris: Presses Universitaires de France, 1963), p. 1398 [184]. (*An Introduction to Metaphysics,* trans. T. E. Hulme [Indianapolis: The Bobbs-Merrill Co., 1955], p. 26: "A consciousness which could experience two identical moments would be a consciousness without memory. It would die and be born again continually. In what other way could one represent unconsciousness?")

57. An important artery in Madrid.

58. Later we shall see what this sense is. [This is a remark by the author. Cf. what follows immediately in the text.]

59. Cf. supra, "Problems," pp. 38–39.

60. "Existence," [another such expression,] cannot be regarded as technical. [Moreover,] let it be clearly understood that I use the word "exist" in its most traditional and even most common acceptation. [This remark is the author's.]

61. Cf. supra, p. 40 and infra, Part IV, pp. 156ff. and 158ff.

62. Cf., e.g., Aristotle, *Metaphysics,* trans. W. D. Ross, rev. J. O. Urmson in *The Complete Works of Aristotle,* rev. Oxford ed., ix, 6–8, 1048 a 25–1051 a 33, II, pp. 1655–1659.

63. Here I have translated *ejecución* literally, though normally I render it as "performance" (as I usually do with its derivatives by means of the derivatives of the English word). My purpose is to give expression, as idiomatically as possible, to Ortega's notion of life—and its "ingredients"—as radical, unmediated being, as opposed to the mediated sense it possesses in this context, namely, that of bringing about something pre-conceived.

64. Cf. supra, n. 63.

65. Cf. Aristotle, *Metaphysics* in op. cit., i.3, 983 a 30 (II, p. 1555); 983 b 16 (II, p. 1556); iv.8, 1017 b 23–26 (II, p. 1607); vii.13, 1038 b 5 (II, p. 1639); *Physics,* trans. R. P. Hardie et al. in ibid., i.7, 190 a 33–35 (I, p. 325) and 9, 192 a 32 (I, p. 328).

66. Cf. Aristotle, *Metaphysics* in op. cit., v.4, 1015 a 11 and 16 (II, pp. 1602–1603); *Physics* in ibid., ii.1, 193 b 7–8 (I, p. 330).

67. Cf. Aristotle, *Metaphysics* in op. cit., ix.8, 1050 a 15–16 (II, p. 1658) and xii.10, 1075 b 22 (II, p. 1700); *On Generation and Corruption,* trans. H. H. Joachim in ibid., i.7, 324 b 18 (I, p. 530); and *On the Soul,* trans. J. A. Smith in ibid., ii.1, 412 a 9–10 (I, p. 656).

68. G. W. Leibniz, *The Principles of Nature and Grace,* §1 in *Die philosophischen Schriften von G. W. Leibniz,* ed. C. I. Gerhardt, VI, p. 598; *A New System of Nature,* ibid., IV, pp. 478–479; *New Essays Concerning Human Understanding,* trans. A. G. Langley, 2nd ed. (Chicago: The Open Court Publishing Co., 1916), Appendix, p. 702 in ibid., p. 396.

69. Cf. supra, "Problems," §9, pp. 38–39 and this course, p. 68.

70. Cf. J. Ortega y Gasset, *Meditaciones del Quijote,* OC I, p. 322 (trans., p. 45 and J. Marías, n. 8, pp. 173–174; *vide* J. Marías, "Comentario," pp. 266ff.).

71. Cf. J. Ortega y Gasset, *Unas lecciones de metafísica,* iii, OC XII, pp. 39ff. (trans., pp. 79ff.).

72. Cf. A. Rodríguez Huéscar, op. cit., ii, chap. 4, §1, pp. 83ff. and particularly pp. 85f.; see also pp. 62ff.

73. Cf. supra, p. 60 and p. 227, n. 40.

74. Cf. A. Rodríguez Huéscar, op. cit., ii, chap. 4, §8, pp. 132ff.; see also his *Éthos y lógos,* ed. J. Lasaga (Madrid: Universidad Nacional de Educación a Distancia, 1996), i, chap. vi, §2, pp. 105ff.

75. Cf. supra, "Problems," §7, pp. 34–35.

76. Cf. supra, n. 53.

77. Cf. supra, "Problems," §7, p. 34.

78. Cf. ibid., p. 35.

79. Cf. ibid., p. 222, n. 10.

80. Cf. ibid., p. 35 and pp. 222–223, nn. 11 and 12.

## II. Concerning Radical Reality

1. *Ed.'s N.* : From this point to the end of the lecture, the original manuscript is identical with the text published as article No. 1 of the series, "What Is Knowledge?," except for slight emendations, as well as for certain passages that were omitted and which are presently restored, as will be indicated [in notes].

2. Cf. M. Heidegger, *Sein und Zeit,* "Einleitung," chap. 2, §5–6.

3. Cf. Charlton T. Lewis et al., *A Latin Dictionary,* p. 500.

4. Cf. Joan Corominas, *Breve diccionario etimológico de la lengua castellana,* 2nd ed. (Madrid: Gredos, 1967), p. 184.

5. Cf. *curo* in Charlton T. Lewis et al., *A Latin Dictionary,* p. 502.

6. "To endeavor," "to make sure," " to procure."

7. "Legal guardian" or "caretaker."

8. "Procurator."

9. The Latin words *incuria* and *securitas* are used as such in the original text. Cf. Charlton T. Lewis et al., op.cit., pp. 930 and 1656, respectively.

10. Cf. Charles F. Peirce, "The Fixation of Belief," §4, *Pragmatism and Pragmaticism*, II, iv, §374 in *Collected Papers*, ed. Ch. Hartshorne et al. (Cambridge, Mass.: The Belknap Press/Harvard University Press, 1963), V (No. 1), p. 232: "But the mere putting of a proposition into the interrogative form does not stimulate the mind to any struggle after belief. There must be a real and living doubt, and without this all discussion is idle" and (No. 3), p. 233: "When doubt ceases, mental action on the subject comes to an end; and, if it did go on, it would be without a purpose." *Vide* J. Ortega y Gasset, *La idea de principio*, pp. 264 and 291 (trans., pp. 267 and 302–303), and "Ideas y creencias," pp. 392ff. (Cf. infra, "Appendix," pp. 185ff.)

11. Cf. J. Ortega y Gasset, *Unas lecciones de metafísica*, pp. 67ff. (trans., pp. 81ff.).

12. Cf. J. Ortega y Gasset, *En torno a Galileo*, i, OC V, p. 16. (*Man and Crisis*, trans. M. Adams [New York: W. W. Norton & Co., 1958], p. 13.)

13. Cf. J. Ortega y Gasset, "Meditación preliminar," §2 in *Meditaciones del Quijote*, OC I, pp. 331ff. (trans., pp. 61ff.), and J. Marías, "Comentario," pp. 291f.

14. Cf. J. Ortega y Gasset, op. cit., § 4, p. 335 (trans., p. 67 and n. 12 on p. 176 by J. Marías). *Vide* J. Marías, *Ortega. I. Circunstancia y vocación* (Madrid: Revista de Occidente, 1960), iii, §vi, pp. 463ff. (*José Ortega y Gasset. Circumstance and Vocation,* trans. F. M. López-Morillas [Norman: University of Oklahoma Press, 1970]), and his "Comentario," pp. 295ff.). See also J. Ortega y Gasset, *Origen y epílogo de la filosofía*, pp. 385ff. (trans., pp. 61ff.), and M. Heidegger, *Sein und Zeit*, §44 and "Vom Wesen der Wahrheit," §§5ff. (and particularly §6), *Weg-marken* in GESAMTAUSGABE (Frankfurt am Main: V. Klostermann, 1976), I.9, pp. 192ff.

15. Cf. M. Heidegger, "The Origin of the Work of Art," trans. A. Hofstadter in *Basic Writings*, ed. D. F. Krell (New York: Harper & Row, 1977), pp. 151f.

16. This paragraph had been omitted. Cf. supra, n. 1.

17. This is the origin of the commonplace locution *quisicosa* [which means "riddle." This remark is by the author.]

18. Cf. E. Husserl, *Logical Investigations*, v, chap. 2ff., trans. J. N. Findlay, II, and *Ideas*, I, trans. F. Kersten, Part III, chap. 3, pp. 211ff.

19. This line had been omitted. Cf. supra, n. 1. *Vide* J. Ortega y Gasset, *La idea de principio*, §18, p. 161 (trans., p. 136).

20. Cf. M. Heidegger, *Sein und Zeit*, §§9 and 12.

21. Cf. J. Ortega y Gasset, "Filosofía pura," OC IV, pp. 55ff.

22. Cf. supra, Part I, "Problems," §§4ff., pp. 33ff., and Antonio Rodríguez Huéscar, *José Ortega y Gasset's Metaphysical Innovation,* trans. J. García-Gómez, ii, chap. 4, §2, p. 87. Concerning the translation of *nos encontramos a nosotros mismos* as "we encounter ourselves," see my n. 6 to that page (which is found on p. 171), the following in particular:

"... what it means is simply that, in coming across something, or in realizing or becoming aware of something, ... [we] would be undergoing an experience containing an implicit component of self-'knowledge' or, more exactly, that in such an experience there would be a spontaneous and reciprocal givenness of self-'knowledge' and æknowledge' of 'things,' though, to be sure, my 'cognitive' action would be focused on the latter only."

23. Cf. supra, Part I, pp. 66ff.

24. Cf. supra, n. 18.

25. This paragraph had been omitted. Cf. supra, n. 1.

26. Cf. supra, pp. 77f.

27. Literally, the "Gate of the Sun." Today it is a small square at the heart of Madrid, serving as the arterial center of the city.

28. Cf. Heraclitus, Fragments 54, 72, 108, and 123 in *Ancilla to the Pre-Socratic Philosophers,* trans. K. Freeman, pp. 28, 29, 32, and 33.

29. Cf. Jean-Baptiste Molière, *Le médecin malgré lui* in *Oeuvres Complètes,* ed. M. Rat (Paris: Bibliothèque de la Pléiade/Nouvelle Revue Française, 1938), II, pp. 109ff. (*The Doctor in Spite of Himself* in *The Plays of Molière,* trans. K. P. Wormeley [New York: The Athenaeum Society, 1897], VI, pp. 211ff. [e.g., Act II, Scene IV]).

30. Aristotle, *Metaphysics,* I.1, 980 a 22 in op. cit., II, p. 1552.

31. Ibid., 22–23.

32. Cf. Plato, *Politeia* in *Platonis opera,* v, 475 d, ed. J. Burnet (Oxford at the Clarendon Press, 1972), IV. Paul Shorey translates the word as "lovers of spectacles" (*Republic* in *The Collected Dialogues of Plato,* ed. E. Hamilton et al. [New York: Pantheon Books, Random House/Bollingen Series LXXI, 1961], p. 714), while B. Jowett prefers "lovers of sights" (*Republic* [Oxford at the Clarendon Press, 1888], p. 173).

33. Aristotle, *Posterior Analytics,* trans. J. Barnes, ii, 19, 99 b 35ff., op. cit., I, pp. 165–166.

34. Cf. Aristotle, *Physics,* ii.1, 192 b 21, trans. R. P. Hardie in op. cit., I, p. 329: "... nature *[phúsis tinos]* is a principle or cause of being moved or of being at rest in that to which it belongs primarily in virtue of itself and not accidentally."

35. Cf. supra, n. 32.

36. Cf. supra, pp. 78ff.

37. Cf. supra, p. 78, and Plato, *Republic,* v, 475 d, trans. B. Jowett, p. 173:

"If curiosity makes a philosopher, you will find many a strange being will have a title to the name. All the lovers of sights have a delight in learning, and must therefore be included. Musical amateurs, too, are a folk strangely out of place among philosophers, for they are the last persons in the world who would come to anything like a philosophical discussion, if they could help, while they run about at the Dionysiac festivals as if they had let out their ears to hear every chorus; whether the performance is in town or country—that makes no difference—they are there."

38. Ferdinand de Saussure, *Cours de linguistique générale* (Paris and Lausanne, 1916), ii, chap. 4, §§2 and 4 and chap. 5, §1; Émile Benveniste, "Nature du signe linguistique," *Problèmes de linguistique générale* (Paris: Gallimard, 1966), I, chap. 4, p. 54; and Oswald Ducrot and Tevetan Todorov, *Dictionnaire encyclopédique des sciences du langage* (Paris: Éditions du Seuil, 1972), pp. 32ff.

39. Cf. supra, Part 1, pp. 60 and 227 (n. 40).

40. Cf. J. Ortega y Gasset, "Comentario al 'Banquete' de Platón," i, OC IX, pp. 751 ff. and particularly p. 764, where he says that "*the surroundings of a word are an essential part thereof . . . and the word is an activity,* something purely dynamic, a pressure exerted by the surroundings on it and by it on the surroundings."

41. *Ed.'s N.:* From this point to the end of the lecture, I am reproducing the third article of the above-mentioned series. [Cf. supra, n. 1.] The reason for this is the same as in the case of the second article.

42. Cf. supra, n. 39.

43. Miguel de Cervantes y Saavedra, *Don Quijote de la Mancha,* II, iii and lxxi in *Obras Completas,* ed. A. Valbuena Prat (Madrid: Aguilar, 1962), pp. 1283 and 1515.

44. Cf. M. Heidegger, *Sein und Zeit,* §35, pp. 223ff. [168ff.]; trans., pp. 211ff.

45. Cf. supra, nn. 12–14.

46. Cf. John 18:38 in *The Interlinear Greek-English New Testament,* 2nd ed., ed. A. Marshall (Grand Rapids: Zondervan, 1975), p. 447: *tí èstin àlétheia?,* or *Quid est veritas?* in *Biblia Sacra iuxta Vulgatam Clementinam,* ed. A. Colunga, 4th ed. (Madrid: Biblioteca de Autores Cristianos, 1965), p. 1061.

47. Cf. M. Heidegger, "Vom Wesen der Wahrheit," §7, pp. 196f.

48. Cf. supra, pp. 89–90.

49. Ortega normally employs the Spanish word *enigma* in the acceptation of riddle, which is its Greek-etymological sense. Cf. *aínigma* in *A Greek-English Lexikon,* by Henry George Liddell and Robert Scott, rev. ed. by H. A. Jones (Oxford at the Clarendon Press, 1966), p. 39, col. 2.

50. Cf. supra, n. 10.

51. Cf. J. Ortega y Gasset, *Investigaciones psicológicas,* ivff., pp. 370ff. (trans., pp. 79ff.), and *¿Qué es filosofía?,* iv, pp. 319ff. (trans., pp. 77ff.)

52. The Spanish locutions *realidad* ["reality"] and *cosa* ["thing"] at first had the same meaning, namely, that which one must discuss, that which one must clarify by means of words. *Res* [a "thing," "object," "matter," "affair," or "circumstance"] possibly signified originally "something one contests at law," "a matter to be cleared up before a judge"; hence [the Spanish word] *reo* ["defendant" or "accused"] would refer to someone whose behavior is not clear. A whole series of old expressions concerning legal procedure serves to indicate that (e.g., *rem habere cum aliquo* ["to litigate something with someone"], *rem dicere* ["to contest something in court"], and *res capitales* ["capital crimes"]). The same holds for the Spanish word *cosa,* which derives from [the Latin] *causa,* when taken in a juridical sense [i.e., when it means a lawsuit]. (This note is by the author).

53. In other words, it is a prologue, an expression etymologically signifying that which precedes speech.

54. Cf. supra, pp. 80ff.

55. Insofar as "is" conveys the active sense of "be" or "being," corresponding to *ser,* the word actually employed by Ortega in the original.

56. For the following analysis of the significance of our living experience (or the handling) of a hammer, cf. J. Ortega y Gasset, "Lector," *Meditaciones del Quijote, OC* I, p. 321 (trans., p. 44): "The hammer is the abstraction of each one of its hammerings . . ." (*vide* J. Marías, "Comentario," pp. 254–255), and M. Heidegger, *Sein und Zeit,* p. 69 (trans., p. 98: "The hammering itself uncovers the specific 'manipulability' ['Handlichkeit'] of the hammer").

57. Cf. J. Ortega y Gasset, *El hombre y la gente,* pp. 109–110 (trans., pp. 52–53).

58. Cf. ibid., chap. 1; "Sobre el estudiar y el estudiante," *OC* IV, pp. 545ff.; and *Unas lecciones de metafísica,* chap. 1.

59. Cf. supra, pp. 82–83.

60. Cf. J. Ortega y Gasset, "Lector," *Meditaciones del Quijote, OC* I, p. 322 (trans., p. 45; see J. Marías's n. 8, which is found on pp. 173–174 of the translation). *Vide* J. Marías, *Ortega. I. Circunstancia y vocación,* Section III, iv, §71.

61. Cf. J. Ortega y Gasset, *El hombre y la gente,* chap. 2, p. 111. Trans., p. 55:

    "Science is only one of the countless activities, actions, operations that man *practices* in his life. . . . Man *practices* science, as he *practices* patience, as he *attends to* his affairs *[hacienda],* as he *practices* poetry, politics, business, *makes* journeys, *makes* love, *makes believe, marks* [or kills] time, and above all, man *conjures up* illusions."

    As the translator points out in his note (*) on the same page, ". . . all the italicized verbs in . . . [the] passage are expressed in Spanish by the verb *hacer,* 'to do, to make' . . . ," which leads him to refer us to a relevant prior text (p. 102; trans., p. 43), to wit: ". . . we have something to do or have to be doing something *always;* for this life that is given us is not given us ready-made, but instead everyone of us has to make it for himself, each his own."

62. Cf., e.g., J. Ortega y Gasset, "Kant. Reflexiones de centenario," *OC* IV, p. 44, and *Origen y epílogo de la filosofía,* i-iii. *Vide* A. Rodríguez Huéscar, *Perspectiva y verdad,* 2nd ed. (Madrid: Alianza Editorial, 1985), p. 155.

63. Cf. supra, p. 97.

64. Cf. Heidegger's notion of *"Als-Struktur"* in *Sein und Zeit,* §32.

65. Cf. A. Rodríguez Huéscar, *José Ortega y Gasset's Metaphysical Innovation,* Part I.

66. Cf. "madera" in J. Corominas, *Breve diccionario etimológico de la lengua castellana,* p. 372, col. 2, and *"húle"* in H. G. Liddell and R. Scott, *A Greek-English Lexikon,* pp. 1847–1848.

67. Cf., e.g., Empedocles, Fragment 17 in *Ancilla to the Pre-Socratic Philosophers,* pp. 53–54 and infra, Part IV, pp. 158ff.

68. Cf. supra, Part I, pp. 70 and 228–229 (nn. 65–67).

69. Cf. Anaximander, Fragment 1 in *Ancilla to the Pre-Socratic Philosophers,* p. 19.

70. *Ed.'s N.:* It seems that this university course was interrupted at the conclusion of this lecture. Classes did not resume until the fall.

## III. What Is Life?

1. In what follows, cf. the relevant notion of "dialectical series" as found in J. Ortega y Gasset, *Origen y epílogo de la filosofía,* i-iv, pp. 349ff. (trans., pp. 13ff.).

2. Cf. Immanuel Kant, *Kritik der reinen Vernunft,* B 211–212, 233ff., and 275ff.

3. Cf. Henri Bergson, "Introduction à la métaphysique," pp. 1397–1398 (trans., pp. 25–26).

4. Cf. supra, Part II, pp. 77–78.

5. Cf. ibid., p. 85.

6. Cf. ibid., p. 87.

7. Cf. ibid.

8. Cf. ibid., p. 88.

9. Cf. ibid., p. 89.

10. Cf. ibid., p. 93.

11. *Ed.'s N.:* The concluding portion of the manuscript version of this lecture, as well as that of the Fourth Lecture, are missing.

12. Cf. J. Ortega y Gasset, "Sobre el estudiar y el estudiante," pp. 54ff. *Vide* also *Unas lecciones de metafísica,* i, pp. 15ff. and vi, pp. 105–106 (trans., pp. 13ff. and 129).

13. Cf. J. Ortega y Gasset, *Meditaciones del Quijote, OC* I, pp. 312ff., 320, and 322 (trans., pp. 32ff., 43, and 45); *Introducción a los problemas actuales de la filosofía (Conferencias en Buenos Aires: 1916),* ix in *Meditación de nuestro tiempo. Las conferencias de Buenos Aires: 1916 y 1928,* p. 167; and *Meditación de nuestro tiempo (Conferencias en Buenos Aires: 1928),* i in ibid., p. 189. *Vide* also J. Marías, "Comentario," pp. 227ff., 252, and 266ff., and *Ortega. I. Circunstancia y vocación,* §71, pp. 408–410 (trans., pp. 382–383).

14. Cf. René Descartes, *Les Méditations touchant la première philosophie* in *Oeuvres de Descartes,* IX-1, p. 21 (trans., p. 152); *Discours de la Méthode,* iv, ed. and comm. É. Gilson (Paris: J. Vrin, 1962), pp. 32–33 and "Commentary," p. 307, to p. 33, l. 17 (trans., p. 101).

15. Cf. I. Kant, *Kritik der reinen Vernunft,* B 155ff.; B 399f./A 341f.; B 428ff.; A 443/B 471; and B 520–521/A 492.

16. Cf. E. Husserl, *Logical Investigations,* v, §§6, 8, and 12 (b), II, pp. 543–544, 548–549, 551, and 561–562; *Ideas,* I, §§37, 53, and 92, pp. 75ff., 124ff., 132f., and 225f.

17. Cf. supra, pp. 106 and 108.

18. Cf. J. Ortega y Gasset, *Investigaciones psicológicas,* v, pp. 375–376 (trans., pp. 85–86).

19. Cf. E. Husserl, *Ideas,* I, §27, p. 52.

20. Cf. supra, p. 108.

21. Cf. supra, Part II, pp. 230–231 (n. 22).

22. The literal meaning of *implicite(r)* is "implicitly," and yet, as used here, it does not refer, strictly speaking, to what is derivable by logical implication, but rather to something more basic, namely, to the opposite of *explicite* or "explicitly," i.e., "in the manner or in the sense of . . . unfolding.". In other words, it seems to give expression to what is given "in a contained manner, intricately, in an envolved way." (Cf. *explico* and *implico* in R. J. Deferrari, *A Latin-English Dictionary of St. Thomas Aquinas,* pp. 377 and 492, respectively; *vide* the category of "complexity" or *complicatio* in A. Rodríguez Huéscar, *José Ortega y Gasset's Metaphysical Innovation,* pp. 95 ff.). Accordingly, in the text, the phrase, "involve, *impliciter,* its existence" appears to mean "implicate its existence."

23. Cf. R. Descartes, *Principia philosophiae,* I, li in *Oeuvres de Descartes,* VIII-1, p. 24 (*Principles of Philosophy,* p. 239, in *The Philosophical Works of Descartes,* trans. E. S. Haldane and G.R.T. Ross [New York: Dover, 1955], I).

24. Cf. supra, Part II, p. 233 (n. 60).

25. *Vide* "Ideas y creencias," p. 400; cf. infra, "Appendix," p. 194.

26. Cf. *Unas lecciones de metafísica,* pp. 77 and 111 (trans., pp. 94 and 139–140); *El hombre y la gente,* pp. 128 ff. (trans., pp. 77 ff.)

27. Cf. J. Ortega y Gasset, *La idea de principio,* §4, pp. 71 ff. (trans., pp. 22 ff.).

28. Cf. supra, pp. 112 ff.

29. Cf. supra, Part I, pp. 46 ff. and 59.

30. Cf. M. Heidegger, *Sein und Zeit,* §12.

31. Cf. supra, pp. 114 ff.

32. Cf. J. Ortega y Gasset, "Sensación, construcción e intuición," pp. 487 ff. (trans., pp. 79 ff.).

33. Cf. J. Ortega y Gasset, *El hombre y la gente,* chap. 4, p. 128 and n. (trans., p. 78).

34. *Vide* J. Ortega y Gasset, "[Prólogo] A 'Historia de la Filosofía' de Émile Bréhier," *OC* VI, pp. 409 ff. (particularly pp. 413 f.). Cf. Aristotle, *Physics,* v, 5, 257 b 7; *Metaphysics,* ix, 1048 b 33 and 1050 a 17 and 21–22; and *On the Soul,* II, 5, 417 b 3.

35. Cf. supra, Part II, pp. 79–80 and 84.

36. Cf. M. Heidegger, *Sein und Zeit,* §17, p. 78 [105] (trans., p. 109).

37. The equivalent of the phrase "But this" has been added by the Spanish editor.

38. Cf. A. Rodríguez Huéscar, *José Ortega y Gasset's Metaphysical Innovation,* Part I.

39. The distinction made here by Ortega between "because of" *("porque")* and "because" understood as "in view of the fact that" *("porque"* or *"en vista de que")* is similar to the one he drew before between "because of" *("por algo")* and "being for the sake of" or "in order to" *("para algo").* Cf. supra, Part I, pp. 60 f. and p. 227 (n. 40).

40. Cf. M. Heidegger, *Sein und Zeit,* §12, p. 55 [74–75] (trans., pp. 81–82); and § 22.

41. Cf. supra, Part II, pp. 80 ff., 84, and 85 ff.

42. Cf. supra, n. 38.

43. Cf. R. Descartes, *Discours de la Méthode,* iii in *Oeuvres de Descartes,* pp. 32–33; *Meditationes de prima philosophia* in ibid., pp. 25 and 27; J. Ortega y Gasset, *¿Qué es filosofía?,* pp. 394ff. (trans., pp. 186ff.).

44. Cf. supra, Part I, pp. 55ff.

45. Cf. supra, p. 115.

46. Cf. supra, pp. 118ff.

47. Cf. E. Husserl, *Ideas,* I, §27, 81, 118, and 150 (pp. 358–359), and *On the Phenomenology of the Consciousness of Internal Time,* trans. J. B. Brough (Dordrecht: Kluwer, 1991), A, First Part: Introduction, §1 and Second Section; B, II, §19.

48. Cf. supra, pp. 127ff.

49. Cf. supra, Part I, "Problems," §8, pp. 35ff. and "The 1929–1930 Course," pp. 63ff. and 66ff.; A. Rodríguez Huéscar, *José Ortega y Gasset's Metaphysical Innovation,* Part II, §§1–5.

50. Cf., e.g., Plato, *Charmides,* 165 a and *Protagoras,* 343 b in *Platonis opera,* ed. J. Burnet (Oxford at the Clarendon Press, 1903; reprinted: 1974), III: *Gnothi sautón;* trans. B. Jowett and W. K. C. Guthrie, respectively, in Plato, *The Collected Dialogues,* ed. E. Hamilton et al., pp. 111 and 336.

51. The equivalent of the phrase "The procedure in question" has been added by the Spanish editor.

52. Cf. J. Ortega y Gasset, *El hombre y la gente,* pp. 101, 103, and 191ff. (trans., pp. 40–41, 43–44, and 162ff.), and "Preludio a un Goya," §3 in *Goya, OC* VII, pp. 548ff.

53. The locution Ortega employed here was *consistencia,* which he proceeded to characterize, in a parenthetical remark not included as such in the English version, as " = *consistir,*" i.e., as "deriving from *consistir.*" The context seems to rule out several possible meanings of the word, namely, "consistency" (whether in the logical, physical, or even ontological sense) and that which would correspond to the nominalized form of "consisting in," apparently leaving us only with the acceptation proper to the nominalized form of "consisting of." This would account for my translation of the word as "makeup."

54. For the notions of project *("Entwurf")* and possibility *("Möglichkeit"),* cf. M. Heidegger, *Sein und Zeit,* §31, pp. 145ff. [192ff.] (trans., pp. 184ff.).

55. Dante Alighieri, *La Divina Commedia,* "Inferno," Canto V, l. 103 in *The Divine Comedy.* "Inferno," trans. and comm. Charles S. Singleton (Princeton: Princeton University Press/Bollingen Series LXXX, 1970), I, pp. 52 and 53: "Love, which absolves no loved one from loving. . . ." Ortega's text has been slightly emended in order accurately to reflect the punctuation and spelling of the original. Cf. II (Commentary), p. 90: according to Singleton, the line quoted serves to state "Francesca's second law of love" that "echoes a dictum which the code of courtly love characteristically had taken from Christian doctrine." Singleton provides the following sources for it: I John 4:19; Fra Giordano da Rivalto, *Prediche,* 1831 ed., II, p. 78; and Andreas Capellanus, *De amore,* II, 8, p. 311.

56. *Vide* J. Ortega y Gasset, "Lector," *Meditaciones del Quijote, OC* I, p. 322 (trans., p. 45, and J. Marías's n. 8 to this edition on pp. 173–174; cf. J. Marías, "Comentario," p. 266ff.)

57. Cf. supra, Part I, "Problems," §7, p. 34 and "The 1929–1930 Course," p. 74.

58. Cf. supra, pp. 114ff.

59. Cf. E. Husserl, *Ideas,* I, §27, pp. 51 and 53.

60. Cf. Jean-Paul Sartre, *L'existentialisme est un humanisme,* p. 22.

61. *Ed.'s N.:* The development of the course, then, did not take place normally either.

62. Cf. supra, Part II, pp. 78ff.

63. Cf. supra, Part II, p. 91 and p. 232 (nn. 45–46).

64. Cf. supra, n. 62.

65. Cf. supra, Part II, pp. 87–88 and 232 (nn. 38–40).

66. Cf. supra, n. 62.

67. Cf. Nicolai Hartmann, *Grundzüge einer Metaphysik der Erkenntnis,* 2nd ed. enl. (Berlin/Leipzig: Walter de Gruyter, 1925).

68. For the connection and distinction between the concepts of being and thing, cf. *La idea de principio,* pp. 161, 208, and 211 (trans., pp. 136, 195, and 198); "Comentario al 'Banquete' de Platón," p. 773; and infra, Part IV, pp. 157–167.

69. Cf. Nicolas Malebranche, *Recueil de toutes les réponses du P. Malebranche, prêtre de l'Oratoire, à M. Arnauld, Docteur en Sorbonne,* ed. David, 4 vol. (1709), vol. I, p. 415; *apud* Martial Gueroult, *Malebranche* (Paris: Aubier/Éditions Montaigne, 1955–1959), I (1955), p. 157: "In accordance with St. Augustine, I have maintained that matter was nothing but extension in terms of length, width, and depth; but I have never entertained the thought that the *idea* of length, width, and depth were long, wide, and deep, or that the intelligible body were material, being larger in a larger than in a smaller space."

70. *Ed.'s N.:* After this point, the rest of the lecture is identical with articles iv and v (or last) of the series, "What Is Knowledge?" The reasons explaining this have already been given. [Cf. supra, Part II, iii, p. 84, n.(*)].

71. Cf. supra, Part II, pp. 85ff.

72. Cf. supra, n. 63.

73. Cf. supra, Part II, p. 92.

74. Cf. supra, p. 106.

75. Cf. E. Husserl, *Ideas,* I, §28, p. 54.

76. Cf. supra, Part II, pp. 78–79.

77. Cf. J. Ortega y Gasset, "Sobre el estudiar y el estudiante," pp. 545ff.; *Unas lecciones de metafísica,* chap. 1; and *El hombre y la gente,* chap. 1.

78. Cf. supra, Part II, p. 98.

79. Cf. supra, Part II, p. 79 and p. 230 (n. 10).

80. Cf. Plato, *Symposium,* 200 b and e.

81. Cf. supra, p. 107.

82. Cf. E. Husserl, *Ideas,* I, §27, pp. 51 and 53.

83. Cf. J. Ortega y Gasset, "Ideas y creencias," pp. 386 and 399f. (see infra, pp. 180 and 193f.), and *El hombre y la gente,* pp. 109–110 (trans., pp. 52–53).

84. Cf. J. Ortega y Gasset, *El tema de nuestro tiempo,* chaps. 6 and 10; "Reforma de la inteligencia" in *Goethe desde dentro, OC* IV, pp. 493ff.; "Ensimismamiento y alteración," *OC* V, pp. 309–310; "Guillermo Dilthey y la Idea de la Vida," pp. 192 and 207ff. (trans., pp. 161 and 175ff.); "Ideas y creencias," p. 387 (see infra, p. 181); *El hombre y la gente,* pp. 93f. (trans., pp. 30f.).

85. Cf. supra, nn. 14 and 43.

86. [Descartes's] *cogito ergo sum* [I think, therefore I am] is one of the most brilliant ideas which have occurred to a human being, but it is, as well, one which is riddled with errors. [This note is the author's.]

87. Stylistically and even conceptually, something is lost here in the translation, for, while "numbered" and "counts" are both seemingly needed in English (however interconnected their meanings may be), in Spanish it is possible to use only different forms of the verb *contar* in order to convey, in this case, both senses— to "number" and to "count—which are signified by the two different English words.

88. Cf. J. Ortega y Gasset, "Meditación preliminar," §11, *Meditaciones del Quijote, OC* I, p. 355 (trans., pp. 95–96): ". . . the preoccupation which, like a new tremor, begins to rise in the breasts of the Greeks and spreads later to other peoples of the European continent, is the anxiety for security—. . . *[tò asphalès]*." (*Vide* J. Marías, "Comentario," pp. 352–353.) For the notion of *tò asphalès* ["that which is safe or secure"], see Plato, *Phaedo* 100 c-d and 101 d, *Platonis opera,* ed. J. Burnet, I, and the translation by H. Tredennick in *The Collected Dialogues of Plato,* pp. 82 and 83.

89. Cf. supra, p. 106.

90. Cf. supra, Part II, pp. 85f.

91. In part, these ideas come close to those which have been recently advanced by [Martin] Heidegger in his work, *Being and Time* [ §§39ff.]. I am sorry to say, however, that I cannot grant him priority in having stated them. They form a doctrinal kernel inseparable from my entire work, beginning with my first book (of 1914), namely, *Meditaciones del Quijote* [the title has been added by the Spanish editor], where knowledge—and, formally speaking, philosophical knowledge—is already [shown to] derive from the dimension of insecurity constitutive of life. Some young Spaniards who, quite rightly, are presently enthusiastic over Heidegger would not have found it idle at all to devote five minutes to reflecting just on the meaning of the formula, "living reason," which gives expression, by way of a schematic synthesis, to my book, *El tema de nuestro tiempo.* (Cf. *Meditaciones del Quijote* [cf. supra, n. 88] and *El tema de nuestro tiempo* [pp. 178 and 201; trans., pp. 58–59 and 92]). [These references, except for the bracketed information, were added by the Spanish editor. However, the text of the note is the author's.]

92. Cf. J. Ortega y Gasset, "Filosofía pura. Anejo a mi folleto 'Kant,'" *OC* IV, pp. 54–59.

93. Cf. J. Ortega y Gasset, *Investigaciones psicológicas,* chaps. 4–6.

94. Cf. E. Husserl, "Phenomenology and Anthropology," trans. R. G. Schmitt in *Shorter Works,* ed. P. McCormick et al. (Notre Dame, Indiana: University of Notre Dame Press/Sussex, England: The Harvester Press, 1981), pp. 319ff. and "Phenomenology," trans. R. E. Palmer in ibid., ii, 7–9.

95. Cf. J. Ortega y Gasset, "Sensación, construcción e intuición," pp. 487ff. (trans., pp. 79ff.).

96. Cf. "Ideas y creencias," I, iv, pp. 405ff. (see infra, "Appendix," pp. 199ff.)

97. Cf. ibid., p. 392 (see infra, pp. 185–186).

98. Somebody else can tell me I was born a good day, and I may take him or her at his or her word, as if he or she had spoken to me of an eclipse that took place three hundred years ago. But my birth is not lived by me; it does not belong to my life, which is comprised only of those things I witness and which I, on my own, enjoy or suffer. I also observe somebody else die, but that fact does not belong to the deceased. Birth and death exist only in somebody else's life, not in that of the one who is born or dies. [This note is the author's.]

99. *Ed.'s N.:* Cf. the articles of the series entitled "¿Por qué se vuelve a la filosofía?," which were published in the Buenos Aires daily, *La Nación.* A few paragraphs belonging to this lecture appeared there, and the series in question was reprinted for the first time as an appendix to the fourth edition (1983) of the book, *¿Qué es filosofía?,* published as part of this collection [namely, *Obras de José Ortega y Gasset,* as edited by P. Garagorri, which also included the present book, *¿Qué es conocimiento?,* that is, *What Is Knowledge?*].

# IV. Glimpses of the History of Philosophy

1. Cf. Plato, *Phaedo,* 74ff.

2. Cf. Aëtius, *Placita,* IV.8.10, in *Doxographi Graeca,* ed. H. Diels (Berlin, 1879), p. 395, *apud* C. J. de Vogel, *Greek Philosophy* (Leiden: E. J. Brill, 1969), I, p. 74, §143 a; Alexander of Aphrodisias, *De sensu,* 24.14 and 56.12, in *Commentarii in Aristotelem Graeca* (Berlin); Simplicius, *Physics,* 73 b; Eduard Zeller, *A History of Greek Philosophy,* trans. S. F. Alleyne (London: Longmans, Green and Co., 1881), II, pp. 266 and 268 (n. 2); G. S. Kirk, J. E. Raven, and M. Schofield, *The Presocratic Philosophers. A Critical History with a Selection of Texts,* 2nd ed. (Cambridge: Cambridge University Press, 1983), p. 429; W. K. C. Guthrie, *A History of Greek Philosophy* (Cambridge at the University Press, 1965), II, p. 442.

3. Cf. supra, Part III pp. 106f.

4. Cf. ibid.

5. Cf. Fragment 3, in *Ancilla to the Pre-Socratic Philosophers,* trans. K. Freeman, p. 19.

6. Cf. Fragment 30, in ibid., p. 26.

7. Cf. Aristotle, *Metaphysics,* I.4, 985 b 4; Simplicius, *De caelo,* p. 294, 33, Heiberg, *apud* C. J. de Vogel, *Greek Philosophy,* I, p. 72, §141.

8. Cf. supra, Part III, p. 107.

9. Cf. supra, p. 156.

10. Cf., e.g., Aristotle, *Metaphysics,* V.30, 1025 a 14–15 and VI.2, 1026 b 31–33; *Topics,* I.5, 102 b 4–6 and 8, 103 b 17–19, and IV.1, 120 b 30–35; *Posterior Analytics,* I.4, 73 a 34–73 b 5 and 6, 75 a 18–22.

11. Cf. Empedocles, Fragment 109, in *Ancilla to the Pre-Socratic Philosophers,* trans. K. Freeman, p. 63, and Aristotle, *On the Soul,* I.2, 404 b 17. *Vide* Eduard Zeller, *A History of Greek Philosophy,* II, pp. 165 ff., and W. K. C. Guthrie, *A History of Greek Philosophy,* II, pp. 228 ff.

12. Cf., e.g., Aristotle, *Metaphysics,* III. 5, 1010 a 25; and *On the Soul,* II. 1, 412 a 9–10 and III. 4, 429 a 15 ff. *Vide* David Ross, *Aristotle,* 3rd ed. (London: Methuen & Co., 1966), pp. 146–148.

13. The equivalent of "after the way" was added by the Spanish editor.

14. St. Thomas Aquinas, *Summa theologiae,* Latin/English, Blackfriars ed. (New York: McGraw-Hill), Vol. III (1964), i, q. 12, a. 4, "Responsio," p. 14; cf. ibid., Vol. XIX (1967), q. 50, a. 2, "Responsio," p. 11.

15. Cf. Plato, *Republic,* VI.23, 508 d–509 b, and *Parmenides,* 129, 131–133 b, and 135 a ff.

16. Cf. Parmenides, Fragments 6, 7, and 8, in *Ancilla to the Pre-Socratic Philosophers,* trans. K. Freeman, p. 43.

17. Cf. J. Ortega y Gasset, *El hombre y la gente,* chap. 1, and "Ideas y creencias," p. 401 (see infra, pp. 195–196).

18. The equivalent of "are" was added by the Spanish editor.

19. Plato, *Phaedrus,* 247 c 3 in *Platonis opera,* ed. J. Burnet, II: *dè huperouránion tópon;* as translated by R. Hackforth in *The Collected Dialogues of Plato,* ed. E. Hamilton, p. 494.

20. Cf. supra, Part III, pp. 115–116 and 122f.

21. Cf. supra, p. 155.

22. Cf. J. Ortega y Gasset, *Investigaciones psicológicas,* chaps. 10–14, and "[Prólogo] A 'Historia de la Filosofía' de Émile Bréhier," pp. 394 and 407 ff. (trans. pp. 102 and 110ff.).

23. Cf. e.g., M. Heidegger, *Sein und Zeit,* §§1 (p. 3), 3 (p. 11), and 16 (p. 72); "What Is Metaphysics?," in *Basic Writings,* ed. D. F. Krell (New York: Harper & Row, 1977), pp. 97, 98, and 101; *The Basic Problems of Phenomenology,* trans. A. Hofstadter (Bloomington: Indiana University Press, 1982), §§3–4, 10 b, 12 c, and 22.

24. Aristotle, *Metaphysics,* IV.1–2, 1003 a 21–1005 a 18; VI.1; VII.1; VIII. 1, 1042 a 24–32; XII.6, 1071 b 12ff.; 7, 1073 a 3–4; 9, 1074 b 30ff.

25. The equivalent of "than to say" has been added by the Spanish editor.

26. The equivalent of "by themselves" has been added by the Spanish editor.

27. Cf. Plato, *Republic*, V.19, 477 a and 478 d.

28. Cf. supra, pp. 163–164.

29. Cf. supra, Part III, pp. 146ff.

30. Plato, *Meno*, 81 d. [This reference is by the author; here it appears as translated by W. K. C. Guthrie in *The Collected Dialogues of Plato*, ed. E. Hamilton, p. 364.]

31. Cf. J. Ortega y Gasset, *El hombre y la gente*, chap. 1, and "Ideas y creencias," p. 401 (and infra, pp. 195–196).

32. Cf. Plato, *Meno*, 86 a 9, in *Platonis opera*, ed. J. Burnet, III.

33. Cf. J. Ortega y Gasset, "Sensación, construcción e intuición," pp. 487ff. and, e.g., Kant, *Kritik der reinen Vernunft*, A xvii, B xvi, B 1, A 19/B 29, A 69, B 94, and B 134.

34. This is so according to the etymology of the word, to wit: from the Greek *gè* ("earth") and *metría* ("measuring"). Cf. C. T. Onions et al., *The Oxford Dictionary of English Etymology* (New York and Oxford: Oxford University Press, 1966): "geo-" (p. 394, right column), "geometry" (p. 395, left column), and "metre" (p. 573, right column).

35. This occasion does not seem to arise in the remaining portion of the book.

36. At least in Plato's version of it; we will later try to learn whether or not this is also true of other forms of idealism. [This remark, which in the original appears in the body of the text, is Ortega's. The topic, whose discussion he anticipates here, does not appear again in the remaining portion of the book, except in the last paragraph by way of simple re-assertion. Cf. J. Ortega y Gasset, *¿Qué es filosofía?*, pp. 352 and 402; *La idea de principio*, pp. 157ff.]

37. Cf. supra, p. 50.

38. Reading *por tanto* ("therefore") for *tanto* ("so much," "so many"), which makes no sense in this context.

39. Cf. Aristotle, *Metaphysics*, I.9, 990 a 34–b 8.

40. This device, also called Cartesian diver, was employed "in physics laboratories for the experimental study of the suspension, immersion, and flotation of bodies in a liquid medium" (*Diccionario enciclopédico hispano-americano de literatura, ciencias, artes, etc.* [London: W. M. Jackson, n. d.], XII, p. 1176, right column). In its simplified form (ibid., p. 1177, left column), it consists of "a hollow figure, partly filled with water and partly with air, and made to float in a vessel nearly filled with water, having an air-tight elastic covering. This covering being pressed down, the air outside the vessel is compressed, and more water forced through a small aperture into the figure, which consequently sinks, to rise again when the external pressure is removed" (*The Compact Edition of the Oxford English Dictionary* [New York: Oxford University Press, 1972], I, p. 345 [p. 139, right column]).

41. *Ennead* IV.8.4, vv. 33–35, in Plotinus, *Enneads*, Greek/English ed., trans. A. H. Armstrong (Cambridge, Mass.: Harvard University Press/The Loeb Classical Library, 1995), IV, pp. 410 and 411. The reference is given in the text by Ortega himself.

42.  *Ed.'s N.:* The manuscript, as extant, breaks off at this point.

## Appendix

1.  An important play on words is unfortunately lost in the translation, namely, that between "encontrarse *con* " ("to come *upon*") and "encontrarse *en*" ("to find oneself placed *in*"). It would have been ideal to find one and the same English verb, so as to be able to render adequately the two uses of *encontrarse.*

2.  Cf., e.g., René Descartes, *Méditations,* iii, p. 29 (37), trans., I, p. 159; Wilhelm Dilthey, "Vorrede," *Einleitung in die Geisteswissenschaften* in *Gesammelte Schriften* (Stuttgart: B. G. Teubner and Göttingen: Vandenhoeck & Ruprecht), I (1966), p. xviii; Franz Brentano, *Psychology from an Empirical Standpoint,* trans. A. C. Rancurello et al. (New York: Humanities Press, 1973), Book II, vi–ix, pp. 194ff.; E. Husserl, *Ideas,* I, §§ 94–95.

3.  Cf. supra, p. 180.

4.  Cf. The Acts of the Apostles 17:28 in *The New Testament* of *The Holy Bible,* King James Version, 1611 (New York: American Bible Society, 1985), p. 142.

5.  Cf. supra, p. 179.

6.  Cf. J. Ortega y Gasset, *En torno a Galileo,* particularly chaps. 8, 10, and 12.

7.  That is, since 1914. Cf. infra, p. 203, for the date of this essay.

8.  Let me leave the question untouched of whether, beneath this most profound of strata, there is still something else, [namely,] a metaphysical bed that not even our beliefs manage to reach. [This note is the author's.]

9.  Cf. R. Descartes, *Discours de la Méthode* in *Oeuvres de Descartes,* VI, p. 31 (trans., p. 101), and *Méditations,* i, in ibid., IX-1, pp. 17–18 (trans., pp. 148–149); E. Husserl, *Ideas,* I, §31.

10. The locution *terra* derives from *tersa,* meaning dry, solid. [This note is the author's. Cf. Charles T. Lewis et al., *A Latin Dictionary: terra* ("ground, earth"); p. 1861, center column); *tersa* ("clean or dry"; feminine form of the past participle of *tergeo;* p. 1862, left column); *tergeo* ("I wipe dry" or "clean"; p. 1858, center column).

11. Doubt derives from *dubitare,* which means "to vibrate to and fro." (Cf. *dubito* in Charles T. Lewis, ibid., p. 613, center column.) The word involves the Indo-European root *dwo,* meaning "two." See *The American Heritage Dictionary of the English Language,* pp. 555 and 2101.

12. Cf. [Plato,] *Parmenides.* [This reference was given in the body of the text by Ortega himself.]

13. This discussion does not seem to be found in this essay.

14. Cf. J. Ortega y Gasset, "Historia como sistema," viii, p. 41 (trans., p. 217).

15. Cf. *mâter,* no. 5 in *The American Heritage Dictionary of the English Language,* p. 2113, left column.

16. Here lies the origin and justification of Ortega's distinction between "circum-

stance" and "world." Cf. J. Ortega y Gasset, *Meditaciones del Quijote, OC* I, pp. 319–323 (trans., pp. 41–46 and 168–174, nn. 5–8, by J. Marías), and J. Marías, "Comentario," pp. 247–270.

17. Cf. J. Ortega y Gasset, *La idea de principio,* pp. 78–80 (trans., pp. 30–32).

18. Cf. infra, p. 196–197.

19. Max Scheler, *Die Stellung des Menschen im Kosmos* (Bern: A. Francke, 1928). (Translation: *Man's Place in Nature,* trans. H. Meyerhoff [Boston: Beacon Press, 1961]).

20. Cf. J. Ortega y Gasset, *El hombre y la gente,* chap. 1.

21. Cf. supra, p. 195.

22. This essay develops certain of the foundations of what I presented in my lecture, "Ensimismamiento y alteración" [Cf. *OC* V, pp. 293 ff.], while the lecture, in turn, develops what in this section of the essay is only advanced by way of statement. [This note is the author's. *Vide* J. Ortega y Gasset, "En el centenario de Hegel," iv, *OC* V, p. 427 and *El hombre y la gente,* chap. 1.]

23. Cf. St. Thomas Aquinas, *Summa theologiae,* I, q. 16, a. 2, Blackfriars, IV (1964), p. 78: "*veritas est adaequatio rei et intellectus.*"

24. Horace, *Epistulae* 2, 2, 102, *apud* Victor-José Herrero Llorente, *Diccionario de expresiones y frases latinas,* 2nd ed. rev. (Madrid: Gredos, 1985), p. 153, No. 2703.

25. Cf., possibly, St. Teresa de Jesús, *Libro de la vida,* 17.7 in *Obras Completas,* ed. Efrén de la Madre de Dios et al. (Madrid: Biblioteca de Autores Cristianos, 1962), p. 69, right column.

26. This word appears in English in the original. For the preceding distinction between the external and the internal worlds, cf. Alfred Schutz, "On Multiple Realities," *Collected Papers,* I, especially ii–v, pp. 229 ff.; see infra, iv, pp. 199 ff.

27. Cf. J. Ortega y Gasset, "Historia como sistema," viii, pp. 41 ff. (trans., pp. 217 ff.), and "[Prólogo] A 'Historia de la Filosofía' de Émile Bréhier," p. 417.

28. Cf. infra, iv, p. 200.

29. Cf. Baltasar Gracián, *El discreto* (1646) in *El héroe. El discreto* (Buenos Aires/Ciudad México, 1939).

30. Cf. Parts I, *passim* and II, pp. 77 ff.

31. Cf. supra, Part I, pp. 60 and 227 (n. 40); Part III, pp. 124 and 235 (n. 39).

32. Cf. J. Ortega y Gasset, *Investigaciones psicológicas,* chaps. 10–14.

33. However, he did not do so with sufficient thoroughness and committed, as well, a radical error to which I refer in the following paragraphs. [This note is the author's. Cf. Wilhelm Dilthey, *Das Wesen der Philosophie,* I.iii in *Gesammelte Schriften,* V (1968), pp. 366 ff.]

34. This vague designation is sufficient [to allow us] to set such an activity in opposition to all other manners of doing that are "practical" in character. [This remark, Ortega's own, appears parenthetically in the body of the text.]

35. Cf., possibly, Ernst Cassirer, *The Philosophy of Symbolic Forms,* trans. R. Manheim (New Haven: Yale University Press, 1955), vol. II.

36. Cf. Wilhelm Dilthey, *Das Wesen der Philosophie, passim* and J. Ortega y Gasset, "Guillermo Dilthey y la Idea de la Vida," iv–v and p. 203.

37. The Spanish original of this essay can be found in *OC* V, pp. 381–409. For a critical examination of Ortega's theory of ideas and beliefs, see my articles entitled, "La acción y los usos intelectuales. En torno a la problemática de las ideas y las creencias en la filosofía de Ortega," *Torre de los Lujanes* (Real Sociedad Económica Matritense de Amigos del País) 34, October 1997, pp. 117ff.; "Caminos de la reflexión. En torno a la teoría orteguiana de las ideas y las creencias," *Revista de Filosofía* (Universidad Complutense de Madrid), 3rd epoch, 11, nos. 19 and 20, 1998, pp. 5ff. and 113ff.; and "La teoría orteguiana de las ideas y las creencias. Una dificultad interpretativa," *Humanitas* 26 (Universidad Autónoma de Nuevo León, Mexico), 1999, pp. 133–140.

# Bibliography

## A. Primary

Ortega y Gasset, José. *Obras Completas*. Edición del Centenario. Madrid: Revista de Occidente/Alianza Editorial, 1983, 12 volumes:

"Sensación, construcción e intuición" (1913), XII, pp. 487–499. Translated by Philip W. Silver under the title "Sensation, Construction, and Intuition." In *Phenomenology and Art*. New York: W. W. Norton & Co., 1975, pp. 79–94.

*Meditaciones del Quijote* (1914), I, pp. 309–400. Translated by E. Rugg et al. under the title *Meditations on Quixote*. New York: W. W. Norton & Co., 1961.

"Ensayo de estética a manera de prólogo" (1914), VI, pp. 247–264. Translated by P. W. Silver under the title "An Essay in Esthetics by Way of a Preface." In *Phenomenology and Art*, pp. 127–150.

*Investigaciones psicológicas* (1915–1916), XII, pp. 331–500. Translated by J. García-Gómez under the title *Psychological Investigations*. New York: W. W. Norton & Co., 1987, 254 pp.

*El tema de nuestro tiempo* (1923), III, pp. 141–242. Translated by J. Cleugh under the title *The Modern Theme*. New York: Harper & Row, 1961, 152 pp.

"Ni vitalismo ni racionalismo" (1924), III, pp. 270–280.

"Reforma de la inteligencia" (1926), in *Goethe desde dentro*, IV, pp. 493–500.

"Kant. Reflexiones de centenario" (1929), IV, pp. 23–47.

"Filosofía pura. Anejo a mi folleto 'Kant'" (1929), IV, pp. 48–59.

*¿Qué es filosofía?* (1929), VII, pp. 273–438. Translated by M. Adams under the title *What Is Philosophy?* New York: W. W. Norton & Co., 1960, 252 pp.

"En el centenario de Hegel" (1931), V, pp. 411–429.

*Unas lecciones de metafísica* (1932–1933), XII, pp. 143–330. Translated by M. Adams under the title *Some Lessons in Metaphysics*. New York: W. W. Norton & Co., 1969, 158 pp.

"Sobre el estudiar y el estudiante" (1933), IV, pp. 545–554.

"Guillermo Dilthey y la Idea de la Vida" (1933–1934), VI, pp. 165–214. Translated by H. Weyl under the title "A Chapter from the History of Ideas—Wilhelm Dilthey and the Idea of Life." In *Concord and Liberty*. New York: W. W. Norton & Co., 1946, pp. 129–182.

"Prólogo para alemanes" (1934), VIII, pp. 11–58. Translated by P. W. Silver under the title "Preface for Germans." In *Phenomenology and Art*, pp. 17–76.

"Historia como sistema" (1935), VI, pp. 11–50. Translated by H. Weyl under the title "History as a System." In *History as a System and Other Essays Toward a Philosophy of History.* New York: W. W. Norton & Co., 1941, pp. 163–233.

"Ensimismamiento y alteración" (1939), V, pp. 295–315.

*En torno a Galileo* (1939), V, pp. 13–164. Translated by M. Adams under the title *Man and Crisis.* New York: W. W. Norton & Co., 1958, 217 pp.

"[Prólogo] A un diccionario enciclopédico abreviado" (1939), VI, pp. 358–367.

"Ideas y creencias" (1940), V, pp. 377–409. Translated by J. García-Gómez under the title "Ideas and Beliefs" (see supra, pp. 175 ff.).

*Sobre la razón histórica* (1940/1944), XII, pp. 143–330. Translated by Ph. W. Silver under the title *Historical Reason.* New York: W. W. Norton & Co., 1984, 224 pp.

"Apuntes sobre el pensamiento: su teurgia y su demiurgia" (1941), V, pp. 517–541. Translated by H. Weyl under the title "Notes on Thinking—Its Creation of the World and Its Creation of God." In *Concord and Liberty,* pp. 49–82.

"[Prólogo] A 'Historia de la Filosofía' de Émile Bréhier" (1942), VI, pp. 377–418. Translated by H. Weyl under the title "Prologue to a History of Philosophy." In *Concord and Liberty,* pp. 83–128.

"Comentario al 'Banquete' de Platón" (1946?), IX, pp. 749–784.

*La idea de principio en Leibniz y la evolución de la teoría deductiva* (1947), VIII, pp. 59–356. Translated by M. Adams under the title *The Idea of Principle in Leibnitz and the Evolution of Deductive Theory.* New York: W. W. Norton & Co., 1971, 381 pp.

*Una interpretación de la historia universal* (1948–1949), IX, pp. 9–242. Translated by M. Adams under the title *An Interpretation of Universal History.* New York: W. W. Norton & Co., 1973, 302 pp.

*El hombre y la gente* (chap. 1, 1939; 1949–1950), VII, pp. 69–272. Translated by W. R. Trask under the title *Man and People.* New York: W. W. Norton & Co., 1957, 272 pp.

*Goya* (1950?), VII, pp. 503–573.

"Pasado y porvenir del hombre actual" (1951), IX, pp. 645–663. (Cf. *La connaissance de l'homme au XXe. siècle,* Rencontres Internationales de Genève, 1951 [Neuchâtel: Éditions de la Baconnière, 1952] and *Hombre y cultura en el siglo XX,* translated by M. Riazza [Madrid: Ediciones Guadarrama, 1957], pp. 321–347. [Discussion: pp. 349–367]).

*Origen y epílogo de la filosofía* (1960?), IX, pp. 347–434. Translated by T. Talbot under the title *The Origin of Philosophy.* New York: W. W. Norton & Co., 1967, 125 pp.

———. *Meditaciones del Quijote,* with Commentary by Julián Marías. Madrid: Universidad de Puerto Rico/Revista de Occidente, 1957, 446 pp.

———. *Meditación de nuestro tiempo. Las Conferencias en Buenos Aires: 1916 y 1928.* Edited by J. L. Molinuevo. Mexico: Fondo de Cultura Económica, 1996, 295 pp.

———. *Introducción a los problemas actuales de la filosofía (Conferencias en Buenos Aires: 1916)* in ibid., pp. 33–172.

──. *Meditación de nuestro tiempo (Conferencias en Buenos Aires: 1928)* in ibid., pp. 173–286.

──. "Principios metafísicos de la razón vital," Curso de 1933–1934. Universidad de Madrid. Unpublished typescript (Madrid: Fundación José Ortega y Gasset), 124 pp.

──. ¿Qué es conocimiento? *Humanitas*, Revista de la Facultad de Filosofía y Letras. Universidad Nacional de Tucumán (Argentina), 12, no. 17 (1964).

──. *¿Qué es conocimiento?* Edited by P. Garagorri. Madrid: Revista de Occidente/Alianza Editorial, 1984, 184 pp.


## B. Secondary

Abbagnano, Nicola. *Dizionario di filosofia*. Turin: Unione Tipografica Torinese, 1961. Translated by A. N. Galetti under the title *Diccionario de filosofía*, Mexico City: Fondo de Cultura Económica, 1991.

Aëtius. *Placita* in *Doxographi Graeca*. Edited by H. Diels. Berlin, 1879. *Apud* C. J. de Vogel, *Greek Philosophy*, I.

Alexander of Aphrodisias. *De sensu*. In *Commentarii in Aristotelem Graeca*. Berlin, n. p., n.d.

*American Heritage Dictionary of the English Language*. 3rd. ed. Boston: Houghton Mifflin, 1992.

Anaximander. Fragment 1. In *Ancilla to the Pre-Socratic Philosophers*, translated by K. Freeman.

*Ancilla to the Pre-Socratic Philosophers*. Translated by K. Freeman. Cambridge, Mass.: Harvard University Press, 1962.

Aristotle. *The Complete Works of Aristotle*. Revised Oxford ed., edited by J. Barnes. Princeton: Princeton University Press/Bollingen Series LXXI-2, 1984:
  I: *On Generation and Corruption* (translated by H. H. Joachim); *On the Soul* (translated by J. A. Smith); *Physics* (translated by R. P. Hardie et al.); *Posterior Analytics* (translated by J. Barnes); *Topics* (translated by W. A. Pickard-Cambridge).
  II: *Metaphysics* (translated by W. D. Ross); *Nicomachean Ethics* (translated by W. D. Ross; revised by J. O. Urmson).

──. *The Metaphysics*. Greek/English ed., translated by H. Tredennick. Cambridge, Mass.: Harvard University Press/The Loeb Classical Library, 1961, vol. I.

Benveniste, Émile. "Nature du signe linguistique." In *Problèmes de linguistique générale*. Paris: Gallimard, 1966, vol. I.

Bergson, Henri. "Introduction à la métaphysique." *La pensée et le mouvant*, vi in *Oeuvres*. Paris: Presses Universitaires de France, 1963. Translated by T. E. Hulme under the title *An Introduction to Metaphysics*. Indianapolis: The Bobbs-Merrill Co., 1955.

*Biblia Sacra iuxta Vulgatam Clementina*. Edited by A. Colunga, 4th ed. Madrid: Biblioteca de Autores Cristianos, 1965.

Brentano, Franz. *Psychology from an Empirical Standpoint*. Translated by A. C. Rancurello et al. New York: Humanities Press, 1973.

Bühler, Karl. *Sprachtheorie.* Jena: Gustav Fischer, 1934.

Cassirer, Ernst. *The Philosophy of Symbolic Forms.* Translated by R. Manheim. New Haven: Yale University Press, 1955, vol. II.

Cervantes y Saavedra, Miguel de. *Don Quijote de la Mancha.* In *Obras Completas,* edited by A. Valbuena Prat. Madrid: Aguilar, 1962.

*Compact Edition of the Oxford English Dictionary.* New York: Oxford University Press, 1972, vol. I.

Copleston, Frederick. *A History of Philosophy.* London: Burns & Oates, 1965, vol. IV.

Corominas, Joan. *Breve diccionario etimológico de la lengua castellana.* 2nd ed. Madrid: Gredos, 1967.

Coseriu, Eugenio. *Teoría del lenguaje y lingüística general.* Madrid: Gredos, 1967.

Dante Alighieri. "Inferno." *La Divina Commedia* in *The Divine Comedy.* Translated and with commentary by Charles S. Singleton. Princeton: Princeton University Press/Bollingen Series LXXX, 1970, vol. 1, text and translation and vol. II, commentary.

Deferrari, Roy J. *A Latin-English Dictionary of St. Thomas Aquinas.* Boston: St. Paul Editions, 1960.

Descartes, René. *Discours de la Méthode.* Edited and with commentary by É. Gilson. Paris: J. Vrin, 1962.

———. *Oeuvres de Descartes.* Edited by Ch. Adam and P. Tannery. Paris: J. Vrin:
VI (1965): *Discours de la Méthode.* Translated by E. S. Haldane and G. R. T. Ross under the title *Discourse on Method,* in *The Philosophical Works of Descartes.* New York: Dover, 1955, vol. I.
VII (1964): *Meditationes de prima philosophia.*
VIII-1 (1964): *Principia philosophiae.* Translated by E. S. Haldane and G. R. T. Ross under the title *The Principles of Philosopy.* In *The Philosophical Works of Descartes,* vol. I.
IX-1 (1964): *Les Méditations touchant la première philosophie.* Translated by E. S. Haldane and G. R. T. Ross under the title *Meditations on First Philosophy.* In *Philosophical Works of Descartes,* vol. I.

———. *Rules for the Direction of the Mind.* In *The Philosophical Works of Descartes,* vol. 1, translated by E. S. Haldane and G. R. T. Ross.

Dewey, John. *Leibniz's "New Essays Concerning Human Understanding."* New York: Hillary House Publishers, 1961; a re-issue of the 1888 ed.

*Diccionario enciclopédico hispano-americano de literatura, ciencias, artes, etc.* London: W. M. Jackson, n.d., vol. XII.

Dilthey, Wilhelm. *Gesammelte Schriften.* Stuttgart: B. G. Teubner, and Göttingen: Vandenhoeck & Ruprecht:
I (1966): *Einleitung in die Geisteswissenschaften.*
V (1968): *Das Wesen der Philosophie.*

Ducrot, Oswald, and Tevetan Todorov. *Dictionnaire encyclopédique des sciences du langage.* Paris: Éditions du Seuil, 1972.

Duhem, Pierre M. M. *SOZEIN TA PHAINOMENA: Essai sur la notion de théorie physique de Platon à Galilée.* Paris: A. Hermann, 1908. Translated by

E. Dolan et al. under the title *To Save the Phenomena*. Chicago: Chicago University Press, 1969.

Empedocles. Fragment 17. In *Ancilla to the Pre-Socratic Philosophers*. Translated by K. Freeman.

Ferrater Mora, José. *Diccionario de Filosofía*. 5th ed. Buenos Aires: Editorial Sudamericana, 1965, 2 vol.

García-Gómez, Jorge. "Interpretación mundanal e identidad propia. Crítica del experimento mental de Bergson y de Schütz en torno a la naturaleza y los límites de la conciencia. *Revista de Filosofía* (Universidad Complutense de Madrid), 3rd epoch, 3 (1990), no. 4, pp. 111–141.

———. "José Ortega y Gasset's Categorial Analysis of Life," *Analecta Husserliana*, 57 (1998), pp. 135–173.

———. "La acción y los usos intelectuales. En torno a la problemática de las ideas y las creencias en la filosofía de Ortega." *Torre de los Lujanes* (Real Sociedad Económica Matritense de Amigos del País), 34, October (1977), pp. 117–138.

———. "Caminos de la reflexión. En torno a la teoría orteguiana de las ideas y las creencias." *Revista de Filosofía* (Universidad Complutense de Madrid), 3rd epoch, 11 (1998), nos. 19 and 20, pp. 5–35 and 113–148.

———. "La teoría orteguiana de las ideas y las creencias. Una dificultad interpretativa." *Humanitas* (Universidad Autónoma de Nuevo León, Mexico), 1999, 26, pp. 133–140.

Gracián, Baltasar. *El discreto* (1646). In *El héroe. El discreto*. Buenos Aires/Ciudad México, 1939.

Gueroult, Martial. *Malebranche*. Paris: Aubier. Éditions Montaigne, 1955–1959, 3 vol.

Guthrie, W. K. C. *A History of Greek Philosophy*. Cambridge at the University Press, 1965, vol. II.

Hamlyn, D. M. "Epistemology, History of." In *The Encyclopedia of Philosophy*, edited by P. Edwards. New York: Macmillan and The Free Press, 1967, vol. III, pp. 8–38.

Hartmann, Nicolai. *Grundzüge einer Metaphysik der Erkenntnis*. 2nd ed. enl. Berlin and Leipzig: Walter de Gruyter & Co., 1925.

Heidegger, Martin. *The Basic Problems of Phenomenology*. Translated by A. Hofstadter. Bloomington: Indiana University Press, 1982.

———. "The Origin of the Work of Art." Translated by A. Hofstadter in *Basic Writings*, edited by D. F. Krell. New York: Harper & Row, 1977, pp. 143–187.

———. *Sein und Zeit*. In GESAMTAUSGABE, I.2. Frankfurt: V. Klostermann, 1977. Translated by J. Macquarrie et al. under the title *Being and Time*. New York: Harper & Row, 1962.

———. "Vom Wesen der Wahrheit." *Wegmarken* in GESAMTAUSGABE, I.9. Frankfurt: Victor Klostermann, 1976.

———. "What Is Metaphysics?" In *Basic Writings*, pp. 91–112.

Heraclitus. Fragments 1, 54, 72, 89, 108, and 123. In *Ancilla to the Pre-Socratic Philosophers*. Translated by K. Freeman.

Herrero Llorente, Víctor-José. *Diccionario de expresiones y frases latinas*. 2nd ed, revised. Madrid: Gredos, 1985.

Hessen, Johannes. *Erkenntnistheorie* (1926). Translated by J. Gaos under the title *Teoría del conocimiento*. Madrid: Revista de Occidente, 1932.

———. *Lehrbuch der Philosophie, I. Wissenschaftslehre*. Munich: Ernst Reinhardt Verlag, 1950.

*The Holy Bible*. King James Version. New York: American Bible Society, 1985.

Horace. *Epistulae*. In V.-J. Herrero Llorente, *Diccionario de expresiones y frases latinas*.

Husserl, Edmund. *The Crisis of the European Sciences and Transcendental Phenomenology*. Translated by D. Carr. Evanston: Northwestern University Press, 1970.

———. *Formal and Transcendental Logic*. Translated by D. Cairns. The Hague: Martinus Nijhoff, 1969.

———. *Ideas Pertaining to a Pure Phenomenology and to a Phenomenological Philosophy*. Translated by F. Kersten. The Hague: Martinus Nijhoff, 1982.

———. *Logical Investigations*. Translated by J. N. Findlay. New York: Humanities Press, 1970, 2 vol.

———. *On the Phenomenology of the Consciousness of Internal Time*. Translated by J. B. Brough. Dordrecht: Kluwer, 1991.

———. "Phenomenology." In *Shorter Works*, pp. 21–35.

———. "Phenomenology and Anthropology." In *Shorter Works*, pp. 315–323.

———. *Shorter Works*. Edited by P. McCormick et al. Notre Dame, Indiana: University of Notre Dame Press/Sussex, England: The Harvester Press, 1981.

*The Interlinear Greek-English New Testament*. 2nd ed. Edited by A. Marshall. Grand Rapids: Zondervan, 1975.

Kant, Immanuel. *Kritik der reinen Vernunft*. Hamburg: Felix Meiner, 1956. Translated by N. K. Smith under the title *Critique of Pure Reason*. New York: St. Martin's Press, 1961.

Kirk, G. S., J. E. Raven, and M. Schofield. *The Presocratic Philosophers. A Critical History with a Selection of Texts*. 2nd ed. Cambridge: Cambridge University Press, 1983.

Lalande, André. *Vocabulaire technique et critique de la philosophie*. 8th ed., revised and enlarged. Edited by the Société Française de Philosophie. Paris: Presses Universitaires de France, 1960.

Leibniz, G. W. *Die philosophischen Schriften von G. W. Leibniz*. Edited by C. I. Gerhardt, vol. IV, VI, and VII. Hildesheim: Georg Olms Verlag, 1978; a reissue of the 1875–1890 ed.

———. *Discours de métaphysique et correspondance avec Arnauld*. Edited and with commentary by G. Le Roy. Paris: J. Vrin, 1957. Translated by G. R. Montgomery under the title *Discourse on Metaphysics. Correspondence with Arnauld. Monadology*. La Salle: Open Court, 1957.

———. "A New System of Nature." In *Die philosophischen Schriften von G. W. Leibniz,* Edited by C. I. Gerhardt, vol. IV.

———. *Nouveaux essais sur l'entendement humain*. Paris: Garnier/Flammarion, 1966. Translated by A. G. Langley under the title *New Essays Concerning Human Understanding*. 2nd ed. Chicago: The Open Court Publishing Co., 1916.

———. *Opuscules et fragments inédits de Leibniz.* Edited by L. Couturat. Hildesheim: Georg Olms Verlag, 1966; a re-issue of the Paris, 1903 ed.

———. *Philosophical Papers and Letters.* Edited and translated by L. E. Loemker, 2nd ed. Dordrecht: D. Reidel, 1969.

Lewis, Charlton, et al. *A Latin Dictionary.* Oxford at the Clarendon Press, 1966.

Liddell, Henry George, and Robert Scott. *A Greek-English Lexikon.* Revised by H. A. Jones. Oxford at the Clarendon Press, 1966.

Locke, John. *An Essay Concerning Human Understanding.* Edited by J. W. Yolton. London: Dent/Everyman's Library, 1964.

Malebranche, Nicolas. *Recueil de toutes les réponses du P. Malebranche, prêtre de l'Oratoire à M. Arnauld, Docteur en Sorbonne.* Edited by David. 4 vol. 1709, vol I. *Apud* M. Gueroult, *Malebranche.* Paris: Aubier/Editions Montaigne, 1955–1959.

Mann, Wolfgang-Rainer. *The Discovery of Things. Aristotle's Categories and Their Context.* Princeton: Princeton University Press, 2000.

Marías, Julián. "Comentario," in conjunction with J. Ortega y Gasset, *Meditaciones del Quijote.* Madrid, 1957.

———. *Ortega. I. Circunstancia y vocación.* Madrid: Revista de Occidente, 1960. Translated by F. M. López-Morillas under the title *José Ortega y Gasset. Circumstance and Vocation.* Norman: University of Oklahoma Press, 1970.

Molière, Jean-Baptiste. *Le médecin malgré lui.* In *Oeuvres Complètes.* Edited by M. Rat. Paris: Bibliothèque de la Pléiade/Nouvelle Revue Française, 1938, vol. II. Translated by K. P. Wormeley under the title *The Doctor in Spite of Himself* in *The Plays of Molière.* New York: The Athenaeum Society, 1897, vol. VI.

Müller, Aloys. *Einleitung in die Philosophie* (1925). Translated by J. Gaos under the title *Introducción a la filosofía.* Madrid: Revista de Occidente, 1934.

Onions, C. T., et al. *The Oxford Dictionary of English Etymology.* New York and Oxford: Oxford University Press, 1966.

Parmenides. Fragment 8. In *Ancilla to the Pre-Socratic Philosophers.* Translated by K. Freeman.

Peirce, Charles F. "The Fixation of Belief." In *Pragmatism and Pragmaticism* in *Collected Papers.* Edited by Ch. Hartshorne et al. Cambridge, Mass.: The Belknap Press/Harvard University Press, 1963, vol. V.

Plato. *Platonis opera.* Edited by J. Burnet. Oxford at the Clarendon Press, 1900–1907 (reprinted: 1973–1975), 5 vol.: I *(Phaedo);* II *(Phaedrus);* III *(Charmides, Meno,* and *Protagoras);* and IV *(Politeia).*

———. *The Collected Dialogues of Plato.* Edited by E. Hamilton et al. New York: Pantheon Books/Bollingen Series LXXI, 1961: *Charmides* (translated by B. Jowett); *Meno* (translated by W.K.C. Guthrie); *Parmenides* (translated by F. M. Cornford); *Phaedo* (translated by H. Tredennick); *Phaedrus* (translated by R. Hackforth); *Protagoras* (translated by W. K. C. Guthrie); *Republic* (translated by P. Shorey); and *Symposium* (translated by M. Joyce).

———. *Republic,* Translated by B. Jowett. Oxford at the Clarendon Press, 1888.

Plotinus. *Enneads.* Greek-English ed. Translated by A. H. Armstrong. Cambridge, Mass: Harvard University Press/The Loeb Classical Library, 1995, vol. IV.

Reinhold, Karl L. *Versuch einer neuen Theorie des menschlichen Vorstellungsmögen.* Prague and Jena: Mauke, 1789.

Rodríguez Huéscar, Antonio. *Éthos y lógos*. Edited by J. Lasaga. Madrid: Universidad Nacional de Educación a Distancia, 1996.

———. *José Ortega y Gasset's Metaphysical Innovation. A Critique and Overcoming of Idealism*. Translated by J. García-Gómez. Albany, N.Y. : State University of New York Press, 1995.

———. *Perspectiva y verdad*. 2nd ed. Madrid: Alianza Editorial, 1985.

Ross, David. *Aristotle*. 3rd ed. London: Methuen & Co., 1966.

Sartre, Jean-Paul. *L'existentialisme est un humanisme*. Paris: Les Éditions Nagel, 1970.

Saussure, Ferdinand de. *Cours de linguistique générale*. Paris and Lausanne, 1916.

Scheler, Max. *Die Stellung des Menschen im Kosmos*. Bern: A. Francke, 1928. Translated by H. Meyerhoff under the title *Man's Place in Nature*. Boston: Beacon Press, 1961.

Schutz, Alfred. "On Multiple Realities." *Collected Papers*, vol. 1. Edited by M. Natanson. The Hague: Martinus Nijhoff, 1962.

———. "Projects of Action." In *Collected Papers*, Vol. I.

———. *Reflections on the Problem of Relevance*. Edited by R. M. Zaner. New Haven: Yale University Press, 1970.

———. *Der sinnhafte Aufbau der sozialen Welt*. 2nd ed. Vienna: Springer Verlag, 1960; 1st ed., 1932. Translated by G. Walsh et al. under the title *The Phenomenology of the Social World*. Evanston: Northwestern University Press, 1967.

Simplicius. *Physics* and *De caelo*. *Apud* C. J. Vogel, *Greek Philosophy*, vol. I.

Teresa de Jesús. *Libro de la vida*. In *Obras Completas*. Edited by Efrén de la Madre de Dios et al. Madrid: Biblioteca de Autores Cristianos, 1962:

Thomas Aquinas. *Summa contra gentiles*. Rome: Forzani, 1894.

———. *Summa theologiae*. Latin/English ed., Blackfriars. New York: McGraw-Hill, vol. III, 1964; vol. IV, 1964; and vol. XIX, 1967.

Vogel, C. J. de. *Greek Philosophy*. Leiden: E. J. Brill, 1969, vol. I.

Zeller, Eduard. *A History of Greek Philosophy*. Translated by S. F. Alleyne. London: Longmans, Green and Co., 1881, vol. II.

Zubiri, Xavier. *Cinco lecciones de filosofía*. Madrid: Sociedad de Estudios y Publicaciones, 1963.

# Index